Inna Tigountsova

The Ugly in Russian Literature

D1796719

Inna Tigountsova

The Ugly in Russian Literature

Dostoevsky's Influence on Iurii Mamleev, Liudmila Petrushevskaia, and Tatiana Tolstaia

LAP LAMBERT Academic Publishing

Imprint

Any brand names and product names mentioned in this book are subject to trademark, brand or patent protection and are trademarks or registered trademarks of their respective holders. The use of brand names, product names, common names, trade names, product descriptions etc. even without a particular marking in this work is in no way to be construed to mean that such names may be regarded as unrestricted in respect of trademark and brand protection legislation and could thus be used by anyone.

Cover image: www.ingimage.com

Publisher:
LAP LAMBERT Academic Publishing
is a trademark of
International Book Market Service Ltd., member of OmniScriptum Publishing Group
17 Meldrum Street, Beau Bassin 71504, Mauritius

Printed at: see last page
ISBN: 978-3-8383-0356-7

Copyright © Inna Tigountsova
Copyright © 2009 International Book Market Service Ltd., member of OmniScriptum Publishing Group
All rights reserved. Beau Bassin 2009

I am grateful to all my teachers. For their helpful criticism of this work at its earlier stages, I am indebted to Donna Tussing Orwin, Kenneth Lantz, Taras Koznarsky, all of the Department of Slavic Languages and Literatures of the University of Toronto, and Richard Pope (York University).

For their comments on the later version of the text and their support, I would to like to thank Myroslav Shkandrij (University of Manitoba), Norman G.O. Pereira (Dalhousie University), Caryl Emerson (Princeton University), and Mark Lipovetsky (University of Colorado at Boulder).

I thank my parents, Fedor and Ekaterina (neé Romodan) Ischenko, for everything that I haven't thanked them before, but in particular, for giving me an opportunity to pursue my studies. I am also thankful to my colleague, Rolf Hellebust (University of Nottingham) for the ultimate encouragement and generous assistance with editing.

To my beautiful daughter

CONTENTS

Introduction

This book offers a picture of the ugly in the Russian literary and cultural scene, focussing on several major writers. It will demonstrate how the category of the ugly (*bezobraznoe*), employed originally by Dostoevsky, is developed in contemporary Russian literature. My investigation of the phenomenon of the ugly in its manifestations in nineteenth-, twentieth-, and twenty-first century literature will proceed as follows: Chapter 1, "Historical and Theoretical Aspects of the Problem of the Ugly," leads readers through the prolegomena to the aesthetics of the ugly and examines Dostoevsky's definition of ugliness. It also includes a review of major Dostoevsky criticism, mainly as it pertains to his idea of *bezobraznoe*, and sets out the goals of the book.

Chapter 2, "The Ugly in Dostoevsky's "Notes from Underground,"" will investigate the ugly (*bezobraznoe*) in this work: the notions of harmony and disharmony as pertaining to Dostoevsky's aesthetics, the issues of the individualism and egotism of the Underground Philosopher, his failed social contacts, and the oppositions of visual/stable vs. verbal/fluctuating. This chapter will also demonstrate the poetic means and imagery resorted to by Dostoevsky in his depiction of ugliness.

Chapter 3, "Monstrous Mamleev: Death, Dostoevsky, and the Problem of Tradition," will deal with Dostoevsky's *Crime and Punishment*, "*Bobok*," and two works by a twentieth-century writer, Iurii Mamleev: "Diary of an Individualist" ["*Tetrad' individualista*"] and *Shatuny*. It will explore his use of Dostoevskian themes and his intertextual references to Dostoevsky's works, characters, and ideas. My aim in this chapter is to demonstrate this influence on Mamleev's prose, primarily focussing on the issue of *bezobraznoe* in both writers.

Chapter 4, "Beauty of the Word and Ugliness of the World," studies Tatiana Tolstaia's "Notes from Underground," "*Limpopo*," "A Sleepwalker in the Fog" ["*Somnambula v tumane*"], "Night" ["*Noch'*"], and *Slynx* [*Kys'*] in the light of Dostoevsky's aesthetics and poetics of the ugly. This chapter will focus on similarities in treatment of space, as well as thematic similarities between Tolstaia's works and those of Dostoevsky. It will demonstrate that she consciously employs Dostoevsky's poetics of the ugly, alludes to his works, takes in new directions his concept of the underground, and shares his view of *bezobraznaia* Russian reality, the absence of home, and dysfunctional families.

Chapter 5, "Liudmila Petrushevskaia: Urban Dystopia: Spaces and People," charts the ways of the ugly in Petrushevskaia's *Time: Night* [*Vremia Noch'*] and "Our Crowd" ["*Svoi Krug*"]. This chapter will focus on similarities between the works of Dostoevsky and Petrushevskaia, and on deformities on three levels: poetics of the ugly; narrative structure and technique; and the *bezobrazie* of characters as well as their spatial surroundings, featuring home-hearth as a locus of dystopia. It will also demonstrate common thematic preferences of Dostoevsky and Petrushevskaia related to *bezobraznoe*.

Given the large scope of this project, embracing several centuries and multiple writers, my bibliographic preference is to give an account of works cited only. The transliteration system used in this book is that of the Library of Congress, apart from the names of the writers that have conventional spelling familiar to the non-academic reader, i.e. *Dostoevsky* and *Tolstoy*. Bibliography will keep the Library of Congress spelling for these names.

Chapter I: Historical and Theoretical Aspects of the Problem of the Ugly

Croce writes that "beauty gives us beauty in unity, and ugliness gives us beauty in multiplicity."[1] According to him, the flaws of aesthetic works, i.e. their ugliness, exist to emphasise their merits. Perfect works possess a unified aesthetic value, which cannot be reduced to the value of their individual parts. Beauty cannot have degrees; its counterpart, however, can "run from slightly ugly (the almost beautiful) up to the very ugly."[2] If ugliness were perfect, devoid of any element of beauty, it would then stop being ugliness, as it cannot exist without its opposite. Thus there is always an element of beauty in the ugly.[3] In this idea Croce develops Aquinas' view of the ugly as a necessary category in a negative definitional field used to categorise the integrity of perfection.[4]

In exploring the complexities of human psychology, the nineteenth-century Russian novelist Fedor Dostoevsky demonstrates how the ugly and the beautiful intertwine, and shows us the ugly in all its multiplicity. To be precise, the quality in question is that referred to by the term *bezobraznoe* (formed from the prefix *bez-* 'without' and the root *-obraz-* 'image'). This word has specific connotations lacking in the more neutral equivalent for the English 'ugly' – *nekrasivyi* (*lit.* 'unbeautiful'). In Dostoevsky, in particular, *bezobraznoe* is related to the wicked, disgraceful, and (bearing in mind the etymology of the Russian term) the deformed. It received a particular emphasis in

---

[1] Benedetto Croce, "The Beautiful and the Ugly" in *The Aesthetic as the Science of Expression and of the Linguistic in General*, Cambridge: Cambridge U Press, 1992, 87.
[2] *Ibid.*, 88.
[3] *Ibid.*
[4] Lesley Higgins, *The Modernist Cult of Ugliness: Aesthetic and Gender Politics*, NY: Palgrave Macmillan, 2002, 21.

9

Dostoevsky's works beginning in 1864, when he published "A Theory of Ugliness" ["*Teoriia bezobraziia*"] by N.I. Solovev in his journal *Epokha* as well as his own "Notes from Underground" [*Zapiski iz podpol'ia*]. Multiplicity, chaos, and disintegration as characteristics of the ugly are also immediate constituents of the postmodern Russian context. I am thus interested to see how Russian writers of the end of the twentieth century use and develop Dostoevsky's views on the ugly.

Mark Lipovetsky draws parallels between the omnivorous nature of postmodernism and the *menippea*, an ancient genre previously studied by Bakhtin in connection with Dostoevsky.[5] According to Bakhtin, a genre related to *menippean* tradition is that of "conversations among the dead," widespread in European literature from the Renaissance to the eighteenth century.[6] This allows Bakhtin to discuss "*Bobok*" in the light of the tradition of dialogues of the dead.[7] Closeness to the latter genre is mentioned by Bakhtin as a feature of Dostoevsky's *menippea*.[8] This genre both in ancient times and in the works of Dostoevsky combines the depiction of fantastic events and characters with the most extreme and rough naturalism. *Menippea* typically includes scandal scenes, inappropriate speeches, distortions of the normal flow of events, behaviour, and etiquette, including speech etiquette. Scandals and eccentricities in *menippea* demolish the wholeness of the normal world, and make it ugly.[9]

The contemporary (1960s to the present) works I intend to discuss mainly fall under the classification of "alternative prose" which arose in Russia after 1985 with Gorbachev's policy of glasnost. The categories devised for this literature in Russian criticism also include 'other prose' (*drugaia proza*), 'coarse prose' (*zhestkaia proza*), 'new prose' (*novaia proza*), 'new wave' (*novaia volna*), and 'young prose' (*molodaia proza*). Another term is 'underground' (transliterated into Russian as '*andegraund*'), which was used to describe the 'angry young men' in the 60s – Aksenov, Gladilin, Voinovich, and Evtushenko – who were members of the 'young prose' movement.[10] Some critics, perhaps in the search for a more internationally recognisable term for this trend, have dubbed it 'postmodernist'. Ironically, their enthusiastic adoption of this label coincided with its devaluation everywhere outside Russia (and maybe Eastern Europe). According to *Brewer's Dictionary of 20th-Century Phrase and Fable* (1991), "attributes of postmodernist work are a playful ironic style, the embracing of cultural pluralism, and a concentration on style and presentation at the expense of

5 M. Lipovetsky, *Russkii postmodernizm: ocherki istoricheskoi poetiki*, Ekaterinburg: *Ural'skii gosudarstvennyi pedagogicheskii universitet*, 1997, 287.
[6] M. Bakhtin, *Problemy poetiki Dostoevskogo*, Moscow: *Sovetskii pisatel'*, 1963, 191.
[7] *Ibid.*, 191-197.
[8] *Ibid.*, 197.
[9] *Ibid.*, 152-163.
[10] Robert Porter, *Russia's Alternative Prose*, Oxford/Providence, USA: Berg, 1994, 1-2.

substance and context... It is hard not to feel that the term has become a humpty-dumpty word meaning almost anything the user wishes it to mean."[11]

Works of alternative prose are intentionally divorced from social and economic problems; they can be realistic or fantastic in nature – but are in either case highly individualistic. They are also explicit in addressing corporeal reality and other taboo subject matter. According to Oleg Dark, one of the myths concerning Russian alternative prose is that it aims at a break with the native realistic tradition.[12] Sasha Sokolov, in an interview with the journal *Iunost'*, affirms that alternative prose chose the line of Lermontov-Dostoevsky-Garshin, as opposed to nineteenth-century literature which chose Tolstoy over Dostoevsky.[13] Shalamov confirms the line of development suggested by Sokolov, but uses Pushkin in place of Lermontov. Stylistically different from the writing of the literary establishment, 'the other prose' is a literature of 'super-realism' (*sverkhrealism*) – a term used by Shalamov – that recalls Dostoevsky's 'realism in the higher sense.'[14] The ontological and existential darkness reflected in alternative prose persuades Dark that Dostoevskian "'fantastic realism' is still seditious today."[15] The way the twentieth century saw its predecessor allowed for two traditions: the first one Apollonian, that of Tolstoy-Turgenev, known for the 'normalcy' of their poetics, for conservative beauty and clarity; the second one Dionysian, that of Gogol-Dostoevsky, an opposing tradition of the grotesque, ambiguity, and ugliness. The Symbolist poet and literary scholar Viacheslav Ivanov refers to the first tradition as to that of prose and the second – that of poetry.[16] According to Aleksei Kruchenykh, a theoretician of the Russian avant-garde and a poet-Futurist, poetry (as opposed to prose) is at the forefront of avant-garde.[17] The poetic side of the Dionysian, Gogol-Dostoevsky tradition receives more emphasis than the Apollonian one, due to its affinity for experimentation and its greater contemporary relevance. The artistic perfection of Turgenev's prose was a symbol of that old beauty that the alternative prose writers had to reject to create their own. Tolstoy's example was selectively but heavily used in the Soviet educational system, and as a result too closely related with the establishment, which the alternative prose writers did not belong to, and perhaps did not wish to belong. Gogol and Dostoevsky offered more variety in artistic experimentation, a trait that was easily adopted in the end

---

[11] *Ibid.*, 3.

[12] O. Dark, *"Mir mozhet byt' liuboi: razmyshleniia o novoi prose,"* *Druzhba narodov* 6 (1990): 223.

[13] S. Sokolov, Interview, *Iunost'*, (12) 1989: 66-68.

[14] Shalamov characterised 'the other prose' as stylistic opposition (*stylisticheskoe protivostoianie*). For more see Porter, *Russia's Alternative Prose*, 10.

[15] Dark, *"Mir mozhet byt' liuboi,"* 230.

[16] Viacheslav Ivanov, *"Dostoevskii i roman-tragediia,"* *Russkaia mysl'* April (1914), http://www.vehi.net/dostoevsky/ivanov.html; accessed on October 16, 2004.

[17] D. Bulatov, ed., *Eksperimental'naia poeziia: Izbrannye stat'i*, Königsberg/Malbork: Simplitsii, 1996, 226.

of the twentieth century, due to the western postmodern influence, the revival of interest in the heritage of the Russian avant-garde of the beginning of the twentieth century, and the political and economical chaos after the fall of the Soviet Union.

Dostoevsky allusions appear in Viktor Erofeev's *Russian Beauty* [*Russkaia krasavitsa*] (*Crime and Punishment* [*Prestuplenie i nakazanie*], *The Devils* [*Besy*], and *The Idiot* [*Idiot*]), Liudmila Petrushevskaia's "Our Crowd" ["*Svoi krug*"] ("Notes from Underground"), and in the *oeuvres* of E. Popov and D.A. Prigov. Among other themes, Robert Porter touches upon Dostoevsky's *nadryv* (frequently translated as 'psychological lacerations') as the salient feature of Petrushevskaia's prose, the apocalyptic element of which is more horrifying than the current political and economic problems dealt with by other contemporary writers.[18] Epshtein also refers to *nadryv* in his discussion of contemporary Russian prose.[19]

The famed Russian critic Viacheslav Kuritsyn emphasizes the role of "practical schizophrenia" (*prakticheskaia shizofrenia*) (referring to the popular equation of this disease with split personality) as a typical feature of the postmodern literary text.[20] According to the nineteenth-century critic Chizh, published in Zelinsky's critical commentaries on Dostoevsky's works, no other writer of that century has such an abundance of characters who experience some sort of psychological disorder. (At the opposite pole Chizh places Tolstoy and Turgenev, corresponding to the lines of literary development outlined by Sokolov and Shalamov.)[21] Schizophrenia is foregrounded in Russian texts of the last quarter of the twentieth century, particularly in those aiming to be considered as postmodernist. In such texts schizophrenia is often a manifestation of the extreme narcissistic love of the narrator, or a character, toward the multiple personalities s/he possesses. The different personalities of Mamleev's characters, for example, fall in love with each other and feel jealous toward each other, worshipping the ugly idol of solipsism. Here, as in Dostoevsky, the disease becomes transcendental rather than psychological, and mentally ill characters become ugly for metaphysical reasons. The continual dialogues that Dostoevsky's monstrous characters conduct with themselves overwhelm the reader; the heavy sound of their thoughts forms an ugly polyphony. Ugly ideas become fully-fledged characters, or different personalities within a character (Ivan Karamazov, Raskolnikov, the Underground Man, etc.).[22]

---

[18] Porter, *Russia's Alternative Prose*, 63.

[19] M. Epshtein, "*Posle budushchego: o novom soznanii v literature*," *Znamia* 1 (1991): 217-30.

[20] An example Kuritsyn gives is that of Boris Vian's texts, which are written on behalf of different authors. *Russkii literaturnyi postmodernizm*, Moscow: *OGI*, 2000, 10.

[21] V. Zelinsky, ed., *Istoriko-kriticheskii kommentarii k sochineniam F.M. Dostoevskogo*, Moscow, 1885, 1, 91. Microform.

[22] See Bakhtin and Ivanov for more on this issue.

It seems that for Dostoevsky, as for the twentieth-century writers, a personality split is ugly not as a disease – schizophrenia – but as a manifestation of multiple ugly ideas or personalities.

The ugly (*bezobraznoe*) is a category of aesthetics that conveys an evaluation of objects and events as monstrous, low, and opposed to beauty. It expresses a negative aesthetic value.[23] The *Filosofskii entsiklopedicheskii slovar'* is the only reference book on aesthetics that also designates the 'imageless' [*'bezóbraznoe'*] *per se* as ugly.[24] According to another source, the *Filosofskii slovar'*,

> the art of critical realism is preoccupied more with negative than with positive characters and criticises and exposes the inhuman sides of life that destroy the beauty of man. In true art the portrayal of what is aesthetically ugly is a peculiar way of asserting the ideal of beauty.[25]

To understand fully the complex, paradoxical relationship between the beautiful and the ugly in nineteenth-century Russian literature, we need to go back to the history of Western aesthetics. The ancient Greeks did not regard the ugly as a separate aesthetic category. Aristotle, who emphasised the difference between a beautiful face and a beautifully painted face, was the first to pose the problem of the paradoxical relationship of the ugly to the beautiful in art. The paradox of the ugly in art is that an ugly object can be nevertheless beautifully depicted. This gives rise to a duality in the aesthetics of the ugly: aesthetic pleasure from a work of art is coupled with the disgust we feel towards the depicted object. Aristotle writes that "we enjoy imitations of all kinds, even of things which are disgusting, even of dead bodies."[26] Cicero labelled the ugly as a specific artistic realm of the comic: "The place and the sphere of the comic is limited to [spiritual] ugliness and [physical] monstrosity; for laughter either exclusively, or for most part, is caused by what denotes or demonstrates something ugly in a non-ugly fashion."[27]

Along with the Ancient Greek tradition of the aesthetics of the ugly, European literature also profited from the Middle Eastern tradition, primarily from the Old and New Testaments, in which there is no strict aesthetic division between 'high' and 'low' genres. In this tradition, great historical events

---

[23] A.A. Beliaev, et al., eds., *Estetika*, Moscow: *Politizdat*, 1989, 28.
[24] L.F. Il'ichev, P.N. Fedoseev, S.M. Kovalev, and V.G. Panov, eds., *Filosofskii entsiklopedicheskii slovar'*, Moscow: *Sovetskaia entsiklopediia*, 1983, 47. The reference books on aesthetics cited here are those written in Russian, as it is the specific term *'bezobraznoe'* that is at issue.
[25] I. T. Frolov, ed., *Filosofskii slovar'*, English edition, Moscow: Progress, 1984, 435.
[26] *Ibid.* Aristotle, *Poetics*, trans. Kenneth McLeish, New York, Theatre Communications Group, 1999, Part IV.
[27] *On the Rhetor*, II. Translation and emphasis are mine throughout the book unless otherwise noted.

and the details of everyday life are interwoven. European literature, however, mainly appropriated what it viewed as the 'high' within the Middle Eastern tradition, leaving out the everyday ('low'/ugly).[28]

The opposition of form and chaos is highlighted in the Judaeo-Christian tradition, with primordial formlessness transformed into cosmos in the opening lines of the book of Genesis. The darkness and void (Genesis 1:2) become light and a variety of forms (1:3 - 1:31), including the human: "So God created man in his own image" (1:27). A central focus of my book will be the absence of precisely this image.

Medieval European aesthetics viewed the ugly as the opposite of the beautiful, equating it with evil. The aesthetics of Classicism during the Age of Enlightenment (17-18th centuries) also regarded the ugly as opposed to the beautiful, but did not believe it to be an aesthetic category. However, already in the eighteenth century, Lessing in his *Laokoon* (1766) argued that the ugly could be used in poetry as a means of provoking feelings of the "comic and the frightening." Hegel included the ugly in the domain of aesthetics when analysing painting and poetry of the modern age, and related it to the category of the "characteristic".

Romantic aesthetics paid special attention to the category of the ugly. Schlegel in his *Fragmente* (1800) asserted that the "eccentric" and the "ugly" are valuable for art.[29] In his 1797 "theory of ugliness," he examines the category as such.[30] The opposition between the ugly and the beautiful can be shown in art as a contrast between the outer ugliness and inner beauty of the depicted object, as for example, in the image of Quasimodo in Victor Hugo's *Notre Dame de Paris*.[31] In general, Hugo paid considerable attention to the problem of the ugly in art. Thus, in the introduction to his drama *Cromwell* (1827), he writes that the combination of the ugly and the beautiful – i.e., the grotesque – is a characteristic of modern poetry that distinguishes it from Ancient art.[32] A focus on the ugly in art can lead to naturalism; or it may reflect the Romantic cult of the ugly, which tends to turn it into a positive aesthetic value (as it does later in some trends of Modernism).[33] The aesthetics of the nineteenth and twentieth centuries examine the ugly in relation to the artistic depiction of the *realia* of life, and to the poetisation of evil (Baudelaire's *Fleurs du mal*). Modernist theory aestheticises the ugly,

---

[28] A.V. Arkhipova, "*Dostoevskii i estetika bezobraznogo*", *Dostoevskii: Materialy i issledovaniia*, Vol. 12, St. Petersburg: DB, 1996, 53.
[29] *Estetika*, 28.
[30] Higgins, *The Modernist Cult of Ugliness*, 21.
[31] *Estetika*, 28.
[32] F.V. Konstantinov, ed.-in-chief, *Filosofskaia entsiklopediia*, Moscow: *Sovetskaia entsiklopediia*, 137.
[33] *Estetika*, 28.

considering it "the theme of our epoch, a source of rejuvenation of art."[34] The Futurists, in particular, abolished the twin ideals of Woman and Beauty and declared themselves to be "hastening the grotesque funeral of passéist Beauty (romantic, symbolist, decadent)."[35] Thus Marinetti writes on ugliness in literature:

> They shout at us, "Your literature won't be beautiful! Where is your verbal symphony, your harmonious swaying back and forth, your tranquilizing cadences?" Their loss we take for granted! And how lucky! We make use, instead, of every ugly sound, every expressive cry from the violent life that surrounds us. We bravely create the "ugly" in literature, and everywhere we murder solemnity. Come! Don't put on these grand priestly airs when you listen to me! Each day we must spit on the *Altar of Art*."[36]

In the aesthetics of the Decadence of the end of the nineteenth century and the Avant-Garde trends of the twentieth century (i.e., Dadaism, Expressionism, Surrealism, Pop-Art), the ugly is regarded as the only possible aesthetic response to the absurdity of existence.[37] In the Modern world, Higgins writes, "the beautiful has been gradually repositioned: not simply negated or rejected, but supplanted by an enthusiasm for a complex, seemingly new and dynamic category" of the ugly.[38]

Hegel suggests that the ugly is a "species" of beauty,[39] and followers of Hegel's aesthetics such as Ruge, Vischer, and Rosenkranz regard it as one of the negative elements of the beautiful.[40] Ruge opposes the ugly to the sublime.[41] Rosenkranz defines the ugly as "something that as such is equated to evil."[42] Rosenkranz creates a typology of the ugly, classifies it variously as formless, amorphous, asymmetrical, disharmonious, vulgar, low, monstrous, and repulsive:[43]

> Ich rolle gleichsam den Kosmos des Hässlichen auf von seinen ersten chaotischen Nebelflecken, von der Amorphie und Asymmetrie an bis zu seinen intensivsten

---

[34] *Revue d'esthètique*, 1954 (7): 2, 211.
[35] Higgins, *The Modernist Cult of Ugliness*, 137.
[36] *Ibid.*
[37] *Filosofskii entsiklopedicheskii slovar'*, 47.
[38] Higgins, *The Modernist Cult of Ugliness*, 21.
[39] *Ibid.*
[40] F.T. Vischer, *Ästhetik*, Vol. 1, 1846, 246-64, 335-50.
[41] A. Ruge, *Neue Vorschule der Ästhetik*, 1837, 88-107.
[42] K. Rosenkranz, *Ästhetik des Hässlichen*, 1853, 463.
[43] *Ibid.*

Formationen in der unendlichen Mannigfaltigkeit der Desorganisation des Schönen durch die Karikatur. Die Formlosigkeit, die Inkorrektheit und die Deformität der Verbildung machen die verschiedenen Stufen dieser in sich konsequenten Reihe von Metamorphosen aus.[44]

He writes that the place of the ugly is between the beautiful and the comical:

Ich habe mich bemühet, den Begriff des Hässlichen als die Mitte zwischen dem des Schönen und dem des Komischen von seinen ersten Anfängen bis zu derjenigen Vollendung zu entwickeln, die er sich in der Gestalt des Satanischen gibt.[45]

Russian social and democratic aesthetics relates the ugly to contemporary social conditions, and sees broad prospects for realistic art in the depiction of the ugly – for example, in the images of Iudushka Golovlev, Smerdiakov, and Prince Vasilii Kuragin.[46] Belinsky, Dobroliubov, and Chernyshevsky regard the ugly as the reflection of the monstrosities of social life.[47] Chernyshevsky, for example, says that facial features are 'badly organized,' and the face is ugly and repulsive, when "the initial development [of this person] occurred under unfavourable circumstances."[48] Belinsky in his discussion of the Natural school insists on the necessity of depictions of "low nature," and Dobroliubov affirms that art takes after life and life does not depend on art, and all that in art does... not come from life straightforwardly and naturally is ugly and meaningless.[49] Another nineteenth-century critic, V.G. Avseenko, fails to find any depictions of the beautiful in Dostoevsky, and expresses his outrage that:

The reader continues to feel as if he is in the unbearable atmosphere of a filthy and dark underground. He is surrounded by some wild convict's life, where at every step there occur events characteristic of a prison or a brothel – events depicted with that imprint of sincerity from which one eventually feels an indescribable vileness in one's soul.

---

[44] Karl Rosenkranz, *Ästhetik des Hässlichen*, Leipzig: Reclam-Verlag, 1990, 5.

[45] *Ibid.*

[46] *Estetika*, 28.

[47] *Filosofskaia entsiklopediia*, 137.

[48] N.G. Chernyshevsky, *"Esteticheskie otnosheniia iskusstva k deistvitel'nosti,"* in his *Polnoe sobranie sochinenii*, Vol. 2, Moscow: *Gosizdat. khud. lit.*, 1949, 12.

[49] V.G. Belinsky, *"Vzgliad na russkuiu literaturu 1847 goda,"* *Estetika i literaturnaia kritika*, Vol. 2, Moscow: *Khudozhestvennaia literatura*, 1959, 653. N. A. Dobroliubov, *"O stepeni uchastiia narodnosti v razvitii russkoi literatury,"* *Izbrannoe*, Moscow: *Iskusstvo*, 1986, 30.

[*Chitatel' prodolzhaet chuvstvovat' sebia v nesterpimoi atmosfere griaznogo i mrachnogo podpol'ia. Ego obstupaet kakai-to dikaia, katorzhnaia zhizn', gde na kazhdom shagu imeiut mesto iavleniia, prisushchie ostrogu ili domu terpimosti, – iavleniia, izobrazhennye s tem otpechatkom iskrennosti, ot kotorogo pod konets neskazanno gadko stanovitsia na dushe.*][50]

S.T. Gertso-Vinogradsky, a critic close to the democratic circles of that time, expresses similar views on *The Devils* [*Besy*] and *The Raw Youth* [*Podrostok*], stating that upon reading these books

> you seem to be in a world unknown to you, where the protagonists have nothing in common with normal people: they walk on their hands, eat with their noses, and drink with their ears; these are people spat out by hell itself, bastards, anomalies, psychological incongruities.

> [*vy tochno popadaete v nevedomyi vam mir, gde deistvuiushchie litsa ne imeiut nichego obshchego s obyknovennymi liud'mi: khodiat vverkh nogami, ediat nosom, p'iut ushami, eto kakie-to ischadiia, vyrodki, anomalii, psikhicheskie neleposti.*[51]]

A.M. Skabichevsky and N.K. Mikhailovsky charge that Dostoevsky allows his sickly imagination to prevail over his knowledge of real life, yet on the other hand is guilty of the most primitive naturalism.[52] They believe that Dostoevsky is trying to scare the reader, to appeal to his base instincts, to affect his nerves. Thus Skabichevskii compares the impact of Dostoevsky's novels to the irritation caused by "rubbing cork on window-glass," which is able to "drive some nervous people to hysterics."[53] Mikhailovsky expresses a similar view in his "Cruel Talent," saying that the Underground Man "pours out his soul to the reader, trying to dig to its very bottom and to show this bottom in all its filth and abomination."[54] Late nineteenth-century critics did, however, approve of episodes in which they detected direct social criticism, in accord with the literary tendency of the time to depict the

---

[50] *Russkii mir* 55 (1875: February 27), quoted in A.V. Arkhipova, "*Dostoevskii i estetika bezobraznogo*," 51.

[51] *Odesskii vestnik* 58 (1875: March 13), quoted in Arkhipova, "*Dostoevskii i estetika bezobraznogo*," 51.

[52] Arkhipova, "*Dostoevskii i estetika bezobraznogo*", 51.

[53] *Ibid.*

[54] N.K. Mikhailovsky, "Dostoevsky's Cruel Talent," in *Fedor Dostoevsky: Notes from Underground*, A Norton Critical Edition, New York/London: Norton & Company, 141.

hardships of the poor and oppressed as a consequence of social inequality. Thus they found something familiar in 'episode with the girl who hangs herself' (*The Raw Youth*), or the Dickensian motifs of "The Boy at Christ's Christmas Party".[55]

Chernyshevsky, in his dissertation *The Aesthetic Relations of Art to Reality* (1855) and his work *The Sublime and the Comic*, uses the idea that "the beautiful is life" to arrive at a definition of the ugly as an opposition to beauty, a deformation of normal development, a monstrosity, the result of illness, hardships, unfavourable circumstances – i. e., as an objective phenomenon.[56] He describes the relationship of the ugly to the sublime, in which the former is transformed from the repulsive to the horrible.[57] For Chernyshevsky, the ugly in art is most frequently manifested in the comic. He writes that "in the comic the ugly is unpleasant for us; what is pleasant is that … we come to the realisation that the ugly *is* ugly" [*Nepriiatno v komicheskom nam bezobrazie; priiatno to, chto my … postigaem, chto bezobraznoe – bezobrazno.*][58]

The ugly (*bezobraznoe*) differs from the low (*nizmennoe*) which, as an aesthetic category, is opposed to the sublime (*vozvyshennoe*). The ugly is "dead, pathological, non-spiritual, unwholesome, lacking integrity, inner light and richness. [*Bezobraznoe – iavlenia mertvennye, patologichnye, neodukhotvorennye, lishennye tselostnosti, vnutrennego sveta i bogatstva.*] The low, for its part, is the ugly and the horrible taken to the extreme; it is, in contrast to the ugly, not merely the result of necessity.[59] It is that part of the ugly which is commonly associated with evil. Again, Aristotle was the first in the history of aesthetics to use the category of 'the low', in describing Menalaeus from Euripides' *Orestes*.[60] Jackson, in his chapter "The Sentencing of Fedor Karamazov" from his *Art of Dostoevsky*, discusses the classical Greek elements in the aesthetics of *The Brothers Karamazov*.[61] He emphasises the tragic role of fate in the lives of Dostoevsky's evil and ugly protagonists; for example, Jackson compares the role of fate in the portrayal of Agamemnon's life (*Oresteia*) to its role for Fedor Karamazov.[62]

---

[55] Arkhipova, *"Dostoevskii i estetika bezobraznogo"*, 51.

[56] N.G. Chernyshevsky, *Izbrannye filosofskie sochineniia*, Vol. 1, Moscow: *Gosizdat. polit. lit.*, 1950, 62-63.

[57] *Ibid.*, 66-67.

[58] *Ibid.*, 293.

[59] A.A. Beliaev, et al., eds., *Estetika*, Moscow: *Politizdat*, 1989, 28, 235.

[60] Aristotle, *Poetics*, Part XV.

[61] Bakhtin also focuses on classical Greek elements in Dostoevsky's art, his main interest being the Menippean satire and the carnival culture, the immediate constituents of which are the low and the comical as aesthetic elements. See his *Problemy poetiki Dostoevskogo*.

[62] R. L. Jackson, *The Art of Dostoevsky: Deliriums and Nocturnes*, Princeton, New Jersey: Princeton U Press, 1981, 305.

The horrible as an aesthetic category embraces events over which people possesses no control, and which bring misfortune and death.[63] It is associated with disasters, frightening events and with the death of the beautiful; and it leaves one without hope.[64] The tragic differs from the horrible in that it always involves a degree of hope for a positive solution in the future. It derives its grandeur from the fact that the tragic hero retains some control over his circumstances – from which his death eventually frees him.[65] In the horrible, the hero is enslaved by circumstances, and has no power over them. The horrible is typical of eschatological conceptions – of the eternal tortures of hell, and the like.[66] It conveys a feeling of global catastrophe and despair.

Richard Pope in his article on evil in *The Devils* refers to Hannah Arendt's view of the horrible as something which "can be not only ludicrous but outright funny."[67] He links evil with the ugly, writing that Dostoevsky reduced evil to "something ugly, banal, and ludicrous, though still pre-eminently dangerous."[68] Pope also refers to the "carnival tradition" which Dostoevsky drew upon in his depictions of evil.[69] In defining evil by means of the ugly and comic, and referring to Bakhtin's argument based on the study of the characteristics of Ancient literature, Pope treats the ugly along the lines of Greek and Roman aesthetics – i. e., as primarily a category of the comic.

Ugliness forms a binary opposition with beauty, and Jackson affirms that Dostoevsky does not consider beauty ambivalent – but his characters do, since it is they who find beauty in Sodom.[70] Vasilii Zenkovsky, too, emphasises the ambiguity of the human perception of beauty:

> This is what Dostoevsky understood by his thought that "the aesthetic idea has grown dim in humanity" – to be precise, that we can find beauty in sin and (moral) ugliness: "what seems a disgrace to the intellect (that is, to moral consciousness) seems to the heart to be nothing but beauty."

---

[63] *Ibid.*, 363.
[64] *Ibid.*
[65] *Ibid.*
[66] *Ibid.*
[67] Richard Pope, "Peter Verkhovensky and the Banality of Evil," *Dostoevsky and the Twentieth Century*, Nottingham: Astra Press, 1993, 45.
[68] *Ibid.*, 39.
[69] *Ibid.*, 45.
[70] R.L. Jackson, *Dostoevsky's Quest for Form: A Study of his Philosophy of Art*, New Haven: Yale U Press, 1966, 64.

[Eto i est' to, chto Dostoevskii ponial v svoei mysli, chto "esteticheskaia ideia pomutilas' v chelovechestve" – a imenno, chto my mozhem nakhodit' krasotu v grekhe i bezobrazii (moral'nom): "chto umu (to est' moral'nomu soznaniiu) predstavliaetsia pozorom, to serdtsu splosh krasotoi."][71]

On the other hand, Jackson admits that Dostoevsky *de facto* recognised the beauty of Sodom, one which is "indifferent to moral context and experienced by man as pleasurable disharmony."[72] The dimming of the aesthetic idea is shamelessly worded by Fedor Karamazov in his statement "my mind has never been so darkened before..."[73] Dostoevsky's ugly characters live in a world of "unprecedented eclipse," a universe without sun or morality.[74]

As Jackson affirms, Dostoevsky's de-formed characters are searching for form and moral structure.[75] The form or image (*obraz*) in Dostoevsky's Christian aesthetics is an ideal of beauty. Accordingly, *bezobrazie* is the antithesis of that which has form or image.[76] In Russian, *obraz* can mean "form," "shape," "image," and "icon." In Dostoevsky, the problem of the lack of *obraz* is frequently touched upon. The dark characters who discuss it include Ippolit Terent'ev in *The Idiot*. Ippolit expresses doubts about the possibility of conceiving "a beautiful or spiritual image that is ugly or lacking in spirituality."[77] Jackson also asserts the centrality of the problem of *obraz* and *bezobrazie* in Dostoevsky's practical poetics, in which *bezobrazie*, ugliness, includes crime (desecration) and punishment (retribution) as well as "moral and aesthetic shapelessness and the loss of all sense of measure and form."[78] The ugly in Dostoevsky's art is a negatively realised "worship of aesthetic and spiritual beauty" that includes sensualism.[79] According to Jackson, the syndrome of evil in Dostoevsky is constituted by "unbridled sensuality, the craving for absolute power, and possessiveness (the acquisitive instinct)," often developing into a habit of tyranny.[80] For the 'reptiles' and sensualists of Dostoevsky's novels, the ugly and evil are "rampant, evil is unpunished, evil prevails."[81] Dostoevsky

[71] V.V. Zen'kovsky, "*Problema krasoty v mirosozertsanii Dostoevskogo*," *Russkie emigranty o Dostoevskom*, ed. Belov, S.V., St. Peterburg: *Andreev i synov'ia*, 1994, 233.
[72] Jackson, *Dostoevsky's Quest for Form*, 65.
[73] Dostoevsky, *Brothers Karamazov*, "Over Brandy," (III,8).
[74] Jackson, *The Art of Dostoevsky*, 311.
[75] Jackson, *Dostoevsky's Quest for Form*, 1966, 65.
[76] *Ibid.*, 68.
[77] R.L. Jackson, *Dialogues with Dostoevsky: The Overwhelming Questions*, Stanford U Press: Stanford, 309.
[78] Jackson, *The Art of Dostoevsky*, 304-305.
[79] *Ibid.*, 308-310.
[80] *Ibid.*, 82-83.
[81] *Ibid.*, 310.

himself insists on the inner beauty of the Russian people that counteracts their superficial, circumstantial ugliness:

> Where the Russian common man of the people is concerned, one must be able to abstract his beauty from the alluvial barbarism. Owing to the circumstances of almost our entire history, our people have been subjected to depravity and have been debauched, tempted, and constantly tortured to such an extent that it is still amazing how they managed to survive and still preserve a human image as well. A true friend of humanity ... will excuse all the impassable alluvial filth in which our people are sunk and will be able to seek out diamonds in this filth.[82]

The innate beauty (image) of the Russian people is darkened by their surface ugliness (*bezobrazie*). Dostoevsky tries to solve the dilemma of human nature. It is not only beauty that seems to be innate, but also ugliness, the potential for evil: "man is made in the image of God; but the potential for evil in him, like the potential for good, Dostoevsky clearly implies, is rooted in his nature."[83] It is probable that he arrived at his views on ugly as evil not without the influence of Schelling, a protean philosopher, at some point a Kantian, whose major work is called *A Treatise on Evil* (Böse). Jackson (like Pope) suggests that since beauty has religious and moral connotations for Dostoevsky, what is ugly also becomes evil.[84] He also insists that "*obraz* and *bezobrazie* enter deeply into the artistic fabric and design of *The Brothers Karamazov*."[85] These are central concepts for a number of other works as well; the present study will be primarily focussed on *bezobrazie* and *bezobraznoe* in Dostoevsky's "Notes from Underground" and *Crime and Punishment*.[86]

I will examine Dostoevsky's poetics to see how he depicts ugliness artistically, beautifully, and by which means his aesthetic views are reflected in his works. Dostoevsky's poetics of the ugly and evil are rich; at moments of the triumph of ugliness in his works, space becomes suspended and time circumscribed.[87] I will also acknowledge the connection between Dostoevsky, Mamleev, and Petrushevskaia through humour. The individual in his ugliness is alienated in this time and space; he is

---

[82] Dostoevsky, *PSS* [henceforth D-*PSS*], Vol. 11, Leningrad: *Nauka*, 1973, 187.
[83] Jackson, *The Art of Dostoevsky*, 78-80.
[84] *Ibid.*, 23-24.
[85] *Ibid.*, 18.
[86] This is not to say that Jackson thinks that *The Brothers Karamazov* is the only work in which *obraz* and *bezobrazie* are central concepts. See, for instance, his study of *The House of the Dead* [*Zapiski iz mertvogo doma*]
[87] Jackson, *The Art of Dostoevsky*, 95.

"vanishing into the blindness and darkness of his ice-bound self."[88] I am mostly interested in disharmonious images of harmony envisioned by Dostoevsky's characters, the moments when they enjoy ugliness, when "there is no form or beauty – *obraz*; there is only shapelessness – *bezobrazie*."[89]

The problem of ugliness in art is a classical question of aesthetics. Ippolit seems to be voicing his creator's own concerns when he asks: "Can one realize in an image that which is ugly? Can that which is monstrous and evil, full of disharmony and discord, be depicted in an aesthetically attractive way?"[90] According to Jackson, supreme artists like Turgenev, Dostoevsky, or Tolstoy are capable of both looking at and into ugliness (*bezobraznoe*), depicting it so that it "reveals its meaning in the larger frame of moral truth or image (*obraz*) – that is, the truth of man created in the image and likeness of God."[91] For Dostoevsky as for many other nineteenth-century Russian writers, this discussion relates to Hugo's ideas on ugliness in art. Hugo's formula – "le laid, c'est le beau" – was understood literally by social and democratic critics who used it as a foundation for the Natural School. What Hugo actually means, however, is that even truly ugly people or events can be beautifully depicted. Thus his focus is more on the issue of artistic mastery, and less on social injustice. As for Dostoevsky, he understands Hugo's formula as "a Christian and supreme moral idea."[92] For him *bezobraznoe* is not the norm, but a deviation from it. And Hugo, in his opinion, does not consider the ugly to be beautiful, but is merely accepting it into the domain of aesthetics.[93]

Dostoevsky holds that the visual arts are unable to depict the ugly from the 'redeeming' perspective (Holbein's painting of Christ in the tomb, Klodt's painting of a consumptive girl); his own practical poetics, however, allows for the depiction of ugly character types as long as the aim of these depictions is redemption. Jackson says that the theme of restoration of the fallen man in Dostoevsky "points to its aesthetic premises, or its poetic."[94]

Beauty and ugliness – the ideal and the vile – co-exist in the hearts of Dostoevsky's characters and form the notion of *homo duplex* expressed in his works. Arkadii Dolgoruky (*A Raw Youth*) observes:

---

[88] *Ibid.*
[89] *Ibid.*, 331.
[90] *Ibid.*
[91] Jackson, *Dialogues with Dostoevsky*, 37.
[92] Jackson, *Dostoevsky's Quest for Form*, 68.
[93] *Ibid.*, 69.
[94] Jackson, *The Art of Dostoevsky*, 39.

A thousand times I have been amazed at this faculty of man (and, it seems, chiefly the Russian man) to cherish in his soul the most lofty ideal side by side with the most extreme vileness, and all this absolutely sincerely. Whether this is a special breadth in the Russian which will take him far, or simply vileness – that is the question.[95]

A tragic paradox of the ugly (*bezobraznoe*) in Dostoevsky's Russia is that the environment in which everybody with a bit of power beats his nearest neighbour is also the environment in which the icon (*obraz*) hangs in everybody's house.[96] Another tragedy Dostoevsky discusses is that of the underground, about which he writes in his notebook for *The Raw Youth*:

I take pride in the fact that I was the first to bring forth the real man of the *Russian majority* and was the first to expose his disfigured and tragic side. The tragedy consists in the consciousness of disfiguration ... I alone brought into the open the tragedy of the underground, consisting in suffering, self-punishment, the consciousness of something better and the impossibility of achieving that something, and chiefly consisting in the clear conviction of these unfortunate people that all are alike, and hence it is not even worth trying to improve! What is there to support those who wish to reform themselves? Consolation, faith? There is consolation from no one, faith in no one! But another step from here and one finds depravity, crime (murder). Mystery.[97]

Strakhov writes about the spiritual abysses of moral corruption in Dostoevsky's works, stating that: "he comes out of them unharmed, that is, without losing the measure of good and evil, of the beautiful and the monstrous."[98] A separate element of evil is violence, which is connected with the issue of guilt and suffering: "We are all guilty because in one way or another we are making other people suffer and enjoying that suffering; we are guilty because in each of us lies the propensity for violence and evil."[99]Goncharov blamed Dostoevsky for depicting the "disfigured world of the underground and the formless life of contemporary 'accidental families.'"[100] According to Morson, the dispute between

---

[95] *The Raw Youth*, (III, 3).
[96] Jackson, *The Art of Dostoevsky*, 103.
[97] D-*PSS*, 16:329.
[98] *Istoriko-kriticheskii kommentarii k sochineniam F.M. Dostoevskogo*, 1, 91.
[99] Jackson, *Dialogues with Dostoevsky*, 5.
[100] Gary Saul Morson, *The Boundaries of the Genre: Dostoevsky's "Diary of a Writer" and the Traditions of Literary Utopia*, Austin: U of Texas Press, 1981, 8.

"conventional descriptions of a beautiful past" and Dostoevsky's depictions of contemporary disfigured society "can be taken as emblematic of that between nineteenth-century realism and twentieth-century modernism."[101] My book will attempt to take this emblem further in time, to the twentieth and twenty-first centuries.

Chapter II: The Ugly in Dostoevsky's "Notes from Underground"

Despite the famous statement – often ascribed to Dostoevsky personally – in *The Idiot* about beauty saving the world, he is best known for his depictions of the ugly and monstrous sides of life and the human soul. It seems that it is the dark, evil, and sensual beauty of Sodom that Dostoevsky is most interested in – or, perhaps, most successful at portraying. The moment he focuses on is often the one of victory of the ugly side of the human heart. This chapter will investigate the ugly (*bezobraznoe*) in "Notes from Underground:" the notions of harmony and disharmony as pertaining to Dostoevsky's aesthetics, the issues of individualism and egotism of the Underground Philosopher, his failed social contacts, and the opposition of visual/stable vs. verbal/fluctuating. The chapter will also demonstrate the poetic means and imagery resorted by Dostoevsky, when it comes to ugliness.

The ugly in Dostoevsky is indirectly formulated either by his fictional narrators and characters, or by the author himself in his letters, articles, and the Writer's Diary [*Dnevnik pisatelia*]. *Bezobraznoe* in all his various works has the same broad definition: it refers to that which is lacking in harmony, order, morality, religious feeling, stable structure, or form; to the chaotic and asocial. In Dostoevsky's later works (beginning with *Raw Youth*), *bezobraznyi* is opposed to *blagoobraznyi*, thus, emphasising the amorality and the lack of religious feeling that is included in the polysemantic meaning of the ugly.[102] *Bezobraznyi* [imageless] is used along with *otvratitel'nyi* [repulsive], and *urodlivyi* [ugly], which are employed interchangeably. It is peculiar that Dostoevsky almost never uses the common Russian word '*nekrasivyi*' [unbeautiful]; it is too weak, too morally neutral for Dostoevsky as beauty

---

[101] *Ibid.*

[102] "*Blago*" is Russian for "grace," immediately suggesting "God's grace" to the reader, and "*obraz*" is "image," from Greek "εἰκών," an icon (archaic). M. Fasmer, *Etimologicheskii slovar' russkogo iazyka*, Vol. 2, Moscow: Progress, 1964, 106. "*Blago*" is often used in words with two roots and corresponds to the Greek "εὐ-," for example, "*blagochestivyi*," "*blagonravnyi*," "*blagorodnyi*." M. Fasmer, *Etimologicheskii slovar' russkogo iazyka*, Vol. 1, Moscow: Progress, 1964, 170.

for him has moral and religious connotations. This is also the reason why he employs the word for ugliness that with its root "*obraz*" emphasises the lack of the *image* of God – of moral and religious value.

In his note to N.I. Solovev's article "Theory of the Ugly" ["*Teoriia bezobraziia*," *Epokha* 1864 (7), section 5, page 8] directed against D.I. Pisarev and V.I. Zaitsev, Dostoevsky agrees with the author's main idea: "if the ideal of morality and beauty is taken from humanity, the **ugly** is all that is left to it" [*esli otniat' u chelovechestva ideal nravstvennosti i krasoty, to ostanetsia tol'ko bezobrazie.*][103] Here, *bezobrazie* implies more than just ugliness; in its semantics, it includes a lack of order and a moral ugliness; and *bezobraznoe* denotes disorder and amorality as opposites of beauty. Solovev, a medical doctor by training, was enthusiastically supported by Dostoevsky as an editor of the journal *Epokha*. Among the ideas which Dostoevsky shares with Solovev is a view of art as a development of nature, essentially the Romantic view expressed by the scholar Haeckel, who regarded nature as art, and by Goethe, whose Doctor Faust is both a poet and a scientist.[104]

A quintessence of the ugly is the figure of the Underground Man: he is maximally non-harmonic, chaotic, and inconsistent. Besides, he is asocial, although he cannot bear the fact that he needs others for his self-affirmation.[105] As portrayed in Dostoevsky's fiction (i.e. "Notes from Underground," *The Devils, The Brothers Karamazov, Crime and Punishment*), unsociability, lack of social skills, and opposing oneself to society, are ugly (*bezobrazny*), since society's approval is vital for the individual. One could argue that in Dostoevsky's works, the subject needs another subject to affirm itself; the second subject is needed to reflect the best sides of the first subject's ego. The Underground Man reveals his ugliness in his failed relationship with real life; he is unable to have working social contacts with other people. This problem is also reflected in his speech, which presupposes an interlocutor but does not have one. Compare Dostoevsky's attempt at a positive, 'beautiful' hero, Alesha Karamazov, who has to return to the secular world in order to test his virtues there, since the beauty of this character can only be valid in the context of society.[106] Dostoevsky depicts recluses and those 'living in corners' as ugly; the loners in his works also typically have dwellings with disproportionate, distorted interiors which reflect the lack of harmony, the ugliness, of their inner

---

[103] D-*PSS*, 20:228, 417.
[104] *Ibid.*, 418. David Lebrun, *Proteus*, USA, 2003, film.
[105] This is seen in the episode with Liza, for example.
[106] Potentially, Alesha would have to become a great sinner before he becomes a "saint" again. This is a typical Dostoevskian way of testing his characters by sending them of a quest full of temptations. It's their choice that makes them saint-like.

world. The assumption that reality is a window to this inner world was a basis of Romanticism.[107] The influence of European Romanticism, as well as that of Nikolai Gogol's native combination of romanticism and realism, are among the reasons for Donald Fanger to classify Dostoevsky as an inheritor of the romantic realists.[108]

The focus on buildings and apartments is not incidental for Dostoevsky; he had studied architecture as a student of the St. Petersburg Academy of Military Engineers. It was one of his favourite subjects, and its lessons remained with him throughout his writing career, as we see from the sketches of architectural details that he left in his notebooks.[109] The Underground Man complains that his schoolfellows "must have despised me for ... my having let myself sink so low, going about badly dressed..."[110] [*dolzhny byli prezirat' menia ...za to, chto ia uzh ochen' opustilsia, khodil v durnom plat'e...*][111] He needs his comrades' approval; otherwise he would not be so worried about his clothes at the farewell dinner with Zverkov. This is also another proof of the fact that in Dostoevsky a subject needs to be mirrored in another subject as a confirmation of his or her existence.

Alienated existence is related to the famous concept of the underground developed by Dostoevsky in his "Notes." Jackson writes in his *Dostoevsky's Underground Man in Russian Literature* that the "landscape for the tragedy of the 'underground' is Russian reality."[112] He emphasises the reality of the underground for Dostoevsky and quotes his Notebooks for *The Raw Youth* to highlight his point about the Underground Man being a representative of the disfigured Russian majority, living in the "tragedy of the underground."[113] The underground is in the focus of my research, inasmuch as it reflects the ugliness of the "consciousness of disfigurement."

In Jackson's opinion, the underground has a two-fold nature: it is the real world of St. Petersburg, and also the Underground Man's inner world. "It is a 'misfortune' to live in Petersburg," says the Underground Man; "Petersburg is a silent grave," says Jackson.[114] The fantastic, premeditated city twists its dwellers and deforms them. In the Underground Man's inner world, self-consciousness

---

[107] Lebrun, *Proteus*.

[108] Donald Fanger, *Dostoevsky and Romantic Realism: A Study of Dostoevsky in Relation to Balzac, Dickens, and Gogol'*, Cambridge: Harvard U Press, 1965, 101.

[109] See Konstantin Barsht's article on the Gothic drawings of Dostoevsky ("*Goticheskii ieroglif Dostoevskogo*," *Novoe literaturnoe obozrenie*, 39 (1999)).

[110] Fyodor Dostoevsky, *Notes from Underground. Poor People. The Friend of the Family*, trans. Constance Garnett, New York: Dell Publishing Co., 1960, 76. Further English-language references to the "Notes" will follow the Garnett translation, modified where necessary for accuracy and clarity.

[111] D-*PSS*, 5:135.

[112] R.L. Jackson, *Dostoevsky's Underground Man in Russian Literature*, The Hague: Mouton & Co, 1958, 28.

[113] *Ibid.*, 28-29.

[114] *Ibid.*, 29.

prevails over the "relationship with the real world."[115] Dostoevsky thought about the relationship between real life and inner life and the necessity of balance between the two prior to writing "Notes from Underground." While working on the novella "The Landlady" ["*Khoziaika*"], Dostoevsky develops his ideas about "dreamers" and writes to his brother Mikhail about the loss of the "equilibrium" between the individual inner and social life in Russian society of the time:

> Of course, terrible is the dissonance, terrible is the imbalance that society presents to us. The external should be in equilibrium with the internal. Otherwise, in the absence of external phenomena, the internal gains a too-dangerous upper hand. Nerves and imagination take up too much place in one's being. Every external phenomenon seems, from our unfamiliarity with it, to be colossal and is somehow frightening. We begin to fear life.

> [*Konechno, strashen dissonans, strashno neravnovesie, kotoroe predstavliaet nam obshchestvo. **Vne** dolzhno byt' uravnovesheno s **vnutrennim**. Inache, s otsutstviem vneshnikh iavlenii, vnutrennee voz'met slishkom opasnyi verkh. Nervy i fantaziia zaimut ochen' mnogo mesta v sushchestve. Vsiakoe vneshenee iavlenie s neprivychki kazhetsia kolossal'nym i pugaet kak-to. Nachinaesh' boiat'sia zhizni.*][116]

"Notes from Underground" demonstrates this lack of equilibrium/harmony in St. Petersburg society, and portrays the underground as the conception of all reality as "a prison of reason and logic."[117] Dostoevsky describes the underground as a product of the Underground Man's consciousness, his inner state: "A grim **idea** came into my brain and passed all over my body, as a horrible sensation, such as one feels when one goes into a damp and mouldy **cellar**" [*Ugriumaia **mysl'** zarodilas' v moem mozgu i proshla po vsemu telu kakim-to skvernym oshchushcheniem, pokhozhim na to, kogda vkhodish v **podpol'e**, syroe i zatkhloe ...*][118] Even if the Underground Man happened to live in a crystal palace, he would still have carried his underground with him. In Dostoevsky's conception, the ugly (*bezobraznoe*) is most repulsive and dangerous when it is an aspect of one's inner world; he focuses on the ugliness of the distorted dreams and twisted consciousness of his characters, and of the

---

[115] *Ibid.*, 30.
[116] D-*PSS*, 28.1:137-38. Letter 71 (1847). Emphasis by Dostoevsky.
[117] Jackson, *Dostoevsky's Underground Man*, 30.
[118] D-*PSS*, 5:152. Garnett translation, 101.

Underground Man in particular. The thought of this character becomes the underground; its ugliness is the ugliness of the thought. The underground is ugly in its separation from the rest of the world. It is also a characteristic of the Underground Man's soul:

> And so, **furtively**, timidly, **in solitude**, at night, I **indulged in** filthy **vice**, with a feeling of shame which never deserted me, even at the most loathsome moments, and which at such moments nearly made me curse. Already even then I had my **underground world** in my soul.

> [*Razvratnichal ia **uedinnenno**, po nocham, **potaenno**, boiazlivo, griazno, so stydom, ne ostavliavshim menia v samye omerzitel'nye minuty i dazhe dokhodivshim v takie minuty do prokliatiia. Ya uzh i togda nosil v dushe moei **podpol'e**.*][119]

The Underground Man complains that he is always alone: "*Voobshche zhe ia vsegda byl odin.*"[120] He steadily grows uglier and uglier while remaining by himself:

> One longed for **movement** in spite of everything, and I **plunged** all at once **into** dark, underground, loathsome **vice** of the pettiest kind ... I had an hysterical craving for **incongruity** and for **contrast**, and so I took to **vice**.

> [*Vse-taki khotelos' **dvigat'sia**, i ia vdrug **pogruzhalsia** v **temnyi**, **podzemnyi**, **gadkii** – ne **razvrat**, a razvratishko ... iavlialas' istericheskaia zhazhda **protivorechii**, **kontrastov**, i vot ia i puskalsia razvratnichat' ...*][121]

The disintegration of the individual, the chaos in which he finds himself, is frequently associated with the notion of "*razvrat*" in Dostoevsky. The sinful nature of the underground is hinted at in the Underground Man's remark regarding his amorality (*razvrat*). This is in addition to the obvious association with the forces of evil, whose traditional habitat is the underworld (*podpol'e/podzemel'e*).

The Underground Man ruins the harmony that is idealised as beauty in Dostoevsky; consequently, he is actively ugly in his destruction:

---

[119] D-*PSS*, 5:128. Garnett translation, 65.
[120] D-*PSS*, 5:127.
[121] D-*PSS*, 5:127. Garnett translation, 64-65.

It really is stupid. We have met here, a company of friends, for a farewell dinner to a comrade and you carry on an altercation," – said Trudoliubov [an overtly positive last name], rudely addressing himself to me alone. "You invited yourself to join us, so **don't disturb the general harmony.**"

[*Deistvitel'no, glupo, my sobralis' v druzheskoi kompanii, chtob provodit' v voiazh dobrogo priiatelia, a vy schitaetes', – zagovoril Trudoliubov, grubo obrashchaias' ko mne odnomu. – Vy k nam sami vchera naprosilis', ne rasstraivaite zhe obshchei garmonii.*][122]

It is very likely that the idea of harmony as beauty came to Dostoevsky from Friedrich Schiller, for whom beauty was a harmonious development of emotional and spiritual elements, and for whom harmonious unity was crucial in aesthetic perception.[123] Schiller also emphasised the priority of form over contents, writing that

In einem wahrhaft schönen Kunstwerk soll der Inhalt nichts, **die Form aber alles tun**; denn durch die Form allein wird auf das Ganze des Menschen, durch den Inhalt hingegen nur auf einzelne Kräfte gewirkt. Der Inhalt, wie erhaben und weitumfassend er auch sei, wirkt also jederzeit einschränkend auf den Geist, und nur von der Form wahre ästhetische Freiheit zu erwarten.[124]

Edmund Kostka, in his excellent study of Schiller's heritage in Russian literature, affirms that there was no other Western writer who influenced Dostoevsky as much as the German poet. At the age of ten, Dostoevsky saw a performance of *Die Räuber* [*The Robbers*] with Mochalov in a leading role and recalled that the impression of this play "acted as an enormous stimulation for my entire spiritual development."[125] Schiller was Dostoevsky's major source of youthful enthusiasm and "with his aestheticism and his unshakeable faith in the essential identity of the Good and the Beautiful, had

---

[122] *Ibid.*, 144. Garnett translation, 89.
[123] F. Schiller, "Über die notwendigen Grenzen beim Gebrauch schöner Formen," *Ausgewählte Werke*, Vol. 5, Darmstadt: Wissenschaftliche Buchgemeinschaft E. V., 1954, 143.
[124] Friedrich Schiller, *Ausgewählte Kostbarkeiten*, Lahr: SKV-Edition, 1981, 14.
[125] F.M. Dostoevsky, *Polnoe sobranie sochinenii*, St. Petersburg, 1883-1904, I, 119 (Appendix), quoted in Edmund K. Kostka, *Schiller in Russian Literature*, Philadelphia: U of Pennsylvania Press, 1965, 215.

inspired [Dostoevsky] to occupy himself with these problems of aesthetics."[126] In his *Critique of Judgement*, Immanuel Kant states that "that proportionate accord [*Stimmung*] (mood, atmosphere) which we require for all cognition", i.e. harmony (order, form), is the essential component of beauty.[127] Kant's heritage is evident in Schiller's aesthetics. Schiller, as a son of the Age of Enlightenment, was convinced that all necessary knowledge had already been discovered by humanity, and that in order to transform it morally, art should be used. Art and aesthetics would educate people, who would become moral, and the natural state (based on the rule of force) would become the moral state (based on moral law).

In the article "Mr. – bov and the Question of Art", Dostoevsky expresses a view on the aesthetic education of man similar to that of Schiller. He mentions that seeing a beautiful work of art could effect one's whole life; this work of art is an ideal of beauty, a standard that could be used in relation to other works of art to decide whether they are beautiful or not. Without identifying Dostoevsky with his characters, I ought to mention that in "Notes from Underground," the Underground Man has few illusions as to the possibility of transforming life with the help of art. He does not believe that art, even great art, can save humanity on its own and confesses that the more he "became conscious of the Good and of all that Beautiful and Sublime,' the deeper [he] sank into [his] mud."[128] Dostoevsky supplements Schiller's idea of the superiority of the aesthetic man with the religious element; his positive character is not the aesthetic man but the religious man (Father Zosima, Alesha).[129] Basing his argument on what one can infer from Dostoevsky's fiction, and cautiously attempting to avoid fusing the views of the writer and his protagonists, Kostka suggests that Dostoevsky considers the idea of the aesthetic man as a concept dangerous to the idea of God and a moral world order. This viewpoint is justified by twentieth-century philosophy (Nietzsche's "Übermensch").[130] As opposed to Schiller, Dostoevsky (in his later years) does not seem to believe that beauty *by itself* can "create a stable equilibrium [harmony] between the forces of good and evil struggling in the soul of man."[131]

The original musical concept of harmony refers to the aesthetic effect of notes that are played at the same time, i.e., as chords. In this sense, I could describe the Underground Man's note as being out of accord with those of his so-called friends. Dostoevsky, in his debate with the ideas of N.G.

---

[126] Kostka, *Schiller in Russian Literature*, 217.
[127] Berys Gaut and Dominic McIver Lopes, eds. *The Routledge Companion to Aesthetics*, London/New York: Routledge, 2001, 55.
[128] Dostoevsky, *Polnoe sobranie khudozhestvennykh proizvedenii*, Vol. 4, Moscow/Leningrad: *Khudozhestvennaia literatura*, 1926-28, 112.
[129] Kostka, *Schiller in Russian Literature*, 247-248.
[130] *Ibid.*
[131] *Ibid.*

Chernyshevsky's *What Is To Be Done*, argues that "science itself will teach man ... that he himself is something of the nature of a piano-key or the stop of an organ ..." [*sama nauka nauchit cheloveka ...chto on sam ne bolee, kak nechto vrode fortep'iannoi klavishi ili organnogo shtiftika...*][132] The Underground Man is opposed to any idea of using mathematical formulae to calculate all human desires and caprices which, as he states, may be a logical development of the ideas of rational egotists.[133] The commentary to the Academy edition mentions that the Underground Man's statement – "I am a man and not a piano key" [*Ia chelovek, a ne fortep'iannaia klavisha*] – refers to Diderot's *Conversation between D'Alambert and Diderot* (1769), in which it is stated: "We are instruments gifted with the ability to feel and remember. Our feelings are keys which hit the nature surrounding us and which often hit themselves."[134] Joseph Frank argues that the musical imagery comes directly from Fourier and that the commentary attempts to make "The Notes" "more easily assimilable in a Soviet Russian context."[135] Vladimir Seduro, a scholar of the Russian and Soviet reception of Dostoevsky, writes that it is impossible to understand Vladimir Ul'ianov-Lenin's attitude towards Dostoevsky without an understanding of Maksim Gor'ky's view of this nineteenth-century novelist, and that Lenin's understanding of Dostoevsky "to a great extent determined the subsequent development of Soviet criticism" of him.[136]

Leonid Grossman's criticism of Dostoevsky is an example of how critical ideas changed under official party influence: his *Path of Dostoevsky* [*Dostoevsky: Put', Poetika, Tvorchestvo*], dating from the NEP period, defends "Dostoevsky's work in its entirety as a philosophical drama," whereas his later "Dostoevsky and Government Circles in the 1870s" ["*Dostoevsky i pravitel'stvennye krugi 1870-kh godov*"] attacks Dostoevsky's ideology and Dolinin's view of Dostoevsky (based on the latter's fiction) as a mirror of the Russian revolution in the manner of Lenin's Tolstoy. Grossman bases his conclusions on Dostoevsky's non-fiction (his description of socialism as a "visionary evil," for example), and reflects the general change in Dostoevsky criticism determined by party policy at the time.[137] Gor'ky, for his part, claimed that all of Friedrich Nietzsche could already be found in "Notes

---

[132] D-*PSS*, 5:112. Garnett translation, 44.
[133] Here Dostoevsky prefigures the mathematical calculations of E. Zamiatin's anti-utopia *We*. J. Stalin's "screws of a joint mechanism" may also be a historical descendent of the ideas of rational egotism.
[134] D-*PSS*, 5:384.
[135] Joseph Frank, *The Stir of Liberation: 1860-1865*, Princeton: Princeton U Press, 1986, 325.
[136] Vladimir Seduro, *Dostoevsky in Russian Literary Criticism: 1846-1956*, NY: Octagon Books, 1969, vii. A practical explanation of Maksim Gor'ky's influence on Ul'ianov-Lenin is that the former had a house on the island of Capri in Italy, where the latter stayed 'hiding from arrest' for prolonged periods of time.
[137] Vladimir Seduro, "Leonid Petrovich Grossman (1888-): From Apologetics to Accusation," *Dostoevsky in Russian Literary Criticism: 1846-1956*, NY: Octagon Books, 1969, 183-185.

from Underground." He saw the "Notes" as a universal and, particularly – European, justification of nihilism and anarchism. And although Gor'ky considered Dostoevsky more subtle than Nietzsche, he still associated the author with his protagonist, and was highly critical of what he believed to be Dostoevsky's "aestheticization of the Underground Man's rebellion."[138] After Lenin's use of the piano key metaphor in his "Materialism and Empiriocriticism" (1908), it frequently appeared in Soviet writings as a mechanistic metaphor for the material nature of human feelings; and the Underground Man's extreme individualism – his refusal to participate in the 'harmony' of society – was not welcomed by Soviet writers and critics, for whom individualism was a sign of disorder.

Although the issue of whether or not Dostoevsky was familiar with Immanuel Kant is still being debated, he was certainly influenced by Friedrich Schiller, in whose works Kant's legacy is well established.[139] Kant affirmed the principle of the unintelligibility of God and immortality, as they do not belong to the sphere of empirical knowledge, but to the sphere of "things in themselves," ready-made forms of being.[140] Music and other arts provide beautiful and ready-made forms of being, says the Underground Man; his escapist fantasies go hand in hand with his disorderly existence. The beautiful forms of being are borrowed from poetry and novels; in the Underground Man's imagination they are a substitute for the ugly chaos he finds himself in:

Everything, however, passed satisfactorily by a lazy and fascinating transition into the sphere of art, that is, into the **beautiful forms of life**, lying ready, **largely stolen from the poets and novelists** and adapted to all sorts of needs and uses.

[*Vse, vprochem, preblagopoluchno vsegda okanchivalos' lenivym i upoitel'nym perekhodom k iskusstvu, to est' k **prekrasnym formam bytiia**, sovsem gotovym, **sil'no ukradennym u poetov i romanistov** i prisposoblennym ko vsevozmozhnym uslugam i trebovaniiam.*][141]

---

[138] D-*PSS*, 5:383.
[139] David A. Goldfarb, "Kant's Aesthetics in Dostoevsky's 'Notes from Undergound'", Mid-Atlantic Slavic Conference, Columbia U, 18 March 1995, http://www.echonyc.com/~goldfarb/u-ground.htm. *The Routledge Companion to Aesthetics*, 55. Anthony J. Cascardi, "Kant, Immanuel," *The Johns Hopkins Guide to Literary Theory and Criticism*, eds. Michael Groden and Martin Kreiswirth, The Johns Hopkins U Press, 1997, http://www.press.jhu.edu/books/guide/. Both websites accessed on September, 29, 2004.
[140] I. Kant, *Sochineniia v 6-ti tomakh*, Vol. 5, Moscow: *Mysl'*, 1966, 469.
[141] D-*PSS*, 5:133. Garnett translation, 73.

Harmony is found in books, whereas at the end of the twentieth century books themselves are a medium of chaos. Creative poetics exists in and is a result of postmodern cultural, linguistic, and ontological chaos – *chaosmos* – probably first expressed in Joyce's *Finnegans Wake*. Joyce's term chaosmos describes "the purest expression of the concept of compromise between chaos and cosmos," the compromise between order and disorder which postmodernism attempts to reach.[142]

In the "Notes," the topic of disorder (*besporiadok*) is closely related to that of the ugly. Disorder is a theme which would become central in twentieth-century literature (Yeats's "widening gyre" and centre that cannot hold, and post-*perestroika* chaos in Russia), and which is frequently treated by Dostoevsky. It receives the most emphasis in the *Diary of a Writer*, in relation to the phenomenon of "accidental families" (*sluchainye semeistva*). Gary Saul Morson confirms that in the *Diary* "the author argues that social 'fragmentation', 'dissociation', and 'isolation' have reached such an extreme that the 'final battle' is almost certainly near."[143] Disorder is an emblematic feature of the Underground Man's existence; it also characterises the environment within which the protagonist of *A Raw Youth* lives. In Dostoevsky's notebooks, the title of this novel was originally *Disorder*:

> Title of the novel: 'Disorder.' The whole idea of the novel is to demonstrate that we now have general **disorder, disorder** everywhere and wherever you go, in society, in business, in guiding ideas (of which – for that very reason – there aren't any), in our convictions (which – for the same reason – we don't have), in the disintegration of the family unit... *Most important*. The idea of disintegration is present everywhere, for everything is falling *apart*, and there are no remaining ties not only in the Russian family, but even simply between people in general. Even children are apart. (*Disintegration is the principal visible idea of the novel*.)[144]

In "Apropos the Wet Snow", the Underground Man himself describes his life as "disorderly": "My life was even then gloomy, **ill-regulated**, and as solitary as that of a savage." [*Zhizn' moia byla uzh i togda ugriumaia, besporiadochnaia i do odichalosti odinokaia*.][145] Disorder (BES*poriadok*) is one of the

---

[142] Mark Lipovetsky, *Russian Postmodernist Fiction: Dialogue with Chaos*, Armonk/London: M.E. Sharpe, 1999, 30.
[143] Morson, *The Boundaries of Genre*, 33.
[144] Francis Spencer, "Form and Disorder in Dostoevsky's *A Raw Youth*" in *F.M. Dostoevsky (1821-1881): A Centenary Collection*, ed. Leon Burnett, University of Essex: Department of Literature, 1981, 37.
[145] D-*PSS*, 5:124. Garnett translation, 60.

characteristics of the ugly (BEZ*ozobraznoe*); the life of the Underground Man without (BEZ) order and form is ugly and lacking in the basic laws he claims he needs to become a better person.

The Underground Man refers to the dreams he has had (*"bezobraznye sny"*); they are called ugly, but no account of them is provided. Instead we have his recollections of his horrible school years. They are so horrible because he thinks of his comrades as being below himself. What is emphasised in these recollections is the amorality of the children at the Underground Man's school; their dreams of a *"teploe mestechko"* in particular.[146] The Underground Man fantasises about sending the officer who has offended him a letter, which he refers to as "the ugliest of anachronisms" [*bezobrazneishii anakhronizm*][147] – i.e., it is ugly precisely because it is too late to send it. The moment when it should have been done has been missed; but the Underground Man tries to reverse the flow of time, to force it to go backwards, distorting its natural form, ruining its harmony. The Underground Man's craving for revenge is ugly because it is ridiculous and disproportionate: he has been feeding on his anger and hurt feelings for a number of years, a curious length of time given the trivial nature of the offence.

The messy state of the Underground Man's clothes sharply contrasts with the military attire of the officer whom he regards as his foe. What bothers the Underground Man most is the *"perekhvat v talii"*, the tight waistline of the officer, which divides his silhouette into two equal parts like the old Russian letter *"fita."* It is the symmetry – order/form – that troubles him more than anything else. The structured look of the officer is also compared with that of the letter *"fert'"*, the old Russian symmetrical "f:" "But of the *ferts* there was one officer in particular I could not endure." [*No iz fertov ia osobenno terpet' ne mog odnogo ofitsera.*][148] The structural stability of the officer's visual image – its symmetry – makes the Underground Man furious. He himself is associated with broken lines; he admits that "I was already longing to expound the cherished ideas I had brooded over in my **corner**." [*ideiki, v **uglu** vyzhitye zhazhdal izlozhit'.*][149] The Russian word for "corner" – *"ugol"* – also means "angle," graphically a broken line. The Underground Man's ideas are supplemented by the *"ugol"* as a sign of disorder. Note that Dostoevsky tends to use the diminutive forms of the common nouns – *"ideiki"* – to bring out a negative connotation in them. Nouns denoting aspects of the ugly are frequently in the diminutive: *"razvratik,"* *"razvtratishko,"* and others. Here Dostoevsky uses diminutive suffixes such as *-ishk-* that tend to lend a negative meaning to a word in Russian. While working on the visual plan, Dostoevsky 'paints' the officer twice as a symmetrical letter; this ligature portrait of the

---

[146] D-*PSS*, 5:139.
[147] *Ibid.*, 129.
[148] D-*PSS*, 5:100. Garnett translation, 26.
[149] D-*PSS*, 5:155. Garnett translation, 105.

officer underlines his inner equilibrium and the Underground Man's chaotic state of mind, his 'formlessness' and disorder.

Another human being with whom the Underground man is in contact is his servant Apollon, whose name is juxtaposed to the mention of "the ugliest dreams" [*bezobrazneishie sny*][150] in the passage where it first occurs. Apollon is extremely self-assured. His inner world also has a rigid structure (form), which the Underground Man desires to ruin but cannot. The comical aspect of this tension is brought out in the appearance of Apollon, who personifies all the features of a misguided attempt at the cultivation of good taste.[151] Some of his characteristics, particularly his obsession with his hairstyle, prefigure Smerdiakov's passion for everything city-like, foreign, and French in *The Brothers Karamazov*. The Underground Man, hiding from all of humanity in his apartment, attempts to fight Apollon (note that the Apollo Belvedere is Dostoevsky's exemplar of the beautiful and beautiful form[152]), under whose thumb he feels himself to be:

> ...my lodging was my private solitude, my **shell**, my **cave, in which I concealed myself from all the mankind**, and **Apollon seemed to me**, for some reason, **an integral part of that flat...**

> [*...moia kvartira byla moi osobniak, moia* **skorlupa**, *moi* **futliar**, **v** *kotoryi ia priatalsia ot vsego chelovechestva, a* **Apollon**, *chert znaet pochemu,* **kazalsia mne** *prinadlezhashchim k etoi kvartire* ...][153]

The Underground Man cannot get rid of his reverse double Apollon, who is juxtaposed with him both as a representative of actual humanity and of Dostoevsky's idea (albeit parodied) of beauty.[154] Apollon seems to the Underground Man to be a *part* of his flat. One imagines him as a statue holding up the ceiling, some sort of an Atlas perhaps (the uglier the apartment the pettier the Atlas). The sculptural image of Liza, this Caryatid of the brothel, makes a nice parallel to the Atlas-like character of Apollon, especially if we bear in mind Dostoevsky's interest in architecture. Besides, Apollon does indeed hold the Underground Man's household upon his shoulders. The all-too balanced Apollon represents the

---

[150] D-*PSS*, 5:139.

[151] Recall the original ancient idea of the ugly as belonging to the sphere of the comic (see Chapter 1).

[152] D-*PSS*, 18:77-78.

[153] D-*PSS*, 5:168. Garnett translation, 125.

[154] One cannot help noticing the idea of the *chelovek v futliare,* successfully used later by Anton Chekhov in his eponymous short story.

worst constituents of stability – stagnation, narrow-mindedness, and arrogance. It seems that in "Notes from Underground" Dostoevsky attempts to defeat stable art forms (the god Apollo is patron of the arts), including conservative narrative techniques, defending his fragmented style, and demonstrating that the ever-fluctuating Underground Man is more versatile than Apollon, and therefore more true to reality.

The Underground Man's opposition to ideals of form and beauty, hinted at in his struggle with Apollon, is reflected elsewhere in the "Notes," e.g. in connection with Shakespeare. In his climactic speech in *The Devils*, Dostoevsky has Stepan Trofimovich Verkhovenskii claim that Shakespeare is one of the highest achievements of humanity, the final result of world cultural development. (Another example of such achievement provided in *The Devils* is the Sistine Madonna.[155]) The playwright's name significantly appears as the culmination of a list of topics of conversation of the Underground Man's 'friends' – all of which irritate him with their focus on the aforementioned ideals:

> They talked of the Caucasus, of the nature of true **passion** … of the extraordinary grace and **beauty** of a Princess D., whom none of them had ever seen; then it came to **Shakespeare's** being immortal.

> [*Oni govorili o Kavkaze, o tom, chto takoe istinnaia* **strast'** … *o neobyknovennoi* **krasote** *i gratsii kniagini D – i, kotoruiu tozhe nikto iz nikh nikogda ne vidal; nakonets doshlo do togo, chto* **Shekspir** *bessmerten.*][156]

The Underground Man loathes the *Stimmung* his friends are in, as manifested in his hatred of their conversation. In the same paragraph, *bezobraznoe,* the ugliness of the Underground Man, becomes low and common, as well as comic:

> I smiled contemptuously and walked up and down the other side of the room, opposite the sofa, from the table to the stove and back again…During those three hours I was three times **soaked with sweat** and **dry** again. At times, with an intense, acute pang I was stabbed to the heart by the thought that ten years, twenty years, forty years would pass, and that even in forty years I would remember with **loathing** and humiliation those

[155] D-*PSS*, 10:265.
[156] D-*PSS*, 5:146. Garnett translation, 93.

filthiest, most ludicrous, and most awful moments of my life... Once – only once – they turned towards me, just when Zverkov was talking about **Shakespeare**, and I suddenly gave a **contemptuous** laugh...

[*Ia prezritel'no ulybalsia i khodil po druguiu storonu komnaty, priamo protiv divana, vdol' steny, ot stola do pechki i obratno ... V eti tri chasa ia tri raza **vspotel i prosokh**. Poroi s glubochaisheiu, s iadovituiu bol'iu vonzalas' v moe serdtse mysl': chto proidet desiat' let, dvadtsat' let, sorok let, a ia vse-taki, khot' i cherez sorok let, s* **otvrashcheniem** *i s unizheniem vspomniu ob etikh* **gryazneishikh, smeshneishikh i uzhasneishikh** *minutakh iz vsei moei zhizni ... Raz, odin tol'ko raz oni obernulis' ko mne imenno kogda Zverkov zagovoril o* **Shekspire**, *a ia vdrug prezritel'no zakhokhotal. Ya tak* **vydelanno i gadko** *fyrknul ...*][157]

The ugly and vulgar situation the Underground Man gets himself into at the hotel is followed by the ugliness of the interior of the brothel, its messiness and disorder, as well as that of his inner state. The description of the room where he is taken to a prostitute echoes his psychological landscape:

It was almost completely **dark** in the **narrow, cramped, low-pitched** room, **cumbered up** with an enormous wardrobe and piles of cardboard boxes and all sorts of frippery and litter.

[*V komnate* **uzkoi, tesnoi i nizkoi, zagromozhdennoi** *ogromnym platianym shkafom i* **zabrosannoi** *kartonkami, triap'em i vsiacheskim odezhnym khlamom, – bylo pochti sovsem* **temno**...][158]

It is narrow, small, and chaotic; it has a low ceiling, possibly a metaphoric reference to the low motives guiding the Underground Man.[159]

The hero of "Notes from Underground" takes revenge for being made fun of, laughing when 'his friends' talk about Shakespeare, and thus changing the direction of the comic vector of the situation from himself towards the 'high and lofty' (an association with Schiller and Kant). He also fights the

---

[157] D-*PSS*, 5:147. Garnett translation, 93-4.
[158] D-*PSS*, 5:152. Garnett translation, 100.
[159] Russian has the expression *'nizmennye pobuzhdeniia'* [low/vile/base motives], almost a cliché.

notion of structure, and of fineness of sculptural form. Stable, regular, and beautiful forms evoke an immediate contemptuous reaction. Liza, whose social status is supposedly lower than that of the Underground Man, irritates him by her wholeness and calmness, that is by her seeming emotional stability. That and her appearance provoke his malice: "Something loathsome stirred within me." [*Chto-to gadkoe ukusilo menia.*][160] Liza's straight eyebrows, her height and strength recall the features of a Caryatid. She remains as motionless as a sculpture; her facial features do not change as they would have, had she proven to be better suited for her profession. She does not smile and does not try any tricks to counterfeit love for her client. In his "Winter Notes on Summer Impressions," written a year before "Notes from Underground," Dostoevsky criticizes French women for their lack of true feelings and their 'professional' adultery, saying that

Ma biche is affected, seasoned, completely unnatural, but this is what so captivating, especially for blasé and somewhat depraved people who have lost their taste for fresh, spontaneous beauty. *Ma biche* was brought up very badly; she has the small mind and the small heart of a bird, but, to make up for it, she is graceful; she has innumerable secrets of such tricks and fancies that you are subdued and follow her around like a savory novelty. She is even rarely attractive. There is something malicious in her face. But that is nothing: it is a lively face, playful, and it possesses the mystery of a counterfeit: rather, it is the very process of counterfeiting that fascinates you; it is the art itself that fascinates you. **For the most part, genuine love and a good counterfeit of love are both the same to the Parisian.**[161]

[*mabish manerna, vylomana, vsia neestestvenna, no eto-to i pleniaet, osobenno blazirovannykh i otchasti razvrashchennykh liudei, poteriavshikh vkus k svezhei, neposredstvennoi krasote. Mabish razvita ves'ma plokho; umishki i serdchishki u nikh ptich'i, no zato ona gratsiozna, zato ona obladaet beschislennymi sekretami takikh shtuchek i vyvertov, chto vy pokoriaetes' i idete za neiu, kak za pikantnoi novinkoi. Ona dazhe redko i khorosha soboi. Chto-to dazhe zloe v litse. No eto nichego: eto litso podvizhno, igrivo i obladaet tainoiu poddelki pod chuvstvo, pod naturu v vysochaishei stepeni. Vam, mozhet byt', nravitsia-to v nei ne to imenno, chto ona etoi poddelkoi*

---

[160] D-*PSS*, 5:151. Garnett translation, 100.
[161] "Winter Notes on Summer Impressions," trans. David Patterson, Evanston, IL: Northwestern U Press, 1988, 68.

*dostigaet natury, no samyi etot protsess dostizheniia poddelkoi vas ocharovyvaet, iskusstvo ocharovyvaet. **Dlia parizhanina bol'shei chastiu vse ravno, chto nastoiashchaia liubov', chto khoroshaia poddelka pod liubov'.***]*[162]

In his damnation of foreign women, Dostoevsky contrasts "fresh, spontaneous beauty" to artificiality. Liveliness of amorphous facial expression of the French women as a sign of amorality – adultery – becomes ugly. Liza lacks precisely "innumerable secrets of such tricks and fancies," she has "fresh, spontaneous beauty," and counterfeit love is beyond her. Constance Garnett emphasises the linear, harmonious, 'graven' image of Liza, consistently translating the Russian *'ser'eznyi'* [serious] as 'grave' in this passage. With Liza, the Underground Man seems to achieve his goal of ruining someone's harmony – even if it is initially merely visual. The straight lines of Liza's face are indeed broken after her first encounter with the Underground Man; neither beauty nor harmony remain in her face; its lines are distorted, twisted:

One moment out of all that had happened last night stood vividly before my imagination; the moment when I struck a match and saw her pale, **distorted face**, with its look of torture. And what a pitiful, what an unnatural, what a **distorted smile** she had at that moment! But I did not know then that fifteen years later I should still in my imagination see Liza, always with the pitiful, **distorted, inappropriate smile** which was on her face at that minute.

[*Imenno odin moment iz vsego vcherashnego mne osobenno iarko predstavlialsia: eto kogda ia osvetil spichkoi komnatu i uvidal ee blednoe, **iskrivlennoe** litso, s muchenicheskim vzgliadom. I kakaia zhalkaia, kakaia nèestestvennaia, kakaia **iskrivlennaia** ulybka u nei byla v tu minuty! No ia eshche ne znal togda, chto i cherez piatnadstat' let ia vse-taki budu predstavliat' sebe Lizu imenno s etoi zhalkoi, **iskrivlennoi, nenuzhnoi** ulybkoi, kakaia u nei byla v etu minutu.*][163]

---

[162] D-*PSS*, 5:93.
[163] D-*PSS*, 5:166. Garnett translation, 122. Auguste Rodin, who is considered a transitional, proto-modern figure in sculpture as Dostoevsky is in literature, has a revolutionary work titled "Caryatid Fallen Under Her Stone." In this work, a traditionally stable female figure is crouching under the weight of a rock she holds. Although Rodin's emphasis is on the body rather than on the face, I suggest a parallel between his piece and the image of Liza after her encounter with the Underground Man.

Where the human face is concerned, what is natural is beautiful and, consequently, what is artificial is ugly; the artificial smile is a distorted, ugly facial expression caused by the Underground Man, whose own face is quite repulsive and totally distorted:

> My harassed face struck me as revolting in the extreme, pale, angry, abject, with dishevelled hair. "No matter, I am glad of it," I thought; "I am glad that I shall seem repulsive to her; I like that."

> [*Vzbudorazhennoe litso moe mne pokazalos' do krainosti otvratitel'nym: blednoe, zloe, podloe, s lokhmatymi volosami. "Eto pust', etomu ia rad, podumal ia, – ia imenno rad, chto pokazhus' ei otvratitel'nym; mne eto priyatno …"*][164]

The harassed face of the Underground Man is anything but harmonious; his hair is chaotic; his face and his whole look are in sharp contrast with the earlier sculptural look of Liza and what turns out to be her fragile tranquillity. Liza's image loses its structural harmony once she is lost in a total chaos of feelings brought out by the Underground Man's false and ugly sentimentality. As the result of her interactions with the Underground Man, she becomes 'formless' and vulnerable. Tzvetan Todorov in his "Genres in Discourse" relates Liza's sudden reaction to the insults of the Underground Man at the close of Part II to the overall message of the story:

> She suddenly jumped up from her chair with a kind of irresistible impulse and, drawn towards me but still feeling very shy and not daring to move from her place, held out her hands to me … It was here that my heart failed me. Then she rushed to me flung her arms round my neck, and burst into tears.[165]

Todorov suggests that Dostoevsky did not reinsert the passage suppressed by the censorship in which he introduces the idea of Christ as a positive principle for the Underground Man precisely because, had he done so, the story would have had two different endings. He suggests that Dostoevsky must have

---

[164] D-*PSS*, 5:151. Garnett translation, 100.
[165] Fyodor Dostoevsky, "Notes from Underground," A Norton Critical Edition. New York/London: W.W. Norton and Company, 2001, 251.

realised that the suppressed passage was redundant, since a dénouement conveyed through Liza's action [that is an averbal dénouement] would have more force.[166]

Later in life, in spite of admiring the art of Schiller's poetry Dostoevsky becomes disappointed with Schiller's humanistic idealism. Nikolai Berdiaev, attempting to look at Dostoevsky and his works as a whole and as a phenomenon of spirit, says that Schiller was Dostoevsky's symbol of the 'high and lofty,' faith in which Dostoevsky loses after the disillusionments of exile.[167] Here Kostka agrees with Berdiaev. In his post-exile "Notes from Underground," Dostoevsky has his protagonist call dreams romantic and repulsive. In this work, the Underground Man attacks Schillerian idealism, and labels mirages and fantasies (typical of idealism) as repulsive and ugly. Criticism and ridicule of Schillerian idealism is expressed already in the *Insulted and Injured*, and continues in "Notes from Underground,"[168] where it combines with the Underground Man's disorderly thoughts of revenge against Zverkov and the rest of humanity:

> They won't go down on their knees to beg for my friendship. That is a mirage, **cheap mirage, revolting, romantic, and fantastical** – that's another ball at Lake Como. And so I am bound to slap Zverkov's face!

> [*Na koleniakh umoliat' o moei druzhbe – oni ne stanut. Eto mirazh, **poshlyi mirazh, otvratitel'nyi, romanticheskii i fantasticheskii**; tot zhe bal na ozere Komo. I potomu ia dolzhen dat' Zverkovu poshchechiny!*][169]

This adds to the Underground Man's negative characteristics: the 'dreamer' side of his character becomes a part of his ugly nature, a significant change in the evolution of the 'dreamer'-type protagonists. Sentimentality, which in general is used as a synonym for Schillerian idealism in "Notes from Underground," is referred to as ugliness, "*poganost'*:" "The **damned romanticism** …Oh, the **vileness** – oh, the silliness – oh, the stupidity of these '**wretched sentimental souls**'!" […*prokliatyi romantizm…O, **merzost'**, o glupost', o ogranichennost' vsekh etikh "**poganykh santimental'nykh dush!**"*][170]

---

[166] *Ibid.*, 252.

[167] N. Berdiaev, *Mirosozertsanie Dostoevskogo*, Moscow: *Zakharov*, 2001, 20.

[168] Kostka, *Schiller in Russian Literature*, 224-225.

[169] D-*PSS*, 5:149. Garnett translation, 96.

[170] D-*PSS*, 5:166. Garnett translation, 122. Note that an archaic meaning of "*poganyi*" is "pagan", "foreign", or "non-Christian." "*Nemets*" ("German," or, in an archaic meaning, a "foreigner" or "pagan") is also frequently

The *"poshlyi mirazh"* [banal/low mirage] that the Underground Man refers to links the realm of fantasies with the low and vulgar. Repulsive, ugly, and chaotic dreams and mirages inhabit the consciousness of the Underground Man, and are a product of his consciousness. He uses beautiful and ready-made art forms that he has borrowed from fiction,[171] but transforms them into ugly and often repulsive nightmares, distorting the ideas of literature by the power of his imagination. The idea of ready-made forms in the dreams was mentioned by Nietzsche in his *The Birth of Tragedy*. In this book, he discusses Apollonian and Dionysian types of art saying that "In our dreams we enjoy an immediate apprehension of form, all shapes speak to us directly, nothing seems indifferent or redundant."[172] Nietzsche associates the forms and shapes of dreams with Apollo and Apollonian art, amorphous art full of motion – with Dionysus.[173] Bakhtin uses a similar distinction between the Apollonian and Dionysian types of art, attributing the Dionysian to Dostoevsky and tending to give it priority as a more dynamic type of art.[174] The amorphous, vacillating Underground Man craves the Apollonian forms of his dreams, but his Dionysian nature prevails and the dreams become misshapen. The contrast between the Underground Man's fantasies about being a hero mounted on a white horse and admired by everyone and the reality of his mouse-hole existence is ludicrous; and, therefore, the ugliness of the fantasies belongs to the sphere of comic. It is reminiscent of Goliadkin's attempt in *The Double* to impress people at the ball at which he appears uninvited. The ugly that could be found in the daily life of the common people – as I discuss in more detail in Chapter 1 – was regarded by the artists of Ancient Greece as "low" and comic. This low category of the ugly became an object of satire, and laughter overcame its disharmony. In Ancient literature, a rigid system of genres determined what was "high" and could be depicted in epos, tragedy, or ode, and what was "low" and would become the theme of comedy or satire. All themes related to daily routine, to every-day, private events were

---

used as a criticism of Schillerian idealism in "Notes from Underground." Viacheslav Ivanov regarded Schiller as "the pagan and dithyrambic poet par excellence," *Po zvezdam*, St. Petersburg, 1909, 81-82, quoted in Kostka, *Schiller in Russian Literature*, 216. Schiller can be looked at as a pagan poet inasmuch he was enthusiastic about the Ancient heritage, and a Christian poet, as a Romantic trying to find the balance between science and religion. The epithet *"poganyi"* (as pagan) fits into Berdiaev's explanation of changes in Dostoevsky's view – from humanistic to religious. Berdiaev, *Mirosozerstanie Dostoevskogo*, 20. In Nikolai Gogol''s "Night before Christmas" [*"Noch' pered Rozhdestvom"*], the devil is called *"nemets."*

[171] D-*PSS*, 5:133.

[172] Friedrich Nietzsche, *The Birth of Tragedy*, trans. Golffing, Garden City, NY, 1956, 20. Original German edition – 1872. Quoted in Elizabeth Cheresh Allen, *Beyond Realism: Turgenev's Poetics of Secular Salvation*, Stanford: Stanford U Press, 1992, 41. Sigmund Freud also studied the forms of dreams in his *Interpretation of Dreams*. Ivanov emphasises the relationship of Dostoevsky's Underground Man, Raskol'nikov, and Kirillov to Nietzsche's Zaratustra. Viacheslav Ivanov, *"Dostoevsky i roman-tragediia,"* *Russkaia mysl'* April (1914), http://www.vehi.net/dostoevsky/ivanov/html, 2, accessed Oct. 16, 2004.

[173] Allen, *Beyond Realism*, 41.

[174] *Ibid.*, 42.

regarded as material for the lower genres. This tradition of depiction of the ugly as low and the low as comic was preserved in European art almost up to the nineteenth century.[175] In both *The Double* and "Notes from Underground," Dostoevsky demonstrates a traditional approach to the comic as the ugly.[176]

Dostoevsky's tribute to the Natural school, a "common" (comic and ugly) everyday detail that the Underground Man notices, is a flaw in his wardrobe – a yellow spot on his trousers.[177] He does not seem to mind, or notice it in his mouse-hole where nobody can see it, but worries about it when he is getting ready for the dinner. He comes to regard the yellow spot as the thing that ruins the impression he wants to make on his 'friends:' "...on the knee of my trousers was a big **yellow** stain. I had a foreboding that that stain would deprive me of nine-tenths of my personal dignity." [. . . *na samoi kolenke bylo ogromnoe **zheltoe** piatno. Ia predchuvstvoval, chto odno uzhe eto piatno otnimet u menya deviat desiatykh sobstvennogo dostoinstva.*][178] Since the Underground Man insists on his superior intellect as his distinguishing quality, it is surprising that it is the state of his garments that receives his chief attention. Yet he returns to the yellow spot once again when the dinner is about to collapse: "Oh, damn my trousers! Zverkov noticed the **yellow** stain on the knee as soon as he came in ..." [*O prokliatye pantalony! Zverkov eshche davecha zametil **zheltoe** piatno na kolenke ...*][179] The Underground Man realises that it should be beneath him '*nizko*' to lose his dignity over a spot on his trousers, but cannot help thinking that it is the yellow spot that has established the distance between his 'friends' and himself, broken the possible *Stimmung*, the harmony of the friendly atmosphere. For the Underground Man, the yellow spot is clearly a crucial element in the failure of the party; the colour yellow brings disorder to his costume and affects his psychological state, forcing him into the depths of hysterics and chaos. In the Underground Man's literary reality, yellow is a sign of *bezobrazie*.

Dostoevsky often uses yellow to denote ugliness in "Notes from Underground." In the last passage of Part I of this text, the colour yellow occurs in an unusual context; it is the sleet (that of the title of Part II) that is given this hue:

---

[175] Arkhipova, "*Dostoevsky i estetika bezobraznogo*," 52-53.

[176] This is also an explanation of why Dostoevsky's works appear comic as well as tragic. As to the question of tragedy and comedy as genres, Ivanov in his discussion of the artistic form of Dostoevsky's works and his *Weltanschauung* calls his novels "novel-tragedies." Ivanov, "*Dostoevsky i roman-tragediia.*"

[177] D-PSS, 5:141.

[178] D-*PSS*, 5:141. Garnett translation, 84.

[179] D-*PSS*, 5:144. Garnett translation, 90.

Snow is falling to-day, **yellow** and **dingy**. It fell yesterday, too, and a few days ago. I fancy it is **the wet snow that has reminded me of that incident** which I cannot shake off now. And so let it be a story apropos of the wet snow."

[*Nynche idet sneg, pochti mokryi, **zheltyi, mutnyi**. Vchera shel tozhe, na dniakh tozhe shel. Mne kazhetsia, ia **po povodu mokrogo snega i pripomnil tot anekdot**, kotoryi ne khochet teper' ot menia otviazat'sia. Itak pust' eto budet povest' po povodu mokrogo snega.*][180]

The Underground Man is affected by the yellow sleet; its ugliness motivates him to tell the reader his story of *bezobraznoe*. The ugly colour is hinted at when the Underground Man introduces himself as a sick man with an ailing liver: "I am a **sick** man … I believe my **liver** is diseased." [*Ia chelovek **bol'noi** … Ia dumaiu, chto u menia bolit **pechen'***.][181] Yellow is also there when the Underground Man's jaundiced condition and envy are mentioned for the second time: "I envy such a man till I am **yellow** in the face." [*Ia takomu cheloveku do krainei **zhelchi** zaviduiu.*][182] Again, yellow in "Notes from Underground" is the colour applied to convey the notion of ugliness, which is in most cases associated with amorality. Yellow is, in fact, the most frequently mentioned colour in "Notes from Underground," (as well as in other Dostoevsky's texts); and every time it occurs, it is used in connection with *bezobraznoe*. Ugly yellow can be found in other Dostoevsky works, i.e. the scarf in the "Weak Heart" ["*Slaboe serdtse*"] and the ugly hue of the buildings in "White Nights" ["*Belye nochi*"]:

It was such a dear little stone house, it looked at me in such a welcoming way, and looked at its clumsy neighbours so proudly, that my heart rejoiced when I happened to go by. Suddenly, last week, I was going along the street and, as I glanced at my friend – I heard a piteous cry: "They're painting me **yellow**!" The criminals! Scoundrels! Barbarians! They had spared nothing: neither columns, nor cornices, and my friend turned as **yellow as a canary**. I nearly overflowed with bile on this occasion, and I have

---

[180] D-*PSS*, 5:123. Garnett translation, 59.

[181] D-*PSS*, 5:99. Garnett translation, 25.

[182] D-*PSS*, 5:104. Garnett translation, 32. The translation here is modified from Garnett's "green in the face," which does not represent the jaundiced condition mentioned in the original. (The Russian "jaundiced" has the same root as "yellow" – "-*zhel-*".)

never yet been strong enough to go and see my poor **deformed** friend, who had been painted from head to foot in the colour of the Celestial Empire.[183]

Another recurrent element in Dostoevsky's poetics of the ugly is the image of the spider:

Now I suddenly realised vividly the hideous **idea – revolting as a spider – of vice**, which without love, grossly and shamelessly begins with that in which true love finds its consummation.

[... *mne vdrug iarko predstavilas' nelepaia,* **otvratitel'naia, kak pauk, ideia razvtrata,** *kotoryi bez liubvi, grubo i besstyzhe, nachinaetsia priamo s togo, chem nastoiashchaia liubov' venchaetsia.*][184]

The Underground Man compares an amoral idea with a spider; the spider is also mentioned in *The Devils* as a symbol of Stavrogin's sin; and in *Crime and Punishment*, Svidrigailov has a vision of hell as a bathhouse with spiders. The Underground Man calls the circumstances he found himself in loathsome/repulsive/ugly ("*gadko*"), using the same epithet as in the beginning of the "Apropos of the Wet Snow" – the ugly ("*gadkii*") yellow sleet – and concludes that was all ugly [*bezobrazno vse eto bylo*].[185] Perhaps it is because he is so disgusted with himself and his ugly situation that he becomes so elaborate in his ornamental speech to Liza on the topics of a beautiful chaste life, motherhood, and 'resurrection.' He does try to take revenge on her, but his initial impulse may have been simply an attempt to beautify, to ennoble ugly reality with ideas borrowed from fiction. This is a parody of the idea of the regeneration of the fallen woman with the aid of the man who loves her, as expressed in Nekrasov's poem "*Kogda iz mraka zabluzhden'ia ...*", part of which is an epigraph for "Apropos the Wet Snow." Written in 1845, this poem fuels the mockery of the Romantic ideas of the 1840s in "Notes from Underground."

Among other peculiarities of Dostoevsky's poetics of the ugly are the Underground Man's dialogical monologues. The Underground Man has no normal contacts with other persons; his relationships with his 'friends', colleagues, and Liza are either ugly or non-existent. He is totally

---

[183] Jacques Catteau, *Dostoevsky and the Process of Literary Creation*, trans. Audrey Littlewood, Cambridge: Cambridge U Press, 1989, 408.
[184] D-*PSS*, 5:152. Garnett translation, 101.
[185] *Ibid.* The Underground Man's "*zhelch'*" is mentioned again in this episode, bringing out the colour yellow.

divorced from life; he himself is his usual environment and interlocutor. Mikhail Bakhtin in his *Problems of Dostoevsky's Poetics* calls Dostoevsky a creator of a new, polyphonic, type of thinking.[186] The discourse of "Notes from Underground," particularly in Part I, illustrates Bakhtin's idea of polyphony in a literary work: a multiplicity of independent and non-amalgamated voices and consciousnesses [*mnozhestvennost' samostoiatel'nykh i nesliiannykh golosov i soznanii*.].[187] "Notes from Underground" is, however, a peculiar polyphonic text, because its polyphony is formed by the multiplicity of voices of one protagonist. According to Bakhtin, double-voiced discourse inevitably appears in dialogic conversation, and is a main object of study of what he calls "meta-linguistics." In differentiating between "pure" linguistics and "meta-linguistics," Bakhtin writes that the latter embraces dialogic relationships including relationships of speaker to discourse ("*slovo*") and the dialogicity of remarks, whereas "pure" linguistics studies language in abstraction from various aspects of the concrete life of the word. In Bakhtin's terms, the Underground Man treats his own discourse as that of a variety of interlocutors. The conversation he engages in is between himself and his imaginary opponents. His polyphonic discourse is a consequence of the Underground Man's split personality, the duality of his character, the topic of the double much favoured by Dostoevsky. The Underground Man has a strange relationship towards verbality and averbality; in his soliloquies, he can hardly stop talking; paradoxically, he does not seem to be able to participate in dialogues with anyone other than himself:

> Here **you and I** ... **came together** ... just now and **did not say one word to one another** all the time, and it was only afterwards you began **staring** at me like a wild creature, and I at you. Is that loving? Is that how one human being should meet another? It's **hideous**, that's what it is!

> [... *vot **my s toboi** ... **soshlis'***... *davecha, i **slova my** vo vse vremia **drug s druzhkoi ne molvili**, i ty menia, kak dikaia, uzh potom **rassmatrivat'** stala; i ia tebia takzhe. Razve etak liubiat? Razve etak chelovek s chelovekom skhodit'sia dolzhny? Eto **bezobrazie** odno, vot chto!*][188]

---

[186] Bakhtin, *Problemy poetiki Dostoevskogo*, 3.

[187] Mikhail Bakhtin, *Problemy poetiki Dostoevskogo*, Moscow: *Khudozhestvennaia literatura*, 1972, 7.

[188] D-*PSS*, 5:155. Garnett translation, 106. Note the stylised folk "*drug s druzhkoi*" as opposed to "*drug s drugom*."

He does not say a word to Liza prior to having sex with her, and fails to communicate with Simonov, even though he prefers him to his other 'comrades.' This lack of words in social contact (since a conversation between two parts of one's personality is not a social occasion) is a sign of the Underground Man's alienation from other people, from the real world, and demonstrates the disintegration of society, its formlessness and disorder, and the ugliness of the Underground Man himself.

The speech habits of Dostoevsky's characters are an absolutely essential part of their makeup. His dreamers (prior to the Underground Man) carry on endless conversations, mostly with themselves. The Underground Man, however, becomes averbal in the company of others; just as a character in *The Devils*, Kirillov, develops his own minimal syntax sufficient to engage in speech on the rare occasions he happens to be in touch with other humans.[189] While Dostoevsky's ugly characters may also be talkative in public, the typical tendency is verbal excess in solipsistic monologues coupled with deficiencies in dialogue with others. Both poles of this communication problem (in which the author anticipates one of the major concerns of the modernists) relate to the absence of normal human contact among Dostoevsky's characters, and are a sign of their ugliness and that of their relationships.

It is noteworthy that in trying to find out about the Underground Man, in searching for his image, Liza starts to "*rassmatrivat'*" him after a silent sex act: the visual element substitutes for conversation. Given Dostoevsky's attitude to the image/icon, visuality in his texts seems to be connected to beauty, whereas verbal characteristics often reflect ugliness. Recalling the sort of sketches he left in the margins of his manuscripts, it seems plausible that Dostoevsky thought in terms of architectural and sculptural drawing. Therefore, the visual aspect of his character sketches bears a particular significance in his works.

The Underground Man says about himself: "I **exaggerate** everything, that is where I go **wrong**…" […*vse-to ia **preuvelichivaiu**, tem i **khromaiu**…*][190] He seems to distort the image of reality, to have a distorted *Weltbild*. The outline of the picture of reality he sees appears fractured, as in the optical experiment with a pencil in a glass of water. His angle of view changes the perspective so much that any "real reality" is seen as ugly. His exaggeration, that is, his distortion of reality through his

---

[189] I use "averbality" to denote both types of speech dysfunctions of Dostoevsky's characters: the lengthy monologues of the Underground Man and the minimal speech abilities of Kirillov being examples of the two. Both poles of this phenomenon involve a problem in communication and an unusual linguistic form of expression.
[190] D-*PSS*, 5:166. Garnett translation, 122.

consciousness and language, is his *bezobrazie*, his sin, since the lameness he attributes to himself is a traditional metaphor for sin.[191]

Such poetic means as the use of the colour yellow, the image of the spider, the polyphonic monologues, and references to broken lines in the depiction of the Underground Man, his dwelling, and the effect he makes on other characters, are employed with particular frequency by Dostoevsky to convey the notion of *bezobraznoe* in "Notes from Underground." The ugly is interwoven into the fictional reality of the "Notes;" in this work we see the variety of meanings it conveys. *Bezobraznoe* in "Notes from Underground" encompasses sentimentality and romanticism, interiors of St. Petersburg and its climate, the Underground Man's messiness and amorality, his lack of normal social contacts and concomitant averbality. It is a work in which *bezobraznoe* is associated with the 'formlessness' of the Underground Man and his existential disorder. Given Dostoevsky's claim about the Underground Man representing the Russian majority, we understand that he attempts to provide the reader with a picture of the chaos and formlessness of the whole of Russian society – perhaps humanity in general.[192]

Chapter III: Monstrous Mamleev: Death, Dostoevsky, and the Problem of Tradition

> *Bo, prostranstvo ekonomia, kak otlit'sia v formu masse,*
> *Krome kladbishcha i krome chernoi ocheredi k kasse...*[193]
>
> I. Brodsky

By the end of the nineteenth century, the underground state of protest and disintegration captured by Dostoevsky in his "Notes" back in 1864 had become the expression of the "often nihilistic protest of the individual against an enveloping isolation, stagnation, and darkness" of the interim period in Russian literature and against the oppressive social and political situation after the assassination of Alexander II (1881).[194] In the twentieth century, Dostoevsky's epigones of the early Soviet era maintained their Underground Man characters in opposition to "the supremacy of the new Soviet man

---

[191] It is noteworthy that the lame Mar'ia Timofeevna, the *khromonozhka* in *The Devils*, is also a character conveying aspects of the religious idea.

[192] Whether true or not, this view was expressed by Dostoevsky in his text as a counter-argument to *What is to Be Done?* (which may excuse the radical form in which he presents it).

[193] For, economizing the space, how can the mass be poured into a form, / Except for at a cemetery and except for in a black queue to the cashiers.

[194] Jackson, *Dostoevsky's Underground Man*, 64, 215.

of action," an unfortunate development of Chernyshevsky's idea of the "new people."[195] In the mainstream socialist realism of Russian literature from the end of 1930s to the beginning of the 1950s, the underground is either not represented, or has negative connotations related to the enemies of the Soviet state. An underground similar to that of the "Notes" of 1864 reappears in Russian literature in the 1960s, some of which was published only much later. Iurii Mamleev, a late twentieth-century writer with a stated interest in Dostoevsky's philosophy and art, depicts an underground of the late-Soviet and post-Soviet period, full of psychic perversions. He essentially develops Dostoevsky's idea but adds a mystical component to it, insisting on its global nature: the state of the world presupposes a conflict between it and the egotistic individual, prone to self-analysis; the underground thus becomes an opposition to reality as such. Mamleev goes to the extreme and transforms Dostoevsky's philosophical and psychological underground into a metaphysical and psychopathic one. What makes this controversial writer particularly important for my thesis is his own admission of Dostoevsky's heritage in his prose, his use of Dostoevskian themes, and his intertextual references to Dostoevsky's works, characters, and ideas. My aim in this chapter is to demonstrate this influence on Mamleev's prose, primarily focusing on the issue of *bezobraznoe* in both writers.

The second half of the 1980s in Russia was marked by an unusually large number of publications in which the use of quotation was the dominant poetic means. Approximately at the same time it became fashionable to talk about postmodernism, intertextuality, and *cento* forms as a newly actualized literary trend. *Cento,* also known as *kento* or *kentho,* is a literary work pieced together from the works of several authors, from Lat. *cento*, quilt or patchwork. *Cento* is close to pastiche "which is also applied to literary patchwork formed by piecing together extracts from various works by one or several authors."[196] Pastiche, however, implies extensive direct imitation. Although the term *cento* is normally used in relation to poetry, Sergei Biriukov affirms that all culture can be looked at as a quilt, or a *cento*. He himself quotes Mandelshtam, who says that a quote is a cricket that calls you, as well as Shklovsky, who liked to repeat in the 1970s that we all use quotes like we used the wall when we were learning how to walk.[197] However, the 'pure' *cento*, as defined by M. Gasparov – one that consists of lines of another text entirely[198] – is quite rare. This is particularly so when the authorship of the lines is known for certain and the compiler of the *cento* only estranges them by putting them in a different context. The inclusion of separate lines of another author or authors into one's own text happens much

---

[195] *Ibid.*, 215.
[196] C. Hugh Holman, *A Handbook to Literature*, N/Y: Bobbs-Merrill, 1972, 380-81.
[197] S. Biriukov, "*Ia napisal stikhotvoren'e,*" *Zevgma: Russkaia poeziia*, Moscow: *Nauka*, 1994, 183.
[198] *Literaturnyi entsiklopedicheskii slovar'*, Moscow, 1987, 492.

more often. Khrustaleva suggests that the end of the twentieth century is characterized by a speeding up of all language processes which compose a dynamic layered model of the world.[199] According to Zubova, such a layered system represents the postmodern *Weltanschauung*; she defines postmodernism as a style of the contemporary epoch, omnivorous when it comes to trends and individual systems.[200] Postmodernism has several interpretations in contemporary criticism: it is an art whose language was formed after modernism (avant-garde), an art of the future, and an eschatological art, that is an art after the end of the world, when the present reality will cease to exist. Among the main principles of postmodernism are: agnosticism; philosophic, ethic, and aesthetic pluralism, denying the existence of a hierarchy of beings; a dismissal of the didactic function of the text; eclectics and dual, or multiple codes; rejection of the author's persona; intertextual interplay; mixing of styles; irony and épatage.

Comparing the understanding of postmodernism in Russia and in the West, Grois states that the western term 'postmodernism' is used in contemporary Russian criticism to describe the gradual liberation of Russian art from the norms of official socialist realism, which happened in Russia in the 1970-80s, and is analogous to the liberation of art from the aesthetic dictatorship of modernism and the transition to cultural pluralism that took place in the West in the 1960-70s.[201] Western postmodernism makes elements of low, mass culture and kitsch a part of high culture, whereas *sotsrealism* was itself mass culture, and this is why trends of Russian postmodernism – *sotsart*, conceptualism – focused on taking clichéd devices of socialist realism to the absurd. Saussure, who attempted to see a system in the multiplicity of phenomena, and to establish a single code to describe individual referents, postulated the subordination of speech to language. The opposite of this view is Derrida's theory, according to which language is subordinated to speech, and all the individual referents in their chaotic variety are foregrounded. Roland Barthes in "From Work to Text" denies a work of art a primary, self-contained nature and suggests that the process of establishing meaning is radically contingent, "the product of a variety of shifting interchanges rather than the divination of the semantic heart of the work."[202] These interchanges or interactions Barthes designates as 'play.' This results in an anti-hierarchical production of meaning; it is the text that speaks rather than the author. Barthes also writes that "the logic regulating the Text is not comprehensive (define 'what the work means') but metonymic; the activity

---

[199] O. Khrustaleva, *"Konets veka," Mitin zhurnal*, 1993 (50): 201-203.

[200] L.V. Zubova, *Sovremennaia russkaia poeziia v kontekste istorii iazyka*, Moscow: *NLO*, 2000, 9.

[201] B. Grois, *"Polutornyi stil': sotsialisticheskii realizm mezhdu modernizmom i postmodernizmom, NLO*, (1995) 15: 44.

[202] *Art in Theory: 1900-1990: An Anthology of Changing Ideas*, Oxford, UK/Cambridge, USA: Blackwell, 1996, 941.

of associations, contiguities, carryings-over coincides with a liberation of symbolic energy…"[203] Such activity is also known as intertextuality, which involves the interplay of allusions, references to a different text or a variety of texts found in one work. Quotations that function as intertextual links can have different meaning-forming functions. According to Kozitskaia there are four of them:

– pure meaning-forming, creating special connotations regarding the pre-text;

– polemic meaning-forming, discrediting the work of a literary forefather, often with elements of parody;

– meaning-forming emphasizing the sacral nature of the quoted text, such as Biblical references;

– and what she calls the retrospective function: quotation that actively forms intertextual links, not just to the pre-text but to other instances of quotation, i.e. references to Dostoevsky as alluded to by Andrei Bely, within a text by Iurii Mamleev.

The criticism on Mamleev is scarce, even for a contemporary writer, and that led me to research all his available interviews and his own literary criticism. My aim has been to elucidate Mamleev's views on Dostoevsky, contemporary literature and the cultural situation in Russia. In his article on Sergei Esenin, Mamleev relates this Russian peasant poet's art to Dostoevsky's, affirming that the writing of both artists touches upon the most mysterious level in the Russian soul, the level that links the Russians with archetypes of the nation and the national character. Dostoevsky's art, therefore, becomes a deeply metaphysical issue, national and universal at the same time. Mamleev focuses on the "unhealthy, feeble, low" ("*Nezdorovoe, khiloe, nizkoe…*") in Esenin's poetry and claims that these characteristics of Russia make it particularly lovable. Mamleev does not see this as a paradox; in his opinion, most negative and devastating images – *obrazy* – in Russian literature, as a rule, conceal unexpected 'light-bearing' phenomena. Again, his examples of such negative *obrazy* – that is of *bezobrazie* – are texts of Dostoevsky and Esenin:

As nostalgia and lack in Esenin only made love for Russia and its land stronger, the cosmic despair of Dostoevsky led to the knowledge of Light, to the final desperate striving to God.

---

[203] *Ibid.,* 943.

[*Kak toska i lishennost' u Esenina tol'ko usilivali liubov' k Rossii i k ee zemle, tak i kosmicheskoe otchaiianie Dostoevskogo velo k poznaniiu Sveta, k poslednemu otchaiannomu poryvu k Bogu.*][204]

Sergei Mikhailov notes a remarkable characteristic of the world of Mamleev's characters: their life resembles a "history of illness of some schizophrenic."[205] Similarly, the protagonist of Dostoevsky's *Crime and Punishment* – Raskol'nikov (a 'descendant' of the Underground Man from "Notes from Underground") – gives the impression of somebody suffering from a mental illness to other characters (including the medical doctor Zosimov) throughout the novel: "...he [Zosimov] has an idea... that you [Raskol'nikov] are crazy.." ["*...u nego ideia...chto ty sumasshedshii...*"] "This Zosimov was recently afraid that he [Raskol'nikov] would go crazy..." ["*Etot Zosimov davecha boialsia, chtob on ne soshel s uma...*"][206] Raskol'nikov himself questions his sanity, dreading the possibility of failing to be one of the chosen few who have a moral right to kill. Such people, according to Raskol'nikov's theory, have no pangs of conscience, as opposed to weak ordinary people who cannot commit a crime without leaving evidence of it. Raskol'nikov explains this by the frantic mental state of ordinary people after the crime; he goes as far as suggesting that ordinary criminals become mentally ill after they commit a crime. The fact that he cannot always remember what he is doing after he kills the pawn-broker and her sister scares him particularly because, according to his own theory, it makes him look like one of the ordinary people. Raskol'nikov's sanity is questionable for his friends and family as well as for himself. He is a moral monster, another anti-hero, whom the novelist occasionally describes as mentally ill *because* Raskol'nikov lacks moral and religious grounds, because the image – *obraz* – of God is dim in this character.

Mamleev's monsters are an ugly "absurd, devil's hallucination," similar to Dostoevsky's moral monsters – only worse, since they are monsters of a parallel surreal world.[207] The term Surrealism, coined by Guillaume Apollinaire (1880-1918), was used by the movement's principal theorist, André Breton. This complex movement included: an opposition to Breton's explicit inscription of Marxism into Surrealism's perspective personified by Georges Bataille (1892-1962), a factual leader of a

---

[204] Iurii Mamleev, "*O Esenine,*" *Nash Sovremennik* 10 (1990): 180.

[205] Sergei Mikhailov, "*O pisatele Iurii Mamleeve*", *Skrizhali* (1999), 1.

[206] D-*PSS*, 6:148, 155. We can look at these two works as a certain unity bearing in mind that *Crime and Punishment* (1865) develops to a logical conclusion the ideas of the Underground Man from "The Notes" (1864). The commentaries to "*Bobok*" in the Academy edition of Dostoevsky also insist on the similarities between "Notes from Underground" and "*Bobok,*" mainly, in the "*emblema 'zagoleniia.'*" See D-*PSS*, 21:407.

[207] Mikhailov, "*O pisatele Iurii Mamleeve,*" 1.

dissident surrealist group in France; a German Surrealist movement, including Siegfried Kracauer, Walter Benjamin, Theodor Adorno, and Ernst Bloch; and an American Surrealist group of Meyer Schapiro, Clement Greenberg, and Harold Rosenberg. Spanish-born Salvador Dali (1904-1989), possibly best known of the Surrealists in Russia, got involved in the movement in Paris in 1929, and although expelled in 1934, continued to have his art exhibitions as a Surrealist until the 1940s. In his essay "The Stinking Ass," evoking a corrosive image from the film *Un Chien Andalou*, on which he collaborated with Luis Buñuel, Dali provides an avant-garde theoretical framework for his otherwise conservative – that is figurative, realistic – technique. He affirms that mental processes of paranoia (hallucinations, unusual juxaposition, and 'doubling' of minutely figuratively images) make it possible "to systematize confusion and thus to help to discredit completely the world of reality."[208] Dali's double image is a representation of an object which is also a representation of an entirely different object, i.e. an image of a woman that may also appear as an image of a horse. The multiplicity of such 'doubling' images can be limited only by one's own paranoia.

Dali's motivation of the 'doubling' of images by paranoia explains why Mamleev's literary works, populated by psychotic monsters and full of such ambiguous, 'doubling' images, have been considered by some critics as surrealistic. According to Nikolai Klimontovich, at the time of the underground Mamleev's *Iuzhinskii* circle in Moscow, that is before his immigration in 1975, surrealism was still popular in Russia. Mamleev's personal life included a direct link to Russian surrealism, as his love interest and one of his disciples was officially the wife of the surrealist artist, V. Piatnitskii.[209] Dali's 'doubling' also links him back to Dostoevsky with his mirroring technique, and particularly with the personae of Goliadkin in "The Double." Mamleev mentions the surrealism of his prose as a reason for it having not been published in the Soviet Union. This prohibition of surrealism in the USSR led him to immigrate to the States, where his books were published both in Russian and English, and to Paris (1983) where they were translated into French and other languages.[210] According to Mamleev, western critics have classified his works as belonging to the tradition of Dostoevsky and Gogol', also underlining the surrealist motifs in his prose.[211] James McConkey has investigated Mamleev's phantasmagoric book *The Sky above Hell* [*Nebo nad adom*] and the roots of his art; in his study he suggests that Mamleev is indeed indebted to Gogol' and Dostoevsky.[212]

---

[208] *Art in Theory 1900-1990*, 225-481.
[209] Nikolai Klimontovich, *Dalee vezde, Oktiabr'* (2000)11: 6.
[210] Mikhailov, *"O pisatele Iurii Mamleeve"*, 1-2.
[211] *Ibid.*, 2.
[212] Iurii Mamleev, *Iznanka Gogena*, Paris/NY: *Tret'ia volna*, 1982, 3.

53

Alexander Glezer writes that in non-conformist Moscow it was hard to find a person unfamiliar with Iurii Mamleev's works. His short-stories, telling us of ugly and fantastic characters and a tragic and surrealist world bereft of the spiritual, were spread through *samizdat* channels.[213] Glezer argues that Mamleev's art also relates to the surrealism of Soviet reality and the new type of man – *homo Soveticus* – lacking moral values and faith, while McConkey affirms that Mamleev, like some American writers, interprets the contemporary world more in a surrealist manner than by means of conventional representations of reality. [214] Mamleev himself writes that his literary goal is the discovery of the inner abysses that are hidden in the soul of wo/men. If a writer expresses these abysses through the behaviour of his characters, says Mamleev, the result would be what Dostoevsky called 'fantastic realism'.[215]

Mikhailov states that some short-stories by Mamleev – "A Living Death" ["*Zhivaia smert'*"], "Abrupt Meetings" ["*Krutye vstrechi*"], or "Will Satisfy Myself!" ["*Udovletvo-rius'!*"] – do meet the criteria of surrealism, while most of his art goes beyond the limits of this category. Parallels to other Russian literary texts drawn by Mikhailov include: "The Portrait" ["*Portret*"] and "The Nose" ["*Nos*"] by Gogol', and *The Master and Margarita* [*Master i Margarita*] by Bulgakov. The Russian writer and critic Iurii Nagibin also discusses Mamleev's short-stories, writing that

> Mamleev is surrealist, if one has to use a relative term to denote the living substance of that sort of literature with which he is involved. But God damn me if I understand why a mundanely realistic story "*Serezha*"[216] about a dying boy whom nobody wants to take to a hospital, or the piercingly precise psychological story "Not Those Relationships" ["*Ne te otnosheniia*"] should be surrealism, while "The Cavalier of the Golden Star" ["*Kavaler Zolotoi zvezdy*"] about a *kolkhoz* heaven is realism, and even with the prefix "*sots-*."

> [*Mamleev surrealist, esli nuzhno oboznachit' uslovnym terminom zhivuiu substantsiiu togo roda literatury, kotorym on zanimaetsia. No ubei menia Bog, esli ia ponimaiu, pochemu zhiteiski pravdopodobnyi rasskaz "Serezha" ob umiraiushchem mal'chike, kotorogo nikto ne khochet otvezti v bol'nitsu, ili pronzitel'no tochnyi psikhologicheskii*

---

[213] *Ibid.*
[214] *Ibid.*
[215] Mikhailov, "*O pisatele Iurii Mamleeve*", 2.
[216] The actual title is "Serezhen'ka."

rasskaz "Ne te otnosheniia" – surrealism, a "Kavaler Zolotoi zvezdy" o kolkhoznom rae – realism da eshche s pristavkoi "sots".][217]

Mikhailov himself insists on the realism of Mamleev's works; but more importantly he emphasizes that it is the dark side of the human soul upon which Mamleev focuses. For Mikhailov, the pivot of Mamleev's art is a synthesis of everything extreme, tragic, irrational, subconscious, and evil.[218] His unworldly images – *obrazy* – form their own mysterious and horrible world, a world consisting only of dark sides that has no place for the normal, for light and kindness. In my opinion, Mamleev's characters live in a world of total pathological ugliness; he does not offer a positive alternative to ugly existence as Dostoevsky does. Mamleev accepts Dostoevsky's *bezobraznoe* in his own writings, but his fiction has no positive religious and/or moral element.

Just as the nature of Dostoevsky's realism has provoked a still ongoing debate amongst critics, so Mamleev's texts are being classified with the help of a variety of "-isms". Alexander V. Suslov, in his doctoral dissertation on the New Art tradition, studies Mamleev's prose as an example of symbolist literature; Suslov uses Merezhkovsky's criteria to prove that Mamleev's works belong to the tradition of New Art with its "mystical content, symbols, and a broadening of the artistic impression".[219] I do agree that the content of most of Mamleev's works is thoroughly mystical, but his technically conservative prose does not seem to broaden the 'artistic impression' in the Symbolists' sense (an example of which is Bely's use of alliteration in his rhythmic prose). Mikhailov mentions in passing the "'kingdom of the absurd' announced by Camus" as characteristic of Mamleev's art; thus, absurdism becomes one more literary trend with which his prose has been linked.[220]

Natalia Mazur adds to the debate on Mamleev and literary tradition, affirming that his artistic system is essentially anti-*sotsrealism*,[221] which makes it postmodern according to Grois (See above). She insists on the lack of philosophical depth in Mamleev's texts, an interesting comment, given that Mamleev's new *Eternal Russia* [*Rossiia vechnaia*] comes with a blurb characterizing him as a philosopher whose books have been translated into all European languages.[222] The ugliness we see in Mamleev's books is petty; in Mazur's opinion, Mamleev's short-stories tell us what Dostoevsky's

---

[217] Mikhailov, "*O pisatele Iurii Mamleeve*", 2.

[218] *Ibid.*, 3.

[219] Alexander V. Suslov, "The New Art Tradition in Modern Russian Prose," *Dissertation Abstracts International*, Vol. 47, No. 1 (July 1986), 175-A.

[220] Mikhailov, "*O pisatele Iurii Mamleeve*", 2.

[221] Natalia Mazur, "*Kobob*", *Literaturnoe obozrenie*, 7-8 (1992): 78.

[222] Iurii Mamleev, *Rossiia vechnaia: Rossiia v proshlom, nastoiashchem, budushchem*, Moscow: *AiF* Print, 2002.

"*Bobok*" would have, had the narrator not sneezed and had the corpses had their say.[223] As Mazur writes about Mamleev's art: "The author has a surprising ability to notice and describe the details of the filth surrounding us." [*Avtor obladaet udivitel'nym umeniem podmetit' i opisat' detali okruzhaiushchei nas gadostnosti.*][224]

Finally, Igor P. Smirnov regards Mamleev's texts as outright postmodern, since they deal with such épatage themes as necromania, schizophrenia, and narcissism in its extreme.[225] Smirnov calls Mamleev's works "*schizoide Postmoderne*" and says that in this type of prose references to death, including the actual physical demise of characters, are omnipresent.[226] According to this critic, the whole "kulturgenerierende Intention der Postmoderne realisierte sich als Nekromanie."[227] Among the various attempts to label Mamleev's art, the suggestion that it is postmodern seems the most justified. For Lipovetsky postmodernism

> operates not by means of one canonic language but of multiple languages and traditions
> of various, chronologically and aesthetically incompatible epochs and cultures, as if
> simultaneously coexisting in a single spiritual space.

> [*...operiruet ne odnim kanonicheskim iazykom, a mnogimi iazykami i traditsiiami
> razlichnykh, khronologicheski i esteticheski nesovmestimykh epokh i kul'tur, kak by
> odnovremenno sosushchestvuiushchikh v edinom dukhovom prostranstve.*] [228]

Bibler even believes, correctly in my opinion, that this peculiarity of postmodernism is a salient feature of twentieth-century culture in general.[229] Such an understanding of postmodernism and the twentieth century brings us back to Biriukov's idea of *cento*, to the quilted nature of contemporary culture. Mamleev's texts have the postmodern ability to absorb features of different literary trends and traditions, perhaps explaining why critics have classified them so variously.

---

[223] *Ibid.*

[224] Mazur, "*Kobob*", 76-78.

[225] Igor P. Smirnov, "Geschichte der Nachgeschichte: Zur russisch-sprachigen Prosa der Postmoderne," Michael Titzmann, ed., *Modelle des literarischen Strukturwandels*, Tübingen: Max Niemeyer, 1991, 206-207, 215-218.

[226] *Ibid.*, 207.

[227] *Ibid.*

[228] M. Lipovetsky, *Russkii postmodernizm*, Ekaterinburg: *Ural'skii gosudarstvennyi pedagogicheskii universitet*, 1997, 16.

[229] V.S. Bibler, *Nravstvennost': Kul'tura: Sovremennost'*, Moscow: *Znanie*, 1991, 37. Quoted in Lipovetsky, *Russkii postmodernizm*, 16.

Mikhailov insists on the significance of the theme of death in Mamleev. He says that death as described by Mamleev disgusts the reader; it is analyzed "from the other world," looked at from the point of view of corpses, vampires, people with psychic problems, and necrophiles.[230] Mikhailov emphasizes the ugliness of death in Mamleev:

> Sometimes his attitude towards death is ironic, even cynical, often death in his works is **ugly, horrible and disgusting**, but never does he create a halo of beauty around it.

> [*Poroi otnoshenie k smerti u nego byvaet ironichnym, dazhe tsinichnym, chasto smert' u nego* **bezobrazna, zhutko-omerzitel'na**, *no nikogda on ne sozdaet vokrug nee oreol prekrasnogo...*][231]

Dostoevsky was very impressed by the depiction of death in Holbein's painting "Christ in the Tomb." His own portrayal of death – an attempted suicide in *Crime and Punishment* – is "an ugly vision:"

> Suddenly he started, saved perhaps from another fainting fit by a strange and **ugly sight**. He felt someone standing beside him, on his right, and looked up; it was a tall woman wearing a kerchief on her head, with a long, **yellow**, hollow-cheeked **face** and red-rimmed, sunken eyes. She was looking straight at him, but apparently without seeing him. With an abrupt movement she rested her right hand on the parapet, raised her right foot and threw it over the railing, followed it with her left, and flung herself into the canal. The **filthy water** parted and engulfed her for a moment, but then she rose to the surface and drifted gently with the current, face downwards, with her head and legs in the water and her skirt ballooning under her like a pillow.[232]

> [*Vdrug on [Raskol'nikov] vzdrognul, mozhet byt' spasennyi vnov' ot obmoroka odnim dikim i* **bezobraznym videniem**. *On pochuvstvoval, chto kto-to stal podle nego, sprava, riadom; on vzglianul – i uvidel zhenshchinu, vysokuiu, s platkom na golove, s* **zheltym**, *prodolgovatym, ispitym* **litsom** *i s krasnovatymi, vpavshimi glazami. Ona gliadela na nego priamo, no, ochevidno, nichego ne vidala i nikogo ne razlichala.*

---

[230] Sergei Mikhailov, "*O pisatele Iurii Mamleeve*", *Skrizhali*, 5.
[231] *Ibid.*, 6.
[232] Fedor Dostoevsky, *Crime and Punishment*, NY/London: W.W. Norton and Co., 1989, 144-145.

Vdrug ona oblokotilas' pravoiu rukoi o perila, podniala pravuiu nogu i zamakhnula ee za reshetku, zatem levuiu, i brosilas' v kanavu. **Griaznaia voda** *razdalas', poglotila na mgnovenie zhertvu, no cherez minutu utoplennitsa vsplyla, i ee tikho poneslo vniz po techeniiu, golovoi i nogami v vode, spinoi poverkh, so vzbivsheiusia i vspukhsheiu nad vodoi, kak podushka, iubkoi.*][233]

The woman survives; however, the ugliness of this near-death makes such an impression on Raskol'nikov that he decides against committing suicide himself. This never happens in Mamleev; his characters take pleasure in the *bezobrazie* of death. Peten'ka, Mamleev's autophague-protagonist in *Shatuny,* is trying to avoid "existential suicide" while literally feeding on his puss, pimples, and fungus infections, and then going on to eat his own flesh:

Meanwhile, Peten'ka already not only scraped pimples and fungi from himself, but really ate himself. And every day – deeper and deeper, more and more real. He himself even did not understand why he lived like that. Although there was, probably, a reason. Its name – his extreme lack of trust in the outside world, from which Peten'ka restrained himself from accepting even food.

Of the world Peten'ka was suspicious as to something limitlessly offensive, arrogant, and would rather let himself be torn to pieces than accept something essential from the world. The latter for him was equivalent to religious, or, rather, existential, suicide.

[*Mezhdu tem Peten'ka uzhe ne tol'ko soskrebyval s sebia pryshchi i lishai, a po-nastoiashchemu poedal samogo sebia. I s kazhdym dnem vse glubzhe i glubzhe, vse deistvitel'nei i deistvitel'nei. On i sam ne ponimal, pochemu on tak zhivet. Khotia prichina, veroiatno, byla. Imia ee – ego kraine nedoverchivoe otnoshenie k vneshnemu miru, ot kotorogo Petia vozderzhivalsia prinimat' dazhe pishchu.*

K miru Peten'ka otnosilsia s podozreniem, kak k chemu-to beskonechno oskorbitel'nomu, khamskomu, i skoree gotov byl dat' razorvat' sebia na kuski, chem

---

[233] D-*PSS*, 6:131. Note the colour yellow, occurring in connection with ugliness.

priniat' ot mira chto-nibud' sushchestvennoe. Poslednee dlia nego bylo ravnosil'no religioznomu ili, skoree, ekzistentsial'nomu samoubiistvu.][234]

The spiritual suicide of Sonia in *Crime and Punishment* is paralleled by the "existential suicide" worrying the pervert Peten'ka in *Shatuny*. Feeding on one's own flesh is also a common twentieth-century metaphor for the phenomenon of *refleksia* – extreme self-analysis – one of the ugliest characteristics of the Underground Man.

In Mamleev's novel *Moscow Gambit* [*Moskovskii Gambit*], his characters – so-called "*tvorcheskie liudi*" – constantly argue about the impossibility of existing in the underground (an allusion to that of Dostoevsky with its *bezobrazie* in "The Notes"). The events in the novel take place at the end of the sixties and beginning of the seventies, when Russia could boast of a number of 'undergrounds:' political, religious, artistic, philosophical and mystical. Knowing Mamleev's interest in mysticism and philosophy, one is not surprised by his writing a novel about a mystical and philosophical underground. A prose writer in *Moscow Gambit* named Muromtsev says that true culture can only be created in the underground, but not when everything is permitted. According to Mamleev, this was the unified opinion of the unofficial intellectual elite of the time.[235] This view is based on the idea that great literature is born in opposition to reality; and it understands the underground not as political or social, but as personal. Such an underground, in Mamleev's opinion, is a counter-reality which people create out of utter dissatisfaction with the existing world.[236] He goes on to develop the concept of a 'cosmic' underground, saying that the contemporary state of the world as a whole causes such a feeling of anxiety and disorder that it could evoke a cosmic resistance to what is happening on Earth – that is, a cosmic underground. Such a global underground, according to Mamleev, is related to a feeling of the end of a certain historical period, not in the sense of an apocalypse, however.[237] In his non-fiction, Mamleev insists on the possibility of the unique role of a future Russian literature written in the cosmic underground, also saying that with the end of the period of "rough" materialism, Orthodoxy is the power that can save Russia from mystical ignorance.[238] This belief in the uniqueness of the role of Russia and the Orthodox Church, making the Russians a special people with a mission for

---

[234] Iurii Mamleev, *Shatuny*, Moscow: Terra, 1996, 150.

[235] Iurii Mamleev, *"Moi geroi zadaiutsia voprosami, na kotorye razum ne v sostoianii otvetit'*, " *Literaturnaia gazeta*, 16.11.94, No. 7 (5487), 3.

[236] *Ibid.*

[237] *Ibid.*

[238] *Ibid.* See also Mamleev, *Rossiia vechnaia.*

the whole world, does of course bring Mamleev close to Dostoevsky's Pushkin Speech of 1881.[239] Mamleev affirms the duality of the powers of evil and God and emphasizes that man was created in the image – *obraz* – of God. In his non-fiction, Mamleev retains Dostoevsky's religious and utopian ideas and has demonstrated his historical hopefulness, first and foremost, by returning to Russia from abroad. In his *belles letters* (which seems an oxymoron when applied to Mamleev's *oeuvre*) Mamleev expands on the 'ideal of Sodom' to no end. Although contemporary clerics may be unhappy with Mamleev as a Christian in the traditional sense, just as Zen'kovsky and Leont'ev were critical of Dostoevsky's Orthodoxy,[240] Mamleev's use of the Biblical terminology so characteristic of Dostoevsky offers yet one more reason to believe that he is consciously recalling Dostoevsky's *bezobraznoe* in his texts.

Smirnov in his "Evolution of Monstrosity" ("*Evoliutsiia chudovishchnosti*") discusses the history of the ugly in world literature, relating the monstrous to the uncanny.[241] He chooses Freud and Bakhtin as his theoretical basis for the ugly and the monstrous in twentieth-century literature.[242] Freud emphasized the role of the uncanny – *das Unheimliche* – to the extent of making it the basis for culture; Bakhtin saw the most significant tendency of culture in carnival, which depicts death giving birth, and inverts corporeal top and bottom.[243] The monstrous and the uncanny in Freud and Bakhtin lead Smirnov to a discussion of the monstrosities of totalitarian Soviet society. The ugly, with its specific constituent the monstrous, has become the norm for the Soviet society, and Mamleev's texts, which he started to write in the end of the 1950s, have the social function of destroying the Stalinist construction of society and returning to the monstrous its own meaning.[244] Smirnov writes about Mamleev's monsters in the context of the postmodern love for the obscene; among postmodern philosophers Derrida, for example in his interpretation of Heidegger's philosophical anthropology, equates the monstrous with the specifically human. According to Smirnov, postmodernism insists on the monstrous as a sole characteristic of the subject, and Mamleev's monsters are not opposed to reality; they are opposed to other monsters in his books.[245] Monstrosity becomes the unifying feature for all Mamleev's characters. His catastrophic world of fantastic reality is inhabited by psychopaths, autocannibals, and

---

[239] This is not to mention Mamleev's membership in a literary committee of the "neo-Eurasia" party. This committee attempts to promote the Russian idea and bases its arguments on the heritage of the classics of Russian literature.

[240] *O Dostoevskom: Tvorchestvo Dostoevskogo v russkoi mysli 1881-1931 godov*, Moscow: *Kniga*, 1990, 407.

[241] I.P. Smirnov, "*Evoliutsiia chudovishchnosti: Mamleev i dr.*", *NLO* 3 (1993): 303.

[242] Note that Dostoevsky attracted the attention of both Freud and Bakhtin.

[243] Smirnov, "*Evoliutsiia chudovishchnosti*", 303.

[244] *Ibid.*, 305. Dating Mamleev's narratives is problematic as in the USSR they appeared only in *samizdat*; his published works appeared only in the 1980s and as *tamizdat*. See David Lowe, *Russian Writing Since 1953: A Critical Survey*, NY: *Ungar*, 1987, 108.

[245] Smirnov, "*Evoliutsiia chudovishchnosti*", 305.

murderers. In the novel *Shatuny*, the conflict is between monsters with differing social and intellectual characteristics. In this novel, Fedor Sonnov, who keeps on murdering people so that he can communicate with corpses, becomes close to the circles of a Moscow group of intellectual monsters philosophizing only on the topic of the dead, but eventually makes them his victims too. The monstrous in *Shatuny* is not only what is accessible to the naked eye: a grotesque body is one of its forms, the other one being the deformed, solipsistic mentality. This brings *Shatuny*'s anti-heroes close to the Underground Man and Raskol'nikov with his philosophy of everything being permissible.

Smirnov thinks that Russian writers in the 1970s modified the notion of the monstrous – thus changing the postmodern understanding of it – by equating the monstrous with the author.[246] In this light, "Notes from Underground" as a confessional narrative becomes ugly by definition. From the viewpoint of what Smirnov calls the second generation of postmodernists (Andrei Bitov, for example), the author may not write about the monstrosity of his characters without admitting his own ugliness.[247] In his article "Between Madness and Magic" [*Mezhdu bezumiem i magiei*], Mamleev traces the disharmony of the world back to the Underground man:

> Dostoevsky's man from the underground meant: Shouldn't we send all this **harmony** ... far away (probably having in mind cosmic harmony in general, not just social harmony). The paradox, however, lies in the fact that **the world** (and all its utopian varieties) **is far from being as harmonious as it seems**, so that there is actually no reason to send anything far away (is it not because of this, that all the theodicies are so limited and imperfectly developed?). The mystery of **"disharmony"** is to my mind absolutely unsolvable on the level of religious conventionality, on the level of ethics, on the level of the human mind in general.[248]

> [*Eshche podpol'nyi chelovek Dostoevskogo govoril, a ne poslat' li nam vsiu etu* **garmoniu** ... *kuda-nibud' podal'she (imeia, veroiatno, v vidu mirovuiu garmoniiu voobshche, a ne tol'ko sotsial'nuiu). Paradoks, odnako, zakliuchaetsia v tom, chto* **mir** *(i vse ego utopicheskie varianty)* **daleko ne tak garmonichen, kak kazhetsia,** *tak chto, sobstvenno, net prichin chto-libo posylat' podal'she (ne ottogo li tak ogranicheny, ne*

---

[246] *Ibid.*, 306.
[247] *Ibid.*
[248] Ulrich Schmid, "Flowers of Evil: The Poetics of Monstrosity in Contemporary Russian Literature (Erofeev, Mamleev, Sokolov, Sorokin)", *Russian Literature XLVIII* (2000): 208.

*dovedeny do kontsa vse teoditsei?). Taina zla, taina **"dizgarmonii"** absoliutno nerazreshima, na moi vzgliad, na urovne religioznoi konventsional'nosti, na urovne morali i chelovecheskogo uma voobshche.]*[249]

Bearing in mind that in Dostoevsky beauty is often associated with harmony and *bezobraznoe* with disharmony (See Chapter 2), I would like to take a closer look at the beginning of Mamleev's *Diary of an Individualist (Tetrad' individualista)*. This work begins with a short foreword providing the details about how the diary, or notebook, was found by a certain Ivan Il'ich Puzankov, a night watchman.[250] Mamleev's apologue – a typical detail of the age of the novel but an unorthodox structural feature for a late twentieth-century text – is an apparent parallel to the beginning of *Notes from the House of the Dead*, with its finding of Gorianchikov's notebook:

This old, ragged notebook was found near the dumpster by Ivan Il'ich **Puzankov**, a night watchman. He considered using it as a wrapping-paper for a herring, but, being drunk, started reading it. Having read a few pages, he gasped, and decided that he was delirious. He was most frightened by the fact that he – this meant – must not drink any more, though he was still missing 200 grams to make a full liter of vodka. But, having decided angrily that we who drink have never yet retreated, Ivan Il'ich nevertheless **crawled** off to the nearest tavern. There he sold this unbelievable notebook for half pint of beer and a pickled smelt to some feeble *intelligent* who was constantly looking around. This *intelligent* was the one who kept the notebook in cobwebs and out of reach.

[*Etu staruiu, dranuiu tetrad' nashel okolo pomoiki Ivan Il'ich **Puzankov**, storozh. On khotel bylo obernut' v nee seledku, no po p'ianomu delu nachal ee chitat'. Prochitav neskol'ko stranits, on akhnul, reshiv, chto u nego belaia goriachka. Ego napugalo bol'she vsego to, chto emu – znachit – nel'zia dalshe pit', a do litra vodki on ne dobral eshche 200 grammov. No, gnevno rassudiv, chto my, p'iushchie, esche*

[249] Iurii Mamleev, *"Mezhdu bezumiem i magiei," Beseda* 6 (1987): 181. Quoted in Schmid, "Flowers of Evil", 208.
[250] Iurii Mamleev, *Tetrad' individualista*, Viktor Erofeev, *Tzvety zla*, Moscow: *Podkova*, 1997, 117. The first name and patronymic are also typical nineteenth-century names directly from classic Russian literature: Tolstoy's *Death of Ivan Il'ich*.

*nikogda ne otstupali, Ivan Il'ich **popolz** vse-taki v blizhaishuiu pivnuiu. Tam on prodal etu neveroiatnuiu tetrad' za polkruzhki piva i kil'ku odnomu oziraiushchemusia, boleznennomu intelligentu, kotoryi i sokhranil ee v pautinakh i nedostupnosti.]*[251]

The last name of the night watchman – Puzankov (Tubby) – is an allusion to the name Polzunkov – the protagonist of the eponymous short-story by Dostoevsky. This connection is etymologically reinforced by the verb used in the same passage: Puzankov crawls into a tavern (*"popolz"*). The name Polzunkov has the same root as *"popolz,"* *"-polz-"* from *"polzat'"* (to crawl). The connection is also magnified by the comic tone of Mamleev's apologue, recalling the fact that Polzunkov is a laughing-stock for everybody in Dostoevsky's story – the ugly in its comic form. Polzunkov seems to be the author's mouthpiece when he calls his story both tragic and comical.[252] Another ugly "P"-character of Dostoevsky – Prokharchin – dies on a mattress filled with change and banknotes. He attempts to deceive other corner-dwellers by drawing their attention to his case, in which they are convinced Prokharchin is keeping his valuables.[253] In a similar fashion, one of the characters in Mamleev's *Diary of an Individualist* enjoys drawing attention to his suitcase full of cash.[254] The protagonist of the *Diary of an Individualist* is a cross between Polzunkov and the Underground Man. Compare the beginning of the *Diary of an Individualist* to the beginning of "Notes from Underground:"

I am yet a filthy little human being. And even more so because I am writing about it – in love with myself; condemning myself – a little rascal, decay-stricken, it's not enough to give me a leg-up – but I am still in love with myself! And how much in love! Heavenly. And yet it is vile to love oneself so…

[*Poganen'kii ia vse-taki chelovechishko. I eshche bolee poganen'kii, chto pishu ob etom – liubia; klianu sebia – negodiaiushko, marazmatik, ushki nadrat' malo – a vse-taki liubliu! I kak liubliu! Po-nebesnomu. No vse zhe eto podlo – tak liubit' sebia…*][255]

---

[251] Iurii Mamleev, *Tetrad' individualista*, in Viktor Erofeev, *Tzvety zla*, Moscow: *Podkova*, 1997, 117. *Cf.* F.M. Dostoevsky, *Zapiski iz mertvogo doma*, *Sobranie sochinenii*, Vol. 4, Moscow: *Khudozhestvennaia literatura*, 1956, 389-394.

[252] F.M. Dostoevsky, *Sobranie sochinenii*, Vol. 1, Moscow: *Khudozhestvennaia literatura*, 1956, 505.

[253] *Ibid.*, 394.

[254] Mamleev, *Tetrad' individualista*, 120.

[255] *Ibid.*, 117.

I am a sick man... I am a spiteful man. No, I am not a pleasant man at all. I believe there is something wrong with my liver. However, I don't know a damn thing about my liver; neither do I know whether there is anything really wrong with me. I am not under medical treatment, and never have been, though I do respect medicine and doctors. In addition, I am extremely superstitious, at least sufficiently so to respect medicine. (I am well educated enough not to be superstitious, but I am superstitious for all that.) The truth is, I refuse medical treatment out of spite. I don't suppose you will understand that. Well, I do.[256]

[*Ia chelovek bol'noi...Ia zloi chelovek. Neprivlekatel'nyi ia chelovek. Ia dumaiu, chto u menia bolit pechen'. Vprochem, ia ni shisha ne smysliu v moei bolezni i ne znaiu naverno, chto u menia bolit. Ia ne lechus' i nikogda ne lechilsia, khotia meditsinu i doktorov uvazhaiu. K tomu zhe ia eshche i sueveren do krainosti; nu, khot' nastol'ko, chtob uvazhat' meditsinu. (Ia dostatochno obrazovan, chtob ne byt' suevernym, no ia sueveren.) Net-s, ia ne khochu lechitsia so zlosti. Vot vy etogo, naverno, ne izvolite ponimat'. Nu-s, a ia ponimaiu.*][257]

An allusion to Dostoevsky's Prokharchin occurs when the Individualist, who mentions his name – Sasha – in passing once in a flirtatious manner, describes his brother-in-law:

That brother of hers was even in a way a pathological personality. A very reserved, **stingy** young man, he deprived himself of everything, only to save money. I remember, one night, when having eaten **a bit of brown bread with an onion**, he went into his **suitcase**, pulled an enormous pile of money from it, and hysterically stroking it, having slobbered all over it, pressed against his heart and muttered: "Only with [money] I can feel myself an *intelligent*."

He needed money not to spend, but to feel himself an human-being, a personality precious in itself, and he put nothing in his life higher than it.[258]

[256] *The Best Short Stories of Dostoevsky*, NY: The Modern Library, 1992, 115-116.
[257] F.M. Dostoevsky, *Sobranie sochinenii*, Vol. 4, Moscow: *Khudozhestvennaia literatura*, 1956, 133.
[258] *Shatuny* starts with a description of a person champing on an onion. See Iurii Mamleev, *The Sky Above Hell and Other Stories*, trans. H.W. Tjalsma. New York: Taplinger Publishing Company, 1980, 73.

[Bratets ee byl dazhe lichnost'iu v svoem rode patologicheskoi. Ochen' zamknutyi,
skarednyi *molodoi chelovek, on otkazyval sebe vo vsem, lish by skopit' den'gi. Ia*
pomniu, kak vecherom, **otkushav korochku chernogo khleba s lukovitsei,** *on polez v*
chemodan, *vytashchil ottuda ogromnuiu pachku deneg i, isterichno poglazhivaia ee,*
obsliuniaviv, prizhal k serdtsu i probormotal: "Tol'ko s nimi ia chuvstvuiu sebia
intelligentom."

Den'gi emu nuzhny byli ne dlia togo, chtoby ikh tratit', a chtoby chuvstvovat'
sebia chelovekom, samotsennoi lichnost'iu, i vyshe ikh on nichego v zhizni ne stavil.]²⁵⁹

Dostoevsky's Prokharchin demonstrates analogous pathological behaviour:

> First thing that everybody noticed was, no doubt, the **hoarding** and **stinginess** of
> Semen Ivanovich [Prokharchin]... Lunch cost half a ruble; Semen Ivanovich always
> used only twenty-five copecks in copper money and never went farther than that, and
> that is why he took either a single serving of cabbage soup with a pie, or a single serving
> of beef; most often he did not eat either soup, or beef, but **ate** his fill of sifted-flour
> **bread with an onion...**

> *[Pervoe, na chto obratili vnimanie, bylo, bez somneniia,* **skopidomstvo i**
> **skarednost'** *Semena Ivanovicha [Prokharchina]...Obed stoil poltiny; Semen Ivanovich*
> *upotreblial tol'ko dvadtsat' piat' kopeek med'iu i nikogda ne voskhodil vyshe, i potomu*
> *bral po portsiiam ili odni shchi s pirogom, ili odnu goviadinu; chashche zhe vsego ne el*
> *ni shchei, ni goviadiny, a s"edal v meru sitnogo s lukom...]²⁶⁰*

Diary of an Individualist, published in the end of the twentieth century, is discussed by Viktor
Erofeev, who distinguishes between different types of Russian literature: Soviet, anti-Soviet, and a-
Soviet.[261] Using his typology, we can say that Mamleev's literature is not just a reaction to Stalinist
literature but a principally different – 'other' – alternative prose that makes a point of being a-Soviet
rather than anti-Soviet.[262] In my opinion, this is correct, as Mamleev's prose does not seem to change

---

[259] Mamleev, *Tetrad' individualista*, 120.
[260] F.M. Dostoevsky, *Sobranie sochinenii*, Vol. 1, Moscow: *Khudozhestvennaia literatura*, 1956, 392.
[261] Viktor Erofeev, *Russkie tzvety zla*, Moscow: *Podkova*, 1997, 12.
[262] *Ibid.*, 17.

much, if at all, after the immediate post-Stalinist period.[263] When Mamleev wrote his texts in the immediate post-Stalinist historical context, they appeared to be part of the polemic with Stalinist literature, but his works since the 1990s do not differ much in their choice of themes or style, and at the end of the twentieth-century and beginning of the twenty-first century they all rather appear a-Soviet, dealing with the monstrous as an aesthetic and literary category. His contemporary characters, although they may now be businessmen and hitmen, are as interested in death and solipsistic monstrosities as ever. Erofeev writes that in the 1980s both Soviet and anti-Soviet literatures have died; and "writers are left with no literature. Not all of them, however."[264] The literature that survives is the a-Soviet, 'the other,' alternative literature which

> learned from a strange (from the point of view of the Russian intelligentsia consciousness) mix of teachers: Gogol' and the Marquis de Sade, decadents of the beginning of the century and surrealists, mystics and the Beatles, Andrei Platonov and the unknown Leonid Dobychin, Nabokov and Borges. It loved Pound and the *zaum'* of the OBERIU, the action movies of Hollywood, pop-art and thieves' songs, Stalin's skyscrapers and western postmodernism.

> [*...uchilas' u strannoi (s tochki zreniia russkogo intelligentnogo soznaniia) smesi uchitelei: Gogolia i markiza de Sada, dekadentov nachala veka i surrealistov, mistikov i gruppy "Bitlz", Andreia Platonova i nikomu ne vedomovogo Leonida Dobychina, Nabokova i Borkhesa. Ona liubila Paunda i zaum' oberiutov, boeviki Gollivuda, pop-art i blatnye pesni, stalinskie neboskreby i zapadnyi postmodern.*][265]

The philosophy of Khrushchev's Thaw, based on a return to humanistic norms, predetermined the choice of the 'theme of the good' for the whole generation of poets and prose writers of the sixties – "*shestidesiatniki*" such as Evgenii Evtushenko, Bulat Okudzhava, Vasilii Aksenov, Fazil' Iskander, Andrei Bitov, Vladimir Voinovich, and Georgii Vladimov.[266] I am convinced that, although chronologically contemporary, Mamleev with his focus on *bezobraznoe* does not belong to this group.

---

[263] See his recent *Bunt luny*, Moscow: Vagrius, 2000.

[264] Viktor Erofeev, *Russkie tzvety zla*, Moscow: *Podkova*, 1997, 11.

[265] *Ibid.*, 12.

[266] *Ibid.*, 11.

The themes of the *shestidesiatniki* and Mamleev are in pivotal opposition: as much as they choose 'the theme of the good', Mamleev chooses the theme of the monstrous and of evil.

According to Erofeev, the starting point for new Russian literature is Hell; two representatives of this literature – Solzhenitsyn and Shalamov – describe the horrors of the GULAG hell. Solzhenitsyn glorifies the Russian soul; Shalamov shows the borderline after which the soul is destroyed, and becomes irreversibly ugly. In his characterization of the new literature, Erofeev affirms that psychopathological prose takes the place of classical Russian psychological prose.[267] This seems to be particularly true for the case of Mamleev, as is Erofeev's general remark about heroes and anti-heroes who easily swap places, or become one.[268] It seems plausible to me that Dostoevsky's controversial Underground Man – although placed by his author among the ranks of the anti-heroes – might represent the beginning of this tendency. Any character in the new Russian prose can become destructive; any feeling expressed by a character untouched by evil is doubted. Erofeev correctly insists that the place of beauty in the alternative literature is taken by *bezobrazie*.[269] Among other tendencies of the new literature are: an aesthetics of épatage and shock; vulgar language as detonator of the text; black despair or cynical indifference.[270] I think Erofeev equates the new Russian literature with *chernukha* (the black literature), in which everything is ugly: death, sex, old age, food, daily routine. New literary texts are full of murders, rapes, seductions, abortions, and tortures. Characters tend to be either insane or mentally deficient, and not just the GULAG but the collapse of all of Russia becomes the metaphor for life.[271] Erofeev emphasizes that Mamleev's narrator begins with a self-definition ("I am yet a filthy little human being") borrowed from Dostoevsky's Underground Man.[272] He also agrees with other critics on the primary importance of the theme of death in Mamleev's writings: "This [death] is an all-consuming obsession, a delighting in the opening of a taboo *sujet*..." [*Eto vsepolglashchaiushchaia obsessiia, vostorg otkrytia tabuirovannogo siuzheta...*][273] Erofeev writes that death in Mamleev's texts is the only true connection between real life and consciousness; death allows for an ugly form of real life.[274] He calls Mamleev's narration conservative (as opposed, one might imagine, to the Moscow conceptualist school, or Dmitrii Bulatov's visual poetry), and emphasizes its similarity to Dostoevsky's prose. He also points out – and I agree – that the lack of thematic variation

---

[267] *Ibid.*, 12-14.
[268] *Ibid.*, 14.
[269] *Ibid.*
[270] *Ibid.*, 14.
[271] *Ibid.*
[272] *Ibid.*, 17.
[273] *Ibid.*
[274] *Ibid.*

in Mamleev comes very close to self-parody.[275] In other words, it is sufficient to read one text to get a good feeling of what the rest are like. Parody and self-parody in Mamleev are related to the polemic function of the quotation in Kozitskaia's system.

L.D. Opul'skaia writes on the connection between "Notes from Underground" and *Crime and Punishment*:

An essential stage on the author's path toward *Crime and Punishment* was his work at "Notes from Underground." The tragedy of a thinking hero-individualist, his proud delight in his "idea" and defeat in the face of "living life," which is personified in the "Notes" by a direct forerunner of Sonia Marmeladova, a girl from a brothel, the image of which, however, does not bear that deep philosophical and ethical load, that the image of Sonia bears, – these basic contours of the "Notes" directly prepare *Crime and Punishment*.

[*Sushchestvennym etapom na puti, priblizivshim avtora k "Prestupleniiu i nakazaniiu", iavilas' rabota nad "Zapiskami iz podpol'ia". Tragediia mysliashchego geroia-individualista, ego gordelivoe upoenie svoei "ideei" i porazhenie pered litsom "zhivoi zhizni", v kachestve voploshcheniia kotoroi v "Zapiskakh" vystupaet priamaia predshestvennitsa Soni Marmeladovoi, devushka iz publichnogo doma, obraz kotoroi, odnako, ne neset eshche toi glubokoi filosofsko-eticheskoi nagruzki, kakuiu neset obraz Soni, -- eti osnovnye obshchie kontury "Zapisok" neposredstvenno podgotavlivaiut "Prestuplenie i nakazanie".*][276]

Grossman thought it possible that Dostoevsky started to work on the idea of *Crime and Punishment* in the beginning of the 1850s, even though his notebooks mention Raskol'nikov only in 1865.[277] This allows us to suggest that *Crime and Punishment* is a development, a continuation of "Notes from Underground," and that we may look at both works as a meta-text.

As *Crime and Punishment*, being a proper novel, has more details of descriptions of interiors of St. Petersburg apartments than "Notes from Underground," I would like to look at the actual space in the novel:

It was a **large room**, but very **low ceilinged**... Sonia's room was rather like a barn; **the irregularity of its angles made it look misshapen**. One wall, with three

---

[275] *Ibid.*
[276] D-*PSS*, 7: 308.
[277] *Ibid.*

windows which gave on to the canal, **was set obliquely**, so that one corner, forming a **terribly acute angle, seemed to run off into obscurity**, and when the light was poor the whole of it could not even be seen properly; the other **angle** was **monstrously obtuse**. There was hardly any furniture in this large room. To the right, **in the corner**, was a bed, with a chair beside it nearer the door. Against the same wall, very close to the door into the other flat, stood a plain deal table covered with a blue cloth, with two cane chairs near it. By the opposite wall, not far **from the narrow corner**, was a small, plain, **wooden chest of drawers, looking lost in the empty space**. This was all there was in the room. The **yellowish, dirty, rubbed wallpaper** was **darkened in the corners**; the **room** must have been **damp and full of charcoal fumes fumes in winter.** Its poverty was evident; the bed had not even curtains.[278]

[*Eto byla **bol'shaia komnata**, **no** chrezvychaino **nizkaia**...Sonina komnata pokhodila kak budto na sarai, imela vid ves'ma **nepravil'nogo chetyrekhugol'nika**, i eto pridavalo ei chto-to **urodlivoe**. Stena s tremia oknami, vykhodivshaia na kanavu, **pererezyvala komnatu kak-to vkos'**, otchego odin **ugol**, uzhasno **ostryi**, ubegal kuda-to vglub', tak chto ego, pri slabom osveshchenii, dazhe i razliadet' nel'zia bylo khoroshen'ko; drugoi zhe **ugol** byl **uzhe slishkom bezobrazno tupoi**. Vo vsei etoi bol'shoi komnate pochti sovsem ne bylo mebeli. **V uglu**, napravo, nakhodilas' krovat'; podle nee, blizhe k dveri, stul. Po toi zhe stene, gde byla krovat', u samukh dverei v chuzhuiu kvartiru, stoial prostoi tesovyi stol, pokrytyi sinen'koiu skatert'iu; okolo stola dva pletenykh stula. Zatem, u protivopolozhnoi steny, poblizosti ot **ostrogo ugla**, stoial nebol'shoi, prostogo dereva komod, kak by **zateriavshiisia v pustote**. Vot i vse, chto bylo v komnate. **Zheltovatye, obshmygannye i istaskannye oboi** pocherneli **po vsem uglam**; dolzhno byt' zdes' byvalo **syro i ugarno zimoi**. **Bednost' byla vidimaia**; dazhe u krovati ne bylo zanavesok.*][279]

The description of Sonia's room includes a striking number of corners/angles: acute and obtuse, ugly and irregular, they are mentioned five times. Just as Raskol'nikov's coffin-like room, Sonia's room has a low ceiling, and although it is large, it is sparsely furnished and disproportionate. The

---

[278] Dostoevsky, *Crime and Punishment*, 266-267.
[279] D-*PSS*, 6:241-242.

69

poverty is apparent; and two different words for "ugly" appear in the same passage: "*urodlivyi*" and "*bezobrazno*." Doors to another apartment lead directly from Sonia's room; there is no feeling of privacy. Similar to old Marmeladov's room, that of Sonia is like a market-place at *Sennaia* Square (a place of chaos and *bezobrazie*). The wallpaper in Sonia's room is yellow, as it is in the pawn-broker's apartment and in the dwellings of many other inhabitants of Dostoevsky's Petersburg. S.M. Solov'ev says that the background of *Crime and Punishment* is exclusively yellow; according to Catteau, "the background of Petersburg is rather whitewashed dusty grey" but yellow "invades" it like a disease. Catteau insists that yellow "establishes the atmosphere of infamy, disgust, spiritual oppression, moral illness and even madness, but chiefly of aggression." [280] From the description of Sonia's room, it seems though that Dostoevsky uses yellow as a sign of *bezobrazie*/ugliness rather than aggression *per se*.

The bedroom in the pawnbroker's apartment is described as "*ochen' nebol'shaia komnata s ogromnym kiotom obrazov.*"[281] The icons in her bedroom do not stop Raskol'nikov from taking the valuables; Dostoevsky's reference to them shows his disapproval of Raskol'nikov's theory. The colour yellow occurs three times in the first description of the pawnbroker's apartment:

> The little room the young man entered, with its faded [**yellow**] wall-paper, geraniums, and muslin window-curtains, was bright with the rays of the setting sun... The **old furniture, all of** painted **yellow wood**, consisted of a sofa with a high curved wooden back, an oval table in front of it, a dresser with a small mirror between the windows, some chairs against the wall, and two or three **cheap** pictures in **yellow frames**, representing **German** young ladies with birds in their hands: that was all... "How do **nasty old widows** contrive to have everything so clean?" he continued to himself... The flat contained only these two rooms.[282]

> [*Nebol'shaia komnata, v kotoruiu proshel molodoi chelovek, s zheltymi oboiami, geraniami i kiseinymi zanaveskami na oknakh, byla v etu minuty iarko osveshchena zakhodiashchim solntsem. . . Mebel', vsia ochen' staraia i iz zheltogo dereva, sostoiala iz divana s ogromnoiu vygnutoiu dereviannoiu spinkoi, kruglogo stola oval'noi formy pered divanom, tualeta s zerkaltsem v prostenke, stul'ev po stenam da dvukh-trekh groshovykh kartinok v zheltykh ramkakh, izobrazhavshikh nemetskikh baryshen' s*

---

[280] Catteau, *Dostoevsky and the Process of Literary Creation*, 409-410.
[281] D-*PSS*, 6:62.
[282] Dostoevsky, *Crime and Punishment*, 4-5.

*ptitsami v rukakh, – vot i vsia mebel'. . . "Eto u **zlykh i starykh vdovits** byvaet takaia chistota", – prodolzhal pro sebia Raskol'nikov. . . Vsia kvartira sostoiala iz etikh dvykh komnat.]*[283]

The wooden picture frames and furniture are yellow; the cheap pictures are of some German girls – another detail with negative connotations for Dostoevsky. Both the pawnbroker and her furniture are called old; she is also rather venomously characterized by a 'formless' Raskol'nikov as an "evil widow."

"Notes from Underground" is a work in which *bezobraznoe* is associated with the 'formlessness' of the Underground Man and his existential disorder. Given Dostoevsky's claim about the Underground Man representing the Russian majority and bearing in mind that Raskol'nikov is an Underground Man-type character, we understand that he attempts to provide the reader with a picture of the chaos and formlessness of St. Petersburg society – perhaps of humanity in general.

In the works of twentieth-century writers (Remizov, Bulgakov, Aksenov, Tolstaia, P'etsukh, etc., or in films such as *Window to Paris*) the house symbolises the nation. These works portray Russia as a country of the Underground people, and although for Dostoevsky the Underground Man does not comprise the whole nation, he is nevertheless believed to be a representative of the educated, alienated majority. It seems to me that we may trace the idea of the house symbolizing the nation back to Dostoevsky, as the apartments and interiors in his works are reflections of his "underground" characters' psychological state.[284] Disorder in the house for Dostoevsky thus serves as a double symbol: on the one hand – of disorder in Russia, on the other – of disorder in his characters' moral and/or religious feelings.

In *Crime and Punishment*, St. Petersburg is the city of jaundiced vision: dirty yellow is the dominant colour in its portrayal. Petersburg dwellings have low ceilings and numerous corners. These 'underground' apartments have irregular shapes; they are either too small (Raskol'nikov's), or too large (Sonia's), but either way disproportionate; and we see that Petersburg, in reality a city dominated by architecture of classical proportions, paradoxically becomes formless/*bezobraznyi* and chaotic in Dostoevsky.

The "underground" characters of contemporary Russian texts oppose themselves to society, indulge in their reflections, and focus on themselves. They do not all suffer from loneliness or

---

[283] D-*PSS*, 6:8-9.

[284] The parallel between psychological state and interiors also has its roots in Gogol', e.g. in his *Dead Souls* [*Mertvye dushi*].

alienation from society. Mamleev's characters, for example, are not suffering because of their solipsism; quite on the contrary, they demonstrate how the *"Iainost"* theory provides a philosophical basis for their perverted way of living and gives them satisfaction. They are not reaching out for other, "normal," individuals as the underground man does, though unsuccessfully as a victim of *"obosoblenie."* In fact, Mamleev's underground characters form sects, which testifies to a multi-layered reception of Dostoevsky in Mamleev's *Shatuny*, including pure meaning-forming and, the more complex retrospective quotation: both directly and through other writers influenced by Dostoevsky such as Andrei Bely, with his portrayal of the highly antisocial sectarians in *The Silver Dove*. There are plenty of "underground" characters in Mamleev; they constitute the society we see in *Shatuny*, for instance. In this novel, the underground man indeed represents the majority.

Dostoevsky affirmed that 'the cause of the underground' is in the lack of faith in common rules: *"net nichego sviatogo"* (there is nothing sacred).[285] The underground in the twentieth century often implies non-conformity to the established social and political order. Kudriavtsev in his book *Tri kruga Dostoevskogo* calls the underground man *"podpol'shchik"* which, whether he is conscious of it or not, distinctly means a member of a political resistance group.[286]

According to the *"Iainost"* theory, professed by the "underground" characters of *Shatuny*, there is nothing sacred; the ego becomes the object of adoration, love, and faith; Mamleev also calls this theory an underground metaphysics and religion:

> Through Glubev's disciples he got introduced, at a certain point, to the religion of "I."
> And he enflamed his soul. He deeply felt some of the theoretical details of this underground metaphysics.
>
> He delighted in, for example, the main thesis of this new religion about the "I" of the believer having to be the object of adoration, love, and hope.
>
> [*Cherez uchenikov Glubeva[287] on poznakomilsia v svoe vremia s religiei Ia. I vozgorelsia dushoiu. On gluboko oshchushchal nekotorye teoreticheskiie niuansy etoi podpol'noi metafiziki.*

---

[285] *Ibid*. See also "Notes from Underground", P.1, Ch. 5.
[286] Iu.G. Kudriavtsev, *Tri kruga Dostoevskogo*, Moscow: *Izdatel'stvo Moskovskogo universiteta*, 1979, 230. Kudriavtsev repeats the word *"podpol'shchik"* after Dostoevsky (See Kudriavtsev, 229), but it does not mean that a twentieth-century critic should not be aware of contemporary connotations.
[287] Again, one cannot help noticing the allusion to Andrei Bely's *Serebrianyi golub'*.

Ego voskhishchalo, naprimer, glavnoe polozhenie novoi religii o tom, chto ob''ektom pokloneniia, liubvi i very dolzhno byt' sobstvennoe Ia veruiushchego.]²⁸⁸

Like the Underground Man writing his notes for himself, or at least, claiming to do so, an underground poet in Mamleev's *Shatuny* writes a collection on the ego, keeping this book to himself and not showing it even to his admirers:

> Gennadii Remin belonged to the same generation as Padov. He was considered one of the best underground poets, but some cycles of his poetry were not even getting to his most unbridled fans; certain things, for example, his collection "Ego – Corpse Lyrics," he kept in a wooden box, not showing it to anybody.

> [*Gennadii Remin prinadlezhal k tomu zhe pokoleniiu, chto Padov. On schitalsia odnim iz luchshikh podpol'nykh poetov, no nekotorye tsykly ego stikhov ne dokhodili dazhe do ego raznuzdannykh poklonnikov; koe-chto, naprimer, sbornik "Ego – trupnaia lirika", on khranil v iashchike, nikomu ne pokazyvaia.*]²⁸⁹

The text of Mamleev's novel *Shatuny* is supersaturated with references to Dostoevsky, particularly having to do with his *bezobrazie*. In the following Table, I would like to show the most apparent parallels between Dostoevsky's and Mamleev's texts – which elements of Dostoevsky's poetics of the ugly Mamleev uses and in what manner:

Page/ comments²⁹⁰	Russian text	English text
87. Death and obscenity.	*Osobenno voskhitilo Padova prevrashcheniie Andreia Nikiticha, kotorogo on tak i nazyval teper':*	Padov was especially taken with the transformation of Andrei Nikitich, whom he immediately dubbed "Chicken-

²⁸⁸ Mamleev, *Shatuny*, 128.
²⁸⁹ *Ibid.*
²⁹⁰ Pagination from Mamleev, *Shatuny*.

	kurotrup.	corpse."
	I vdrug iz-za spiny razdalsia blagostnyi, chut' shal'noi golos Klavy: – Prisusedilis', nebesnye… Nu kak, Annulia, otsosala emu iad nebesnyi iz chlena?..a?.. – I ona laskovo potrepala pukhloi rukoi Aninu grud'. …	Suddenly, Klava's sweet, somewhat demented voice rang out behind their backs: "Angels snuggling side by side… So, Annulia, did you suck God's poison out of his organ good and proper? Huh?" And she patted Anna's chest with her swollen hand…
Death. "Human chicken" in Mamleev and "human louse" in Dostoevsky.	*Nado skazat', chto dva dnia nazad Andrei Nikitich stal uzhe razgovarivat', no kak-to odnoslozhno. Strashno izmennennyi dazhe vneshne, teper', posle neskol'kikh dnei novoi zhizni, on skoree napominal ne zhivuiu kuritsu, a mertvuiu. I teper', v svoikh odnoslozhnykh vyrazheniiakh, on uzhe tak ne upiral na to, chto on – kuritsa, a vyrazhal mnenie, chto on prosto mertv.*	Two days earlier, Andrei Nikitich had resumed talking, albeit in monosyllables. He had changed terribly after these several days of his new life; he sooner resembled a dead chicken than a living one. And now in his monosyllabic utterances he did not insist so much on the fact that he was a hen but rather expressed an opinion that he was simply dead.[291]
90. Underground. Underworld, evil, and uncanny	*Iz-pod zemli donessia Klavin golos, prichem pochemu-to s pokhabnymi intonatsiiami:* - *Da, kazhis', zlymi vsekh*	Klava's answer came from below ground: "Well, seems he thought we were all evil." Padov laughed.

[291] Mamleev, *The Sky Above Hell and Other Stories*, 117-118.

characters. Grave. Obscenity.	*nas schital.* *Padov rassmeialsia.* - Da ved' my ne zlye, my prosto potustoronnie, – skazal on i spriatal golovku v travianuiu mogilu. …	"Come now, we're not evil, we're just ethereal," he said, ducking down out of sight.[292] [into a grass grave]
The other world. Grave. Underground. Metaphysical nightmares. Monstrocity.	*A Padova nedarom nazyvali* *"liubimchik zagrobnogo* *mira"; v travianoi mogilke* *on nadumal takoe pro* *budushchuiu zhizn', chto ne* *reshalsia skazat' ob etom* *dazhe Anne. S* *poblednevshchim litsom on* *vylez iz-pod zemli.* *Voobshche metafizicheskie* *koshmary chasto smenialis'* *v ego dushe, verenitsei, odin* *chudovishchnei drugogo.* *Vozmozhno, chto sygrala* *rol' peremena situatsii . . .*	And not for nothing Padov was called "a favourite of the other world;" in his little grass grave he thought such things about the future life that he did not dare to tell about even to Anna. His face grown pale; he climbed out from under ground. In general, metaphysical nightmares were often interchanging in his soul, one more monstrous than the other. It is possible that a change in the situation played a role…
Grave. Narcissism.	*Anna eshche lezhala v* *mogilke, liubuias' na sebia* *v zerkaltse. V to zhe vremia* *ona iskala nepoznavaemoe v* *samoi sebe.*	Anna was still lying in her little grave and looking at herself with love in her little mirror. She was, at the same time, searching for the unknown in her own self.
Sex with "the	*K tomu zhe Annu*	Besides, Anna could not

---

[292] *Ibid.*, 119.

thing in itself" – parody of Kant's *Ding an Sich*. The horrible. The canny. "Metaphysical courtesan."	*presledovala mysl' o proshedshei nochi: o soedinenii s Padovym i veshchiu v sebe. Do etogo, periodami, ona zhila s Padovym, no s veshchiu v sebe – nikogda. I dazhe fizicheskoe udovletvorenie ot etoi nochi kazalos' ei zhutkim i lezhashchim po tu storonu obychnogo... Ona dazhe ne mogla poniat', udovletvorena li ona ili prosto spokoina – spokoina kholodom neizvestnogo. "Ty u nas metafizicheskaia kurtizanka", – govoril ei neredko Padov."*	stop thinking of the last night: of the intercourse with Padov and the thing in itself. Earlier, from time to time, she did have sex with Padov but never – with thing in itself. And even physical satisfaction from that night seemed to her horrifying and uncanny... She could not even understand if she was satisfied, or rather just calm – calm with the cold of the unknown. "You are our metaphysical courtesan," – Padov often told to her.
92. Metaphysical sex. Surreal window into the Unknown.	*– Klavusha-to naslazhdaetsia, – podmignula Anna Padovu. – Vot tol'ko kak, nikto ne znaet . . . No dusha Anny po-prezhnemu byla zaniata nepoznavaemym; i dazhe litso Padova bylo kak surreal'noe okno v nepoznavaemyi mir. No vneshne Anna byla zdes'.*	– Well, Klavusha has her fun, – Anna blinked to Padov. – Only how she does it, nobody knows... But Anna's soul was still busy with the unknowable; and even Padov's face was like a surreal window into the unknowable world. But in appearance, Anna was here.
95. Dead dish. Sex with a gosling.	*Annu i Padova porazilo stremitel'noe prevrashchenie zhivogo*	Anna and Padov were struck by the speedy transformation of a living gosling into a dead,

Devouring the dead lover – the use of Dostoevky's symbol for ugly sins – spiders.	*gusenka v mertvoe, sochnoe bliudo. Eta istoriia vdrug vnezapno ochen' bol'no kol'nula v serdtse, podcherknuv vsiu illuzornost' zhizni.* *Anna bez sodroganiia ne mogla vziat' kusok miasa v rot. Klavusha zhe dobrodushno i naslazhdenno upisyvala vovsiu.* *– Poliubovnichka svoego zhrete, Klavdiia Ivanovna? – umililsia Padov...*	juicy dish. This story suddenly hurt everybody, having underlined all the illusiveness of life. Anna could not take a slice of meat into her mouth without shuddering. Klavusha, however, was devouring the food whole-heartedly and enjoying herself. - You are eating your paramour, Klavdiia Ivanovna, aren't you? – Padov was moved...
A spiritual disciple named Aleksei – parody of Alesha Karamazov. Stylization of Dostoevsky: *svoebrazno.* Corners.	*Na sleduiuschii den' priekhal Aleksei Khristoforov. . . Annushka tozhe postaralas' zaderzhat' ego do vechera, svoeobrazno prigolublivaia. Khristoforov priatalsia ot nikh po uglam, v sarae, mezhdu drovami.*	Next day Aleksei Khistoforov arrived... Annushka also tried to make him stay till the night, fondling him in her own way. Khristoforov hid from them in the corners, in the shack, in the firewood.
96.Ugly impulses. Holy foolishness. Alesha Khristoforov's religious	On [Aleskei Khristoforov] boialsia Padova, boialsia cherez nego vyzvat' v sebe kakie-to bezobraznye impul'sy. Khotia Padov chasto nes pri nem	He [Aleksei Khristoforov] was afraid of Padov, was afraid to awake some ugly impulses in himself. Although Padov often talked nonsense in his presence, Alesha felt that

feeling.	nesusvetnuiu, iurodivuiu dich, Alesha chuvstvoval, chto za vsem etim skryvaetsia takoe, pri vide chego nado bezhat' v travy i molit'sia.	behind all that there was something that would make you run to the fields and pray, if you saw it.
116. Allusions to Andrei Bely. Sectarians – Rogozhin. Mikhei as an human being un-related to God, i.e. *bezobraznoe.* Low and common.	*Sam Mikhei k sekte otnosilsia ironicheski, schitaia skoptsov ne "belymi golubiami" kak oni sebia nazyvali, a vorobyshkami; Gospoda ili Tvortsa vselennoi Mikhei, obtiraia kroshki so rta, liubovno nazyval "khoziainom". No vnutrenne schital chto sam ne imeet k Tvortsu nikakogo otnosheniia.*	Mikhei himself had an ironic attitude towards the sect, considering the sectarians to be not "the white doves" as they called themselves, but sparrows. Wiping the crumbs from his mouth, Mikhei called the Lord or Creator – the master. Deep in his heart, he, however, did not think that he had any relation to the Creator.
117. Spiritual eunuch. Sectarians. Andrei Bely allusion. Dark, bigoted, yet full of God's grace appearance – evil and good characters of Dostoevsky. The horrible.	*Okazalos', chto Fedoru povezlo: skoptsy pochemu-to ochen' doveriali Mikheiu, i on zaranee dogovorilsia, chto privedet na radeniia, poruchivshis' za nego, svoego starogo druga, kotorogo Mikhei predstavil kak "dukhovnogo skoptsa", to est' fakticheski chlena sekty, no drugogo "korablia" i drugogo*	It turned out that Fedor was lucky: the sectarians for some reason trusted Mikhei, and he agreed with them in advance that he would bring his old friend to the rites, having vouched for him. Mikhei introduced this friend as a "spiritual *skopets*", that is as a factual member of the sect, but from a different "ship" and from a different trend.

Ferociousness. Dostoevsky's stylistics: narrow trail; house lacking air; hidden black bathhouse; small window.	*napravleniia.* *Zhutkii i svirepyi vid Fedora malo napominal vid "dukhovnogo skoptsa" ili "belogo golubia", no Mikhei liubovno prichesal Fedora, staraias' pridat' ego mrako-izuverskomu litsu blagostnyi vid. Potom skazal, chto soidet.* *Pod noch', kogda vse selo spalo, Fedora s Mikheiem vpustili chrez kalitku neveroiatno vysokogo, slovno vechnost' zabora, vo dvor odnogo doma, khoziain kotorogo byl "glavnyi" skopets. Uzkaia, vremenami teriaiushchaiasia tropinka vela v glub' sada, v skrytuiu, chernuiu ban'ku. Zdes' v spertom pomeshchenii s malen'kim odinokim oknom proiskhodili radeniia.* *Mikhei posheptalsia s chelovekom, razvalivshimsia na skameike, pered ban'koi; predstavil Fedora, kotoryi, osklabivshis', proshipel*	The terrifying and ferocious apperance of Fedor only slightly recalled the look of the "spiritual *skopets*", or "white dove," but Mikhei carefully combed Fedor's hair trying to give his dark and bigoted face a decent appearance. Then said that it would do. At night, when the whole village was asleep, Fedor and Mikhei were let in through a wicket-gate of a fence, unbelievably high, like eternity, into the yard of one house whose owner was the "main" *skopets*. A narrow trail, at times disappearing, went into the depths of the orchard, into a hidden, black bathhouse. There, in the stuffy building with a small, lonely window, the rites took place. Mikhei whispered something to a person lounging on a bench in front of the bathhouse and introduced Fedor who, with a distorted grin on his face, hissed out several terms which Mikhei had communicated to him.

	neskol'ko terminov, soobshchennykh emu Mikheiem.	
120. Mamleev's Lebedinoe and Dostoevsky's Lebiadkins. The horror of life. Graveyard. Dead yells. Drinking. Digging the graves. Corners. Blasphemy. Underground. Corpse of a young and holy girl – Dostoevsky's "The Meek." "Padov" derived from "the fall." Necrophilia.	*Kak tol'ko Padov – pochti mesiats nazad – priekhal v Moskvu, pokinuv Lebedinoe, to, chtoby podkrepit' svoi sily pered uzhasom zhizni, on brosilsia na kladbishche, okolo V. Zdes' ego uzhe davno znali. Mogil'shchiki privetstvovali Toliu radostnymi, mertvoutrobnymi krikami. Neskol'ko dnei on provel u nikh, p'ianstvuia, pomogaia ryt' mogily, nochuia gde-to po zakutkam, chut' li ne v samoi tserkvi . . .* *Na etot raz Padov ugovoril ikh ostavit' ego na odnu noch' v podvale vmeste s pokoinitsei, molodoi, blazhennoi devushkoi let semnadtsti. Ot radosti Padov tak napilsia, chto eta noch proshla ne sovsem na urovne.*	As soon as Padov – almost a month ago – arrived in Moscow, having abandoned Lebedinoe, he, in order to reinforce his strength in the face of the horrors of life, rushed into the grave-yard, near V. There they had been long awaiting him. Grave-diggers greeted Tolia with joyful, dead-bellied yells. He spent several days with the grave-diggers drinking, helping to dig graves, sleeping in some chimney-corners, it seemed even in the church itself… This time Padov convinced them to leave him for a night in the cellar together with a deseased young, blissful girl of about seventeen years old. Out of joy, Padov drank so much that that night was not quite at his usual level.
121. Vampire's complexion of Stavrogin and Mamleev's	*Chtob sovsem zakrepit' zhiznestoikoe sostoianie, Padov stal ezdit' na boiniu; zdes', podruzhivshis' s*	To entirely reinforce the state of being able to stand life, Padov started going to a slaughter-house, where, having

"blood-suckers." Life possible with the help of death.	*rezunami, on podstavlial svoi rot pod tepluiu, zhivuiu krov' tela, vypivaia v den' po dve-tri kruzhki krovi.*	made friends with the cutters, he used to put his mouth under the warm and living blood of the body. He had about two or three mugs of blood per day.
126-127: "Bobok" parallel – "empirical" Underworld. Murders (*dushegubstvo* – literally, murder of souls) and Raskol'nikov. Murder, a symbol of killing of the soul as for Dostoevsky. The murderer's name – Fedor. "Empirical and after-death punishment." Underworld. Fedor as the underworld of the underworld.	*Padov otkryl dlia sebia, chto dlia Fedora, veroiatno, ubiistvo bylo simvolom dushegubstva, dusheubiistva; khotia Fedor kak-to po-osobomu veril v inoi mir, no zdes', vidimo, eto bylo dlia nego ubiistvom dushi, popytka dobit'sia raspada zagadki.* *...Fedor nichego ne boialsia i ne zadumyvalsia ob empiricheski-poslesmertnom vozmezdii ...* Padov s radostiu videl, chto Fedora ne strashit nichto empiricheski-zagrobnoe, tak kak ego potystoronnee lezhit po tu storonu nashego soznaniia, a ne po tu storonu zhizni. Krome togo, v kakoi-to stepeni on byl potustoronen samomu potustoronnemu.	Padov discovered for himself that for Fedor, apparently, the murder was a symbol of soul-destroying, soul-killing; although Fedor somehow especially believed in the other world, here, it seems, this was for him a murdering of the soul, an attempt to achieve a breaking apart of the mystery. Fedor feared nothing and did not think of an empirical after-death punishment... To his joy, Padov saw that Fedor was not afraid of anything empirical and having to do with the underworld, as for him the other-worldly was on the other side of our consciousness but not on the other side of life. Besides, he was, to some extent, on the other side of the other world itself.
Fedor –	*Eto vigliadelo i bolee*	This appeared to be both more

majestic murderer as Stavrogin (the horrible from romaticism). Dark madness. Fedor – the Horror of the horrors. Horrors of the after-death everyday life.	*istinnym, i bolee velichestvennym; Padov chuvstvoval, chto Fedor "ikh", chto mrakopomeshatel'stvo – vysokogo kachestva, ...on trepetno oshchushchal, chto Fedor – sam takoi uzhas, chto pred nim melki vse uzhasy poslesmertnoi povsednevnosti, a tem bolee zdeshnie plachi i vozmezdiia.*	real and more majestic; Padov felt that Fedor was "theirs," that dark madness is of a high quality,... he anxiously felt that Fedor was such a horror that all the horrors of the after-death daily life, not to mention this world's cries and punishments, were petty compared to him.
Pettiness of punishment of this world.	*"Chego Uzhasu boiat'sia melkikh uzhasov," – dumal Padov.*	"Why would the Horror be afraid of petty horrors," – Padov thought.
Fedor opposed to world order like the Underground Man and Raskol'nikov.	*Inogda on grozno chuvstvoval, chto Fedor protivopostavil sebia mirovomu poriadku...*	Sometimes he terribly felt that Fedor placed himself in opposition to the world order...
Frenzy (the Underground Man) and rage (Raskol'ni-kov). Tavern. The sun as an	*Nakonets, v isstuplenii, ukhodiashchem vnutr', oba oni – Padov i Fedor – poshli k vykhodu, na ulitsu. Na stenakh pivnushki ostavalis' piatna dum, zhelanii, strastei. Rvano-*	Finally, in an agony directed inwards, both of them – Padov and Fedor – went towards the exit, into the street. On the walls of the little beer-house there remained the spots of thought, wishes, and

ominous augury – use of an overtly positive Dostoevsky's metaphor ("the rays of the setting sun") in most negative, terrifying way.	*izmuchennyi invalid polz za nimi do samogo vykhoda. A potom vdrug poiavivsheesia solntse udarilo im v litso, tochno ono bylo ne teplym, a zloveshchim predznamenovaniem.*	passions. A torn and suffering invalid was crawling after them until the very exit. And then, having suddenly appeared, the sun hit them in the face, as if it were not a warm but a terrifying omen.
131. Tavern. Dim and disproportionately wide windows-eyes. Setting similar to *Crime and Punishment* scene with Raskol'nikov in a tavern before he meets a court clerk. Dishevelled company (the Underground Man). Low ceiling – the company trying to get up to the light and air ("an alive life"). Poet, drunkard.	*Podoidia, glianul v ee mutnye, no neobychaino shirokie okna i uvidel, chto ona pochti pusta. No za odnim stolikom, priamo riadom, u okna, sredi lokhmato-kriklivoi, tochno rvushcheisia na potolok kompanii, Padov uvidel Remina. On sidel, oblokotiv svoiu poeticheskuiu, propituiu golovu na ruku. Drugie byli poluneznakomye Padova: chetyre brodiachikh filosofa, kotorye, vmeste so svoimi poklonnikami, obrazovyvali osobyi zamknutyi krug v moskovskom podpol'nom mire. Vid u nikh byl pomiatyi, izzhevannyi, dvizheniia uglovatye, ne ot*	Having come close, he looked into its dim but unusually wide windows and saw that it was almost empty. But at one table, right there, by the window, among the company, so dishevelled and loud, as if it were trying to reach the ceiling, Padov saw Remin. He sat, having put his poetic, drunken head on his hand. Others were half-unfamiliar to Padov: four wandering philosophers, who, together with their fans, formed a special closed circle in the Moscow underground world. They had a messy, chewed-on appearance, angular, awkward movements not from this world, but a common facial expression they had – unbridled and transcendental.

"Half-non-aquaintances" (Underground Man and his "comrades"), also typical Dostoevskian "loophole" language. Moscow underground world. "Stray Dog" (symbolist reference) Philosophizing – Underground Man, Raskol'nikov. Disorderly, messy, angular, awkward philosophers – Underground Man. Unbridled, transcendent expression – parody of Dostoevsky's aesthetics. Philosopher with all points	*mira sego, no obshchee vyrazhenie litsa – ogoltelo-transtsendentnoe. ...Tretii – Vitia – byl voobshche chert-te chto: vse punkty ego litsa stoiali torchkom, a dusha, po sushchestvu, byla smorshchena.*	...The third one – Vitia – was entirely the-devil-knows-what: all the points of his face were upside-down, and his soul, in essence, was wrinkled.

of his face upside-down, soul wrinkled – disorderly.		
136. Cleopatra of the underworld. (Cleopatra mentioned in "Notes from Underground" and *Writer's Diary* in relation to *bezobraznoe*.)	*Klavusha stoiala velichestvenno, kak nekaia potustoronniaia Kleopatra, i tol'ko ne khvatalo, chtob Igorek tseloval ee pal'tsy.*	Klavusha stood majestically like some Cleopatra of the underworld, and only one thing was missing, that was for Igorek to kiss her fingers.
140. Schizophrenic corners and transcendent dumpster-like cracks-underground. Dostoevskian *bezobraznoe*. "Unseen" creatures from the underworld.	*Da i sam dom Sonnovykh, s ego zakutkami, shizofrennymi uglami i transtsendentno-pomoinymi zanyrami, sposobstvoval poiavlemiiu "nevidimykh."*	And the house of the Sonnovs itself, with its chimney-corners, schizophrenic corners, and transcendental and dumpster-like cracks, assisted in the appearance of those "invisible."
141. Corners. Underground-underworld.	*Snachala emu kazalos', chto iz kakogo-nibud' ugla kto-nibud' vnezapno vyidet, no ne chelovek, a skoree "nechto" ili v luchshem*	In the beginning, it seemed to him that from some corner somebody will come out, but not a human but rather a "something," or in the best

	sluchae vykhodets s togo sveta.	case an apparition.
Emphasis on space and consciousness.	*No on postaralsia sviazat' prostranstvo s svoim soznaniem.*	But he tried to link the space with his consciousness.
Inhuman belonging to the underworld-underground.	*I emu stalo videt'sia chto-to sovsem nechelovecheskoe, no chto zato vtaine predchuvstvovalos' im v dushe.*	And he started to see something totally inhuman, but secretly, he, however, foresaw it in his soul.
Underground-underworld and its inhabitants.	*Snachala smutno proiavilos' kakoe-to podpol'e potustoronnosti; potom stali vyiavliat'sia i sushchestva, obitateli...*	In the beginning, some underground of the other world became visible; then its creatures, inhabitants became apparent...
Right to "squeak" once in a billion years – the Underground Man's verbal frenzy.	*Pervym poiavilsia tip, ch'e sushchestvovanie zakliuchalos' v tom, chto emu odin raz v million let razreshalos' pisknut', prichem ne bolee minuty; vse zhe ostal'noe vremia, promezhdu etikh piskov, on byl v polnom nebytii. Etot zamorochennyi tolstiachok kak raz i poiavilsia na svoiu edinstvennuiu minutu; nesmotria na eto vel on sebia neobychaino mnogoznachitel'no i dazhe napyshchenno; vidno bylo,*	The first to show up was a type whose existence consisted in being given permission once in a million years to squeak, though not longer than a minute; the rest of his time, between these squeaks, he was in complete non-existence. And this confused little fatso did appear right for his single minute; in spite of that, he behaved in an unusually important and even pompous manner; it was evident that he held to his right to squeak very tightly and that it was very significant to him...

	chto on ochen' krepko derzhitsia za svoe pravo pisknut' i kraine dorozhit etim . . .	
142. My own louse. Blasphemy.	*"Luchshe svoia vosh', chem dary svyshe," – vse vremia bormotal on [Evgenii Izvitsky] pro sebia i otkhodil v storonu.*	"One's own louse is better than sacraments," – he [Evgenii Izvitsky] constantly muttered in his mind and kept on moving aside.
143-44: Light vs. rotting. Making sprirituality ugly: "spiritual" girl with pale face (frequent image in Dostoevsky – Nelly, Netochka Nezvanova, Polen'ka, Sonia). Teeth-gnashing, distorted beast-like face of the girl when full of "metaphysical" thoughts.	*Vspominali, chto Izvitskii ne raz govoril pro etu devochku, chto ona "napolnena svetom".* *I vzapravdu, v nekotorom rode devochka deistvitel'no svetilas': ee blednoe litso s chut' vypiachennoi cheliust'iu i gnilymi zubami priamo-taki ozarialos' kakim-to molnienosnym, podprygivaiushchim vdokhnoveniem, a glaza v oshcherennom, odukhotvorennom lichike tochno vylezali iz orbit, kogda ona radovalas' nevidimomu i svoim mysliam.*	They remembered that Izvitsky often talked about this little girl, calling her "filled with light." And, indeed, in some sense, the girl was really emitting light: her pale face with slightly protruding jaw and rotten teeth did get lit up with some instantaneous, leaping-up-and-down inspiration, and the eyes on her distorted, spiritual little face seemed to pop out, when she was enjoying the invisible and her thoughts.
144. Underground bottle of vodka. Corner.	*Zakatannaia, podpol'naia butylka vodki zelenela v uglu…*	The closed, underground bottle of vodka was green in the corner.

145. Human chickens (also in Pelevin). Corner. "*Smerdet*'" (to stink, "*smerd*" – peasant farmer) – Elizaveta Smerdiashchaia, Smerdiakov in *Brothers Karamazov*." Speech as stink – ugliness of Undergound Man's discourse. Mention of Dostoevsky. Rat's squeak of Remin – the Underground Man as mouse. Quickly became embittered – typical of the Underground Man and Raskol'nikov.	*...Remin, kotoryi iz svoego ugla nachal chto-to smerdet' o zhizni Vysshikh Ierarkhii; chto-de po sravneniiu s etim liubye dostizheniia, kak krysinyi pisk po sravneniiu s Dostoevskim...* *Na Padova osobenno podeistvovalo eto napominaniie; "chto nam, kuriam, dostupno!" – slezlivo probormotal on.* *No potom ozlobilsia.*	...Remin, who from his corner began to stink about the life of the Highest Hierarchies, said that in comparison to that all achievements are like a rat's sqeaking compared to Dostoevsky... Padov was especially influenced by his reminder; "What do we, chickens, know!" – tearfully muttered he. But then he got angry.
152. Spiritual suicide and re-birth. Murders.	*Daleko, daleko poidet Petia ... v tom miru, – s penoi u rta bormotal Fedor. – eto ne*	Petia will go far, very far...in that world, – Fedor muttered foaming at the mouth. – This is

	to chto drugikh ubivat' ... *Sam sebia rodil Petia.*	not like murdering others... Petia gave birth to himself.
161. Underworldly ugly figures. Church.	*Osnovnye veshchi vyvezli s vechera, a rano utrom tri nezdeshne-urodlivye figury, nagruzhennye uzelkami, vykhodili iz vorot sonnovskogo doma: odna – deda Koli – nesmotria na tiazhest', radostno podprygivaiushchaia; drugaia – Mily – nelepo-otsutstvuiushchaia; tretia – Mikheia – vazhno sosredotochennaia, kak budto on shel v tserkov'...*	Basic things were taken out yesterday, and early in the morning three figures, ugly and of the underworld, loaded with bundles, were coming out of the gates of the Sonnov house: one figure – belonging to Grandpa Kolia – inspite of the heaviness of the load, was joyfully jumping up and down; the other – belonging to Mila – was ugly and absent; the third – of Mikhei – was significantly focused, as if he was going to a church...
163. Padov – "the fallen" – in the underground (basement) of the Universe.	*– Vot vy menia za penek prinimaete, Klavdiia Ivanovna, – radostno ulybnulsia Padov, – a ia ved' grushchu, ottogo chto ia vsego-navsego – chelovek i zabroshen v etot, po izvestnomu vyrazheniiu, podval vselennoi.*	– Here, you are taking me for a tree-stamp, Klavdiia Ivanovna, – joyfully smiled Padov – but I am sad because I am only a human and I am thrown into this – according to a well-known expression – cellar of the Universe.
164. Roof – Fedor trying to get closer to Heaven – parody of Dostoevsky's	*Vecherkom prizhalis' drug k druzhke. Tol'ko Fedor zalez kuda-to na kryshu.*	In the evening they sat close together. Only Fedor went somewhere onto the roof.

religious ideas.		
165. Kant (see Chapter 2 for discussion of Kant's influence on Dostoevsky). Underworld/ beyond the grave dissertation. The horrible – parody of Dostoevsky (see Chapter 2 for Dostoevsky and romanticism). Metaphysical creatures. Mephistopheles.	*Vse ponemnogo vkhodili v ee bredovuiu i v to zhe vremia real'nuiu ustoichivost'. . . Snachala tantsevali, eshche napominaia prezhnikh metafizicheskikh tvarei. Tantsuiushchii Padov byl voobshche zhutok, kak tantsuiushchaia mefistofel'skaia mysl.' Volosy napominali zagrobnuiu dissertatsiiu. Kazalos', pliasali – na gorizonte, pri lune – sami sushchnosti.*	Step by step everybody entered his nighmarish and at the same time real stability... At first, they danced still resembling the former metaphysical creatures. The dancing Padov was, in general, terrifying like a dancing thought of Mephistopheles. His hair resembled a dissertation from the underworld. It seemed that on the horizon, in the moonlight, it was the essences themselves that were dancing.
166. Irrationality – Underground Man. Irrational world – my fortress where ego is preserved. Madness. Transcendent understanding of the world –	*Padov vkhodil v mir Klavushi i nemnogo zavidoval ei: "ee mir irratsionalen, nelep," – dumal Padov, – "no v to zhe vremia zashchischen i samodovleiushch, ustoichiv imenno svoei nelepost'iu, v kotoruiu ona zamknula real'nost'; nikakie chuzhdye vetry ne vryvaiutsia v nego; moi mir – moia krepost'."*	Padov was entering the world of Klavusha and getting a bit jealous of her: "Her world is irrational, ugly," – thought Padov – "but at the same time it is protected and self-dominant, stable exactly in the ugliness of it, in which she enclosed reality; no foreign winds disturb it; my world – my fortress." Simultaneously, he saw that

Dostoevsky. Darkness and joy (*mrakoradostno*) – parody of Orthodox vocabulary (*svetloradostnyi*).	*Odnovremenno on videl, chto eto ne bezumiie, a sostoianiie, v kotorom "ia" sokhraneno, prakticheskaia orientirovka ne narushena, no zato izmenilos' transtsendentnoe vospriiatie mira i razrushilas' prezhniaia irratsional'naia podopleka veshchei i ikh znachimost'. I chto Klavusha mozhet teper' inache, nelepo i mrakoradostno, vosprinimat' mir.*	this was not madness, but a state in which "I" is preserved, practical orientation is not disturbed, but transcendental perception of the world has changed and the former irrational grounds for things and their significance has been destroyed. And that Klavusha can now in a different way, in the ugly, dark and joyful manner, perceive the world.
Ibid. World as a hut upside-down. Disorder. Emphasis on architectural aspect.	*[Klava] govorila i o mire v tselom, kak o khoroshei-de, letiashchei vverkh tormashkami izbenke, prochno okhvachennoi ee krepkim i vseob''emliushchim razumom.*	[Klava] also talked about the world as a whole, as if the world were a good, flying upside-down hut, tightly held by her thought and all-embracing mind.
167. Combining Satan's pride with a feeling of a mouse – Raskol'nikov/ Stavrogin/Ivan Karamazov and Underground	*– I chtob vyzhit' v zagrobnom sushchestvovanii, pryt' nado imet', sovmeshchat' v sebe sataninskuiu gordyniu s chuvstvom myshki! I Tolia vdrug pliunul v svoiu kruzhku s pivom.*	– And in order to survive in the underworld existence, one has to have liveliness, to combine in oneself Satanic pride and the feeling of the mouse! And Tolia suddenly spat into his own mug of beer. – One has to be Satan and a

Man.	*– Satanoiu nado byt' i myshkoiu! – zalilsia on, podniav glazki k nebu. – Myshkoiu, chtob poprivyknut' k nepolnotsennosti i zashchitit'sia takim putem ot Vysshego, a Gordyneiu, zastilaiushchei svet, chtob ne pogibnut' s toski, ot ushchemleniia "ia".*	little mouse! – he went on, looking up at the skies. – One has to be a little mouse in order to get used to inferiority and defend oneself from the Highest, and Pride, dimming the light, in order not to perish from sadness, from distortion of the "I."
169. Underworld.	*"Skok-skok, ne uidesh, " – krichala Klavusha kakim-to potustoronne-radostnym goloskom. Mir prinimal iavnyi real'no-bessmyslennyi vid. Vdrug zavopiv, Padov skrylsia vo t'mu...*	"Hop-hop, I'll come and get you," – shouted Klavusha in some joyful little voice of the underworld. The world became clearly real and meaningless. Having yelled suddenly, Padov disappeared into the darkness…
169-170. Ugly, philosophical scene. Underground.	*Nautro vse, kazalos' uleglos' v miagkiie provaly myshleniia. Ne tiagoteli v dushe ni pryzhki s sachkom, ni posledniaia bezobrazno-filisoficheskaia stsena po povodu Satany i myshki. Tol'ko Padov ugriumo dumal: "Nu i ogromen zhe seks i ego sdvig u etoi baby. . . K nei s obychnymi merkami ne podoidesh." No kakoi-to vnutrennii*	In the morning, everything, it seemed, settled down in soft abysses of thinking. Neither jumps with the net, nor the last ugly and philosophical scene about Satan and the little mouse. Only Padov was thinking gloomily: "How enormous this woman's sex and its distortion are…She cannot be judged by usual norms." But some inner

Drunken and dim look. All world in chaos and quasi-destruction.	*podzemnyi gul narastal. V dushe Klavushi tochno vzbesilis', vstali na dyby i so strashnoi siloi zavertelis' ee klaven'ko-sonnovskie sily. Eto bylo vidno po dvizheniiam i osobomu p'iano-mutnomu, obnimaiushchemu vzgliadu...* *Sut' sostoiala v tom, chto prezhniaia sushchnost' veshchei upala na dno i sami oni byli onelepeny goloi volei i siloi soznaniia. Ot etogo ves' mir pogruzilsia v khaos i kvaziunichtozheniie, no dusha Klaven'ki za schet etogo priobrela ustoichivost'.*	underground noise was getting louder. In Klavusha's soul, her *klaven'ko-and-sonnov* powers sort of went mad, turned upside-down and started to whirl with a scary speed. This was evident from her movements and a special, drunken and embracing look of hers... The thing was that the former essence of things fell on the bottom, and they themselves were disfigured by the naked will and power of consciousness. As a result, the whole world sank into chaos and quasi-destruction, but at the expense of that Klaven'ka's soul became stable.
174. Ugly city, chaotic, made up of disjunct parts, disharmony. Dirt, dust, no trees – St. Petersburg in *Crime and Punishment.* Ugly dead-ends.	Ponemnogu ogromnyi, vneshne bezobraznyi, tochno sostavlennyi iz loskut'ev gorod, okhvatyval ikh. Oni videli rodnuiu griaz', bezdonnuiu pyl', nelepye pereulochki bez edinogo derevtsa, kak budto stisnutye brakovannym zhelezom. Izredka v takikh pereulochkakh popadalis'	Gradually the city, huge and evidently ugly, as if composed from disjuncted patches, surrounded them. They saw their native filth, bottomless dust, disproportionate lanes without a single little tree, as if squeezed by defective iron. Occasionally, in such lanes one could find beer kiosks that looked like wooden public

Beer kiosks like wooden washrooms. Filth of memory of life. Crowds of underground/ underworld people	pokhozhie na dereviannye klozety pivnye lar'ki, okruzhennye skopishchem obmiagshikh liudishek. Inogda vyryvalis' zelenye sadiki, pogania sertse vospominaniem o zhizni. I, nakonets, liudi – ogromnoe ikh skopleniie, potok; i sredi nikh vdrug – strannye, raduiushchie glaz, igrivo-potustoronnie... *"Shaluny-to vidno u nas opiat' narozhdaiutsia, v Rassei", – ponial ee Izvitskii.*	washrooms, surrounded by an herd of softened-down people. Sometimes, little green orchards stood out in that picture, defiling the heart with a memory of life. And, finally, people – the enormous concentration of them, the flow; and among them suddenly – strange, pleasing the eye, those flirting from the underworld. "The naughty ones apparently are being born here, in Russia, again," – Izvitsky understood her.
Ibid. Individualism (Underground Man, Raskol'nikov). Nightmare-like persons.	*Individuumy... koshmarnye lichnosti*	Individuums...nightmarish personalities
174-175. Dostoevskian *topos.* "Existential" public.	Nakonets, po krainei mere letom, otmechalis' mesta, obychno griaznye, zabroshennye pivnye, tiagoteiushchiie k kladbishcham, gde vremenami sobiralas' vsiakaia ekzistentsial'naia	Finally, at least in the summer, some places were marked, usually filthy, abandoned beer houses, often nearby graveyards, where at times there gathered all sorts of existential public. ...but Anna and Izvitsky

Depths of the underground.	publika. ...*no Annu i Izvitskogo vleklo tol'ko glukhoe podpol'e.*	were only attracted by the deep underground.
Ibid. Extremely ugly little tavern. Heart is softened by ugliness. Ugliness of the broken window – common metaphor for eyes and soul. Ugly (*nelepyi*, hist. *ne lepyi* – not beautiful), strange log out of place. Chaos. "*Smrad*" – stink (*smerdet'* – see comment for p. 145). Graves and wine spirits. Orthodox tavern (beer-house) – ugly. Torn songs – dysfunctional syntax (see Chapter 1 on verbality and	*...pivnushechka byla donel'zia bezobrazna i imenno poetomu tak smiagchala serdtse. Bezobraziie sostoialo v razbitom edinstvennom okne, v nelepom brevne, valiaiushchemsia u vkhoda, i v osobom smrade, kotoryi poluchalsia iz tonkogo smesheniia zapakha bliz' raspolozhennykh mogil i vinnykh parov. V ostal'nom pivnaia byla ortodoksal'na: griaz', blevotina, propitannye chernoi pyl'iu bytylki, p'ianye, poiushchie razorvannye pesni.*	...the little beer house was overtly ugly and, precisely because of that, softened the heart so much. The ugliness consisted of a single widow that was broken, in the out-of-place wooden log lying about by the entrance, and the special stink which resulted from a subtle mix of the smell of stuffy graves and wine vapours. In all other respects the beer house was orthodox: filth, vomit, bottles that had absorbed some black dust, drunkards singing torn songs.

averbality of Dostoevsky's characters).		
176-177. Underground sex.	*Anna znala, chto Izvitskii sil'no liubil (ili liubit) ee; no znala takzhe, chto ne bylo bolee podzemnogo v seksual'nom otnoshenii cheloveka, chem Izvitskii.*	Anna knew that Izvitsky had been (or still was) very much in love with her; she also knew that there was no man more underground in a sexual sense than Izvitsky.
178. Extreme narcissism – jealousy of one to one self. Multiplicity of personalities/ voices – the Underground Man.	*Strashnaia dogadka mel'knula v ume Anny. – Ty revnuesh sebia ko mne! – voskliknula ona.*	A scary guess flickered in Anna's mind. – You are jealous of yourself because of your relationship with me! – She shouted.
Ibid. The underworld and the underground.	*Izvitskii schital, chto chelovek, kotoryi vladeet svoim chlenom, vladeet vsem mirom. Ibo ves' mir, vse potustoronnee i tainoe dlia Izvitskogo boltalos' na nitochke seksa.*	Izvitsky thought that a man who is in control of his organ is in control of the whole world, for the whole world, everything of the underworld and mystery, had for Izvitskii to do with sex.
179. Intercourse of different parts of one's personality and Dostoevsky's doubles.	*...eshche ran'she (no osobenno poslednee vremia) ego chasto tianulo, dazhe vo vremia liubvi s obychnoi, "real'noi" zhenshchinoi, kak by podstavliat' (khotia by chastichno) svoe "ia" v*	...even before (but especially lately) he was often drawn to, even during love-making to a usual, "real" woman, sort of substitute (even if only partially) his own "I" for her body. The degree of his

	ee telo. Ot uspekha etoi operatsii v znachitel'noi mere zavisela mera vozbuzhdeniia. Emu vse chashche i chashche neobkhodimo bylo ili naiti v zhenshchine sebia, ili (bez etogo voobshche ne obkhodilos') dopustit' podlog s pomoshchiu voobrazheniia.	excitement depended very much on the success of this operation. He more and more often had to either find himself in the woman, or (he absolutely could not do without this) allow for a forgery with the help of his imagination.
184. Love as cancer and *Lebiadinoe* alluding to Dostoevsky's Lebiadkins.	*Prezhde vsego potomu, chto eshche ran'she, do vozniknoveniia liubvi k sebe, on ispytyval k nei sil'noe, pogloshchaiushchee chuvstvo. V Lebedinom zhe metastazy etikh chuvstv vnezapno ozhili.*	First of all, because of the fact that even earlier, before his love for himself had appeared, he felt deeply and all-absorbingly for her. In Lebedinoe, the metastases of these feelings suddenly were revived.
193. Narcissism and further development of the theme of the doubles.	*Teper' on polnost'iu oschuschal vidimost' kak prodolzhenie sebia, vernee kak sobstvennuiu ten'. Ten' svoei zakonchennoi i edinstvennoi lichnosti.*	Now he entirely felt the reality as a continuation of himself, to be more precise, as his own shadow. The shadow of his whole and unique personality.
Ibid. Outside world as a dumpster and Narsiccism/ Solipsism. Stylistic parallel to Dostoevsky's	*Nekii svet, kak planeta, vzoshel v nem: to bylo rodnoe, siiaiushchee, nepostizhimoe Ia, tainstvennoe, beskonechnoe i edinstvenno real'noe sredi vsei etoi sheveliashcheisia*	A certain light, like a planet, arose in him: that was his native, shining, unintelligible "I", mysterious, endless, and exclusively real among all this moving dumpster of half-non-existence.

textual loop-holes and diminutives– 'half-non-life.'	*pomoiki polu-nebytiia.*	
195-6. Personified barracks. Filth. Mamleev's occasionalism as stylistic and intertextual reference to Dostoevsky – "*idiotoobraz-nye*" (*bezobraznoe/ blagoobraznoe* and *The Idiot*)	*Raion Moskvy, gde okazalsia Fedor, napominal svoei prelestiu podnozhiie ada. V storone po kholmam vidnelis' prilepivshiesia drug k drugu, slovno v nepotrebnoi, griaznoi seksual'noi laske, baraki. Derevtsa, khoronivshiesia mezhdu, kazalos', davno soshli s uma. Sleva ot Fedora na baraki nastupali beskonechnymi idiotoobraznymi riadami novye, ne otlichimye drug ot druga doma-korobochki.*	The part of Moscow, where Fedor happened to be, resembled the lower levels of hell in its beauty. Aside, spread on the hills, one could see barracks stuck to each other as if in some obscene, filthy sexual play. Little trees hiding among the barracks, it seemed, had gone mad a long time ago. To the left of Fedor, were endless idiotic and ugly rows of new box-houses, indistinguishable from one another.
197. The underworld and underground. The goal of Mamleev's protagonist – to murder metaphysical Napoleons but not old pawn-brokers/lice.	*Emu stiraiushche kazalos', chto ubiistvo etikh naibolee dukhovnykh liudei, mozhno dazhe skazat' napolnennykh dukhom, razreshit kakuiu-to tainu, mozhet byt' tainu sushchestvovaniia dushi, prervet son mira i vyzovet sdvig v zapredel'nom.*	It eliminatingly seemed to him that murdering of these most spiritual people, one can even say, filled with spirit, will solve a certain mystery, maybe the mystery of the existence of the soul, will interrupt the sleep of the world and cause a distortion in the underworld.
198-199.	Tramvai, kazalos', byl vyshe	The tram, it seemed, was

Disproportion-ate dwellings: houses-sheds, also in "The Shed" by Pelevin and in *Andegraund* by Makanin.	raskinuvshikhsia krugom domov – saraiushek s chernymi dyrami vmesto glaz. Iz etikh dyr vykhodili pomiatye, tochno ne ot samikh sebia liudi.	higher than the spread-about houses – sheds with black holes instead of eyes. From these holes, there were coming out people disfigured, as if not being themselves.
Ibid. Ugly interiors: entrance of a barrack. Apocalypse. Rats. Dostoevsky's "evil" and "good" sides of human nature: dumpster-like and light-bearing eyes of a woman.	*V koridore baraka ego vstretili vizg, apokalipticheskii po otnosheniiu k krysam stuk posudy i pugaiushche-nemoi khokhot . . . Zhenshchina, ne otryvaias', smotrela na nego svoimi pomoinymi, no v to zhe vremia udivitel'no svetlymi, vse okhvatyvaiushchimi glazami.*	In the barrack's hall, he was greeted by a loud scream, apocalyptic in relation to the rats clinking of the dishes and scary and numb laughter... The woman was looking at him non-stop with her dumpster-like but at the same time surprisingly light, all-embracing eyes.
202-203. St. Petersburg-style yard. Dostoevsky's poetics of St. Petersburg: ugly and narrow, lacking air ("a living life") yard, ugly	*Vkhod v kvartiry Izvitskogo byl so dvora; dvorik okazalsia pochti peterburgskii: malen'kii, kholodnyi, zazhatyi mezhdu gromadami kamennykh semietazhnykh domov... bezobrazno zagazhennyi mertvoi, sero-ischezaiushchei i vse-taki*	The entrance to the apartment of Izvitsky was through the yard; the little yard seemed almost like those in St. Petersburg: small, cold, squeezed among huge stone seven-storied buildings...it was befouled in an extremely ugly way by a dead, gray and disappearing, and still stinking

dumpster. Dead dumpster.	*voniuchei pomoikoi.*	dumpster.
Ibid. Half-windows, half-cracks. Izvitsky (coiling). Corner. Dostoevsky and Gogol' reference – portrait of Dostoevsky. Dostoevsky's double in the mirror.	*Poluokna... polushcheli... Iz dal'nego ugla v nem otrazhalsia strashnyi portret Dostoevskogo, Dostoevskogo s nepodvizhnym i stradal'cheskim vzgliadom.*	Half-windows...half-cracks... From a far corner, there was reflected in it [mirror] a scary portrait of Dostoevsky, Dostoevsky with a static and suffering look.
205. Izvitsky (coiling). Extreme Narcissism (a parallel to the Underground Man). The other world – underworld. Human toad. Mirror and the double.	*...odnako Izvitskii, pogloshchennyi strastiu k sebe, nichego ne zamechal; kak ogromnaia potustoronniaia zhaba, on polzal po zerkalu, staraias' obniat' svoe otrazhenie...*	...however Izvitsky, absorbed in his passion for himself, took no notice; like a huge toad from the under world, he crawled along the mirror trying to embrace his own reflection...
211. Blasphemy: [The Virgin] Eleousa (*umilenie*) and	*... ona [Anna] podsela i s umileniem pogladila ruku Khistoforova; emu pokazalos', chto gde-to szadi nego, v uglu,*	...she [Anna] sat close and tenderly stroked Khristoforov's hand; it seemed to him that somewhere behind him, in the corner, a dumpster rat started

lamentation in obscene context. Making Dostoevsky's Orthodox vocabulary ugly. Corner, dumpster, rat – borrowings from Dostoevsky's poetics; typical Dostoevskian setting and symbols.	*zaprichitala pomoinaia krysa.*	lamenting.
215. The young ones, names mocking Russian national heroes – Sashen'ka [Aleksandr Nevsky], Vadimushka [Vadim Novgorodsky]. Mocking of Dostoevsky's *pochvenni-chestvo.* Socialist ideas, when young, –	*– Ish, kuda poneslo, – ulybnulas' Anna. – V sotsial'shchinu. . . Nu, eto po iunosti . . . Ty eshche organizui partiiu pod nazvaniem "Zagrobnaia"...*	– See, where it is going, – smiled Anna. – Towards socialist ideas... Well, it is just a youth thing...You can also organize a party called "The Underworld..."

a hint at Dostoevsky. Underworld party.		
216-18. Axe. Lack of proportions: half-corners, half-rooms.	*Topor ...Polyzakutki ... polukomnaty*	Axe... Half-corners...half-rooms

Among the reasons for the particular influence of Dostoevsky on writers and the reading public in the late Soviet and post-Soviet period is the lifting of his virtual ban in the post-Stalin era and consequent republication of his works in 1956, followed by the complete Academy edition (started in 1973). Dostoevsky's works evoked particular interest because of his status as a formerly prohibited writer. His focus on *bezobraznoe*, chaos, and fragmented society also appealed to late twentieth-century Russian writers, as the processes of social disintegration achieved their climax after the devastations of *perestroika*. The numerous references to Dostoevsky in late twentieth-century works can be also explained as an attempt to demonstrate that culture was not wiped out by Bolshevik, Nazi, Stalinist or other Soviet regime, including *perestroika* with its hyperinflation and return to voucher distribution of basic necessities (the first occurrence of which dates back to the 1930s). Dostoevsky's poetics of the ugly is consciously used by twentieth-century authors not only as a sign of influence but also as a part of their intertextual technique. Mamleev, in particular, with his perverse humour, shows a definite preference for an intertextual and often parodic use of Dostoevsky's *bezobraznoe* and its poetics. Mamleev's love of the grotesque, his humour, his solipsistic characters with their extreme self-analysis, and his concept of the underground, make it possible to speak of a Gogol-Dostoevsky tradition reflected in his writings. The vitality of this tradition in late twentieth-century Russia can be explained by the fact that it allows for a link to the Russian classics without its all-too ideological, prophetic, or didactic aspect, which discredited itself during the Soviet era.[293]

---

[293] See more on this issue in Tolstaia's *Pushkin's Children*.

As is evident from the Table, most direct references to Dostoevsky in *Shatuny* have to do with names. For example, the title recalls Shatov, a character in *The Devils* (The word *shatun* itself is the Russian name for a bear whose hibernation has been interrupted, and who wonders around half-asleep, angry, and confused.). The protagonist in *Shatuny* shares his first name Fedor with Dostoevsky himself; his last name Sonnov has a semantic reference to the dream world (*son* = 'dream') which seems to be creating Mamleev's surreal monsters. The narcissism of the Underground Man, as well as Raskol'nikov's Napoleonic ideas, are paralleled by the "*Ia*-theory" in Mamleev's texts (this parallel also occurs in Pelevin's *Life of Insects*). Mamleev's characters gain harmony and order by either literally or figuratively eliminating the world around them; i.e. Klava's soul becomes stable precisely when the surrounding world is in the greatest chaos. Her beauty, however, is a perverse one, the true beauty of Sodom, if ever there was one.

Whereas in the *Diary of an Individualist* the underground is a psychological or psychopathic phenomenon, in *Shatuny* Mamleev understands the underground (*podpol'e*) as the underworld (*preispodniaia/dno obshchestva*), both in the traditional and the "metaphysical" sense of the word, thus comprising an ugliness of cosmic scale. In *Diary of an Individualist*, we can see the incorporation of Dostoevsky's *Notes from the House of the Dead*, "Notes from Underground," "*Polzunkov*," "Mr. Prokharchin*," and "*Bobok*." "*Bobok*" as well as *Crime and Punishment* extensively influenced Mamleev's novel *Shatuny*, particularly in relation to its theme of death, a primary focus of all Mamleev's texts. As the Table shows, there are twenty-one mentions of death, murder, graves, and corpses in *Shatuny* in a Dostoevskian context – that is, occurring together with direct references to Dostoevsky and/or other typically Dostoevskian themes that Mamleev chooses to parody. Similarly, Dostoevsky's use of the image of the underground mouse is paralleled and intensified by Mamleev's frequent depictions of rats in *Shatuny*. Direct and indirect references to the underground, the Underground man, the underworld, to underground mice and rats, and to various underground paraphernalia such as vodka and a political party among others, as seen from the Table, occur in *Shatuny* forty-three times. Mamleev consciously uses the word *bezobraznyi* as relating to Dostoevsky and his aesthetics of the ugly in combination with other words derived from the same root, including his neologism "*idiotoobraznyi*." Mamleev's poetics of the ugly is also indebted to that of Dostoevsky in its use of multiple diminutives and lexemes with the prefix "*polu-*"(half-). The latter occur five times in combination with other references to Dostoevsky, as one can see from the Table. The Table also contains eighteen mentions of the ugly in relation to other Dostoevskian phenomena. In Dostoevskian fashion, Mamleev also employs images of mice and spiders in association with ugliness, sinfulness, and a lack of moral and religious feeling. Space in *Shatuny* is typically Dostoevskian with the same stylistic features: multiple corners, disproportionate dwellings (barracks), small (half) windows, low ceilings (forcing characters to get out onto the roofs), mirrors with doubles/reflections, the underground and underworld, taverns, and dumpsters. The underground does become larger, turning into an underworld in Mamleev; but it also diminishes in size in parallel to the shrinking of residential space in the twentieth century. It turns into cracks and crevices, which are also used as a contemporary, even "narrower," underground symbol by Vladimir Makanin in his *"Laz"* and *Andegraund.*

Mamleev's texts offer the reader an abundance of ugly details of both real and psychological landscapes. He also demonstrates a tendency – recalling Dostoevsky – to assign the psychological landscape the primary role over the real, but with the focus on *bezobraznoe* in both. Mamleev's narrators tell of perverts expressing themselves in "bestial acts and bodily functions," in an emotionally neutral tone and simple language. To quote Lowe, "no other Russian writer, living or dead, has contrived to create as repulsively grotesque a world as Mamleev has."[294]

The use of nineteenth-century literature by late twentieth-century authors appears to be a universal tendency, and can be seen as an example of the first, second, and fourth functions of quotation discussed earlier. In late twentieth-century Russian literature, intertextuality becomes a widespread means of linking back to the texts of the classic age of the novel – 'Great Russian literature', which involves the use of quotation in its third, "sacral" function. At the same time, though, contemporary Russian writing is full of irony towards the classics, based on the postmodern "everything-has-been-said" stance. The particular significance that literature has had for Russian culture and society has stimulated the development of intertextual works, as the level of recognition of references among readers is traditionally high. Cultural archaeology can discover quoted *realia*, not just references to pre-texts. The functions of quotations in late twentieth-century Russian prose intertwine, and frequently lead to the formation of intertextual fields, as, for example, in the case of references to Biblical concepts – e.g., *obraz* – through Dostoevsky in Mamleev's *Shatuny* and the *Diary of an Individualist*. Thus, the *cento* nature of contemporary Russian prose deserves a primary place in literary scholarship of the end of the twentieth and beginning of the twenty-first centuries.

Finally, in Dostoevsky's works St. Petersburg is chaotic and ugly; in twentieth-century narratives such as Mamleev's, Moscow in turn becomes ugly, thanks to the literary image of St. Petersburg as a *bezobraznyi* city. The literary myth of Petersburg influences the consciousness of authors who write about Moscow; after Dostoevsky, any big city has to be ugly. For Mamleev,

---

[294] David Lowe, *Russian Writing since 1953*, NY: *Ungar*, 1987, 108.

Moscow courtyards are as ugly as those of St. Petersburg (See Table). The newest Russian capital is ascribed all the evils of the former one (which was still rather new when Dostoevsky was writing about it). Ugliness becomes a significant characteristic of a new capital city, and whether in real life it is ugly or not, the mythopoetic conventions have to be followed.

Chapter IV: Tatiana Tolstaia: Beauty of the Word and Ugliness of the World

> *Vosem' tysiach dvesti verst pustoty,*
> *I vse ravno nam s toboi negde nochevat',*
> *Byl by ia vesel, esli by ne ty,*
> *Esli by ne ty, rodina-mat'.*[295]

Boris Grebenshchikov

"A controversial figure in her own country," according to Goscilo, Tatiana Tolstaia "impressed Western readers as the uncontested premier Russian prosaist of a new era."[296] Tolstaia comes from a privileged family of writers, poets, and translators, among which are: Lev and Aleksei Tolstoy, Natalia Krandievskaia, and Mikhail Lozinsky. A classicist by education, fluent in English and French, Tolstaia started to write after an eye operation which prevented her from reading. Her debut was remarkably successful; all sixty-five thousand copies of the first collection of stories *Sitting on the Golden Porch They Were* [*Na zolotom kryl'tse sideli…*] sold out in an hour.[297]

The literary atmosphere of her family evidently formed Tolstaia's love for the beautiful word, as an antithesis to and salvation from the absurdity and ideology of the surrounding ugly Soviet reality. Fazil' Iskander believes that "Tolstaia's style, and, above all, her lush language, in a *sui generis* strategy of displacement, compensates the reader for her characters' sorrows and travails."[298]

This chapter on Tatiana Tolstaia will focus on similarities in treatment of space as well as thematic similarities between her works and those of Fedor Dostoevsky. It will demonstrate that

---

[295] Eight thousand two hundred versts of emptiness, / And still you and I have no place to have a night's sleep, / I would have been joyful, if not for you, / If not for you, my motherland.
[296] *Dictionary of Literary Biography*, Vol. 285, Detroit: Gale, 2004, 317.
[297] *Ibid.*, 318.
[298] *Ibid.*, 319.

Tolstaia consciously employs Dostoevsky's poetics of the ugly, alludes to his works, takes his concept of the underground in new directions, and shares his view of *bezobraznaia* Russian reality, the absence of home, and dysfunctional families. Of course the connections between a writer like Tolstaia and the nineteenth-century novelist go far beyond the question of direct influence, since Dostoevsky has permeated contemporary Russian culture to the extent of becoming an icon, a myth, an anti-Pushkin of twentieth-century fragmented narratives.

Tatiana Tolstaia's "*Limpopo*" is included in the collection *Fifth Corner* [*Piatyi ugol*], with a title evoking the search for the fifth corner in a four-cornered room, and emphasizing the problem of space in Russian literature and reality.[299] "*Limpopo*" is a tale with an amorphous plot and burlesque ending; the focus of this story is on the creation of a new Pushkin, who is expected to appear from the union of marginal underground poet Lenechka and Judy, an African student of veterinary science. The *skaz* manner of Tolstaia's "*Limpopo*" brings this short-story close to Dostoevsky's style; in Tolstaia, the narrator's questions to the reader (for example, "But where will you now find him?" [*No gde ego teper' naidesh?*]) are reminiscent of the dialogical monologue in "Notes from Underground." In "*Limpopo*," Tolstaia, like Dostoevsky, focuses on the problem of space and develops his concept of the underground. She describes the late Soviet period, a time when the spiritual elite, the superfluous men, went into the underground:

> Lenechka admired all these professions as the last bastions of the genuine intelligentsia. Because outside, the times were such – in Lenechka's words – that the spiritual elite, no longer able to watch its weak but honest candle crackle and smoke in the foul air of the epoch, had retreated, had turned away, and, accompanied by the hooting of the mob, gone into the basements, the watchmen's lodges, shacks, cracks, and crevices, in order, having hidden itself, to preserve the last candle, the last tear, the last letter of its dispersed alphabet.[300]

> [*Vse eti professii Lenechka uvazhal, kak poslednie platzdarmy, kuda otstupili istinnye intelligenty, ibo na dvore zavislo vremia, kogda – po slovu Lenechki – dukhovnaia elita, ne v silakh bolee vzirat', kak treshchit i chadit v voniuchem vozdukhe epokhi ee slabaia, no chestnaia svechka, otstupila, povernulas' i ushla pod uliuliukan'ie*

---

[299] The title is taken from that of the first short-story in the collection, "*Piatyi ugol*" by Israel Mitter.
[300] Tatiana Tolstaia, *Sleepwalker in a Fog*, trans. Jamey Gambrell, NY: Alfred A. Knopf, 1992, 136.

106

cherni v podvaly, storozhki, vremianki i shcheli, chtoby tam, zataivshis', sberech posledniuiu svechu, posledniuiu slezu, posledniuiu bukvu rassypannogo svoego alfavita.][301]

The suffocating atmosphere of the Soviet state is a typical metaphor for a twentieth-century Russian literary text; it appears in "*Limpopo*" as well as in other contemporary works. The lack of air or the absence of "living life" (*zhivoi zhizni*) in Dostoevsky is a similar metaphor, but an unusual one for the nineteenth century.[302] This lack of air can also be interpreted as a lack of space. Even the metaphysical underground is not spacious. In Tolstaia, people find their underground behind the wallpaper where they exist like cockroaches; a surviving intellectual is as rare as an albino cockroach, and his survival often comes at the cost of mutation. In the Soviet times described by Tolstaia, even a variant of the underground, wallpaper, is scarce: people are lining up for it but cannot get it:

...it took so long that even the newspapers promising that Uncle Zhenia's memory would remain forever in our hearts had been handed over for recycling, to return, in the eternal circulation and transformation of matter, as eighty-kopeck wallpaper, the line for which was long and dismal, as if in mockery of our aspirations.[303]

[*...uzhe i gazety, obeshchavshie, chto svetlaia pamiat' o diade Zhene navsegda ostanetsia v nashikh serdtsakh, byli sdany v makulatyru, chtoby obernut'sia, v vechnom krugovorote prevrashchenia materii, oboiami po vosem'desiat kopeek, ochered' za kotorymi dlinna i pechal'na, slovno nasmeshka nad nashimi chaianiiami.*][304]

Another version of the underground is a hole, a crack, into which people disappear like insects: "time has stopped, space has dried out, people have hidden in the cracks, domes have rusted..."[305] [*...vremia vstalo, prostranstvo vysokhlo, liudi popriatalis' po shcheliam, kupola prorzhaveli...*][306] In the reality of "*Limpopo*," space becomes smaller and narrower (recalling Dostoevsky's treatment of his

---

[301] T. Tolstaia. "*Limpopo*" in *Piatyi ugol: Sbornik sovremennoi prozy.* Moscow: Knizhnaia palata, 1991, 332. On burrows and cracks see Il'ia Kabakov, "On Emptiness," *Re-Entering the Sign,* Ann Arbor: U of Michigan Press, 1995, and Makanin's "*Laz,*" Moscow: Vagrius, 1998.
[302] See also Remizov's *Vzvikhrennaia Rus* for the lack of 'air.'
[303] Tolstaia, *Sleepwalker in a Fog,* 146.
[304] Tolstaia. "*Limpopo*", 338.
[305] *Cf.* Dostoevsky's reference to the condensed moment of time right before an epileptic fit.
[306] Tolstaia. "*Limpopo*", 344.

coffin-like rooms). Even insects are in need of more space in "*Limpopo.*" Church domes are rusted; the "all is permissible" caused by the lack of faith warned about by Dostoevsky becomes permanent. Another allusion to Dostoevsky's reality comes in a reference to the holes of the exile: "*i katorzhnykh norakh...*"[307] His *Notes from the House of the Dead* are the prelude to a long line of twentieth-century exile literature, with, for example, Solzhenitsyn and Shalamov developing this theme.

The underground in Tolstaia serves as a hiding place, and the changes Tolstaia's narrator refers to have to do with the Soviets and the transformations they brought to pre-revolutionary Russian reality. The *intelligentsiia*'s old, now moth-eaten, ideals were kept in the underground, behind the wallpaper, for most of the twentieth century and are now brought back to life. The idea of hiding behind paper – newspapers or wallpaper – reflects Tolstaia's subtle social criticism. The recycling of paper recalls the ease with which political ideas were changed in twentieth-century Russia, as well as the capacity of paper to bear anything. Tolstaia questions the value of the ideals of the *intelligentsia* in hiding:

> And others survived, preserved themselves, guarded against changes, laid low behind the strips of unglued wallpaper, behind the loosened doorframes, under the tattered felt, and now they emerged, honest and old-fashioned, redolent of ancient virtues and devalued sins. They emerged and couldn't understand, they recognized neither the air, nor the streets, nor a single soul – "this is not the same city, nor is the night the same!" They came out, carrying under their arms valuables safeguarded in their lethargic sleep: decayed novelties, frayed audacities, moldy discoveries, expired insights, amen; squinting, strange, rare, and useless, they came out the way an antiquarian, albino cockroach might emerge from a pile of old newspapers, and the hosts, amazed by nature's play, can't bring themselves to raise their slippers and crush the creature, who seems as noble as a Siberian fox.[308]

> [*A inye utseleli, sokhranilis', ubereglis' ot peremen, prolezhali bez dvizheniia za poloskoi otkleivshikhsia oboev, za otstavshim kosiakom, pod prokhudivshimsia voilokom, a teper' vyshli, chestnye i staromodnye, popakhivaiushchie starinnymi dobrodetialiami i utsennennymi grekhami, vyshli, ne ponimaia, ne uznavaia ni vozdukh,*

---

[307] *Ibid.*, 351.
[308] Tolstaia, *Sleepwalker in a Fog*, 138.

ni ulitsy, ni dushi, – ne tot eto gorod, i polnoch ne ta! – vyshli, vynosia pod myshkami
sberezhennye v letargicheskom sne dragotsennosti: sgnivshie novinki, prokhudivshiesia
derzosti, zaplesnevelye otkrytia, prosrochennye prozrenia, amin': vyshli, shchurias',
strannye, redkie i bespoleznye, podobno tomu, kak iz slezhavsheisia bumagi, iz staroi
kipy gazet vykhodit Bely, muzeinoi redkosti tarakan, i izumlennye igroi prirody
khoziaeva ne reshaiutsia pribit' tapkoi blagorodnoe, slovno sibirskii pesets,
zhivotnoe.][309]

She reveals her ironic attitude toward valued spiritual categories ("audacities," "insights," and the like)
by giving them food- or clothes-related epithets. Chaos and ugliness are reflected at the textual level to
mirror ugly reality and also hint at the abundance of words and scarceness of material possessions in
Russian reality of the end of the twentieth century. Right after that, on the same page, occurs the word
"*bezobrazie;*" and the whole passage has a Dostoevskian tint, including similar metaphors for the
depiction of ugliness. On the other hand, unusual epithets are related to estrangement (*ostranenie*) – a
poetic device that impedes our perception and understanding of things we take for granted.[310]
Conceptual and verbal echoes of Dostoevsky are particularly apparent because they are so close to each
other in the text:

> But that's now. Then – it was January, a **black frost**, two-sided, double-lobar
> love, and the two of them, standing opposite each other in the foyer of my old
> apartment, gazing at each other in amazement – oh, to hell with them, I should have
> pulled them apart right away and nipped imminent misfortune and **the whole**
> **disgraceful mess** in the bud.[311]

> [*No eto teper'. A togda – ianvar', **chernyi moroz**, dvykhstoronniaia krupoznaia*
> *liubov'*[312] *i eti dvoe, stoiashchie v prikhozhei moei byvshei kvartiry drug protiv druga i s*
> *izumleniem drug na druga vziraishchie – a nu ikh k cherty, nado bylo nemedlenno*

[309] Tolstaia. "*Limpopo*", 333.
[310] Viktor Shklovsky, *O teorii prozy*, Ann Arbor: Ardis, 1985, 13.
[311] Tolstaia, *Sleepwalker in a Fog*, 138.
[312] Again 'love' is used as an analogy to illness. In Mamleev, it is compared with cancer. See Chapter 3.

rastashchit' ikh v raznye storony i v korne presech griadushchie neschast'ia i bezobraziia.]³¹³

In addition to the 'lack of air' and 'living life', Dostoevsky has another unusual metaphor related to *bezobraznoe* – this is the 'yellow snow' (see Chapter 2). Tolstaia's stylistic parallel in a passage saturated with references to Dostoevsky is 'black frost.' Both of these metaphors are related to the ugliness of city life.

Dostoevsky and Tolstaia both address the theme of literature. The following references to *Insulted and Injured* and to Hugo's *Les Misérables* in "*Limpopo*" relate to the theme of literature in general, and specifically to the search for a new Pushkin, who bears special significance for both Dostoevsky and Tolstaia. For Dostoevsky, Pushkin is an exemplary Russian poet, the "most harmonious form," and for Tolstaia he is a mythical symbol of unattainable artistic beauty.³¹⁴ As such, Pushkin is the leitmotif of "*Limpopo*:"

> It therefore followed that the intellectual [Lenechka] and the black [Judy] should be joined in the bonds of matrimony and this union of the insulted and injured, the wounded and outcast, this minus, multiplied by a minus, would yield a plus – a curly-headed, plump-bellied, swarthy little plus: if our luck holds we'll get Pushkin right off; if not, we'll go at it again and again, or wait for our grandsons, great-grandsons – and going to the grave my blessing will I give – decreed Lenechka.³¹⁵

> [*A posemu intelligent (Lenechka) i negr (Dzhudi) dolzhny soedinit'sia brachnymi uzami, i etot soiuz **unizhennykh i oskorblennykh**, uiazvlennykh i **otverzhennykh** [Hugo], etot minus, pomnozhennyi na minus, dast plius, - kurchavyi, puzatyi, smuglyi takoi plius; povezet – tak srazu budet Pushkin, ne povezet – eshche raz ukhnem, i eshche*

---

³¹³ Tolstaia. "*Limpopo*", 333.

³¹⁴ Dostoevsky, *PSS*, Vol. 18, Leningrad: *Nauka*, 1973, 69. Kenneth Lantz, *The Dostoevsky Encyclopedia*, Westport/London: Greenwood Press, 2004, 338. The famed Russian rock musician and intellectual Boris Grebenshchikov enriched his art by returning to the 'roots,' to Old Russian folklore and language, realizing Dostoevsky's ideal of a Russian poet in the late twentieth century. He also relates to Dostoevsky in his poetry: "…anywhere, as long as the air is fresher there." ["…*kuda ugodno, lish by byl vozdukh svezhei.*"]

³¹⁵ Trans. Jamey Gambrell, quoted in Liudmila Parts, "Pushkin and Company: from Myth to Text in Today's Russia," *Russian Literature* I.II (2002), North-Holland, 464.

*raz ukhnem, a to vnukov dozhdemsia, pravnukov, **i, v grob skhodia, blagoslovliu!** –
postanovil Lenechka.*][316]

Victor Hugo, in his influential introduction to the drama "Cromwell," discusses the issue of ugliness in art and affirms it as a subject appropriate for the artist:

> And so, let addle-pated pedants (one does not exclude the other) claim that the deformed, the ugly, the grotesque should never be imitated in art; one replies that the grotesque is comedy, and that comedy apparently makes a part of art. Tartuffe is not handsome, Pourceaugnac is not noble, but Pourceaugnac and Tartuffe are admirable flashes of art.[317]

Both *Les Misérables* and Hugo's aesthetic views were familiar to Dostoevsky, who touches upon the problem of ugliness in art in his article "Exhibition at the Art Academy for 1860-61" [*"Vystavka v Akademii khudozhestv za 1860-61 god"*]. Dostoevsky denies ugliness a place in the visual arts: "The artist, thus, chose for himself an extremely difficult task: to portray the repulsive beautifully; this can never be achieved by anybody." [*Khudozhnik vybral sebe, takim obrazom, chrezvychaino trudnuiu zadachu: otvratitel'noe predstavit' prekrasno; eto nikoga nikomu ne udaetsia.*][318] In literature, on the contrary, as Dostoevsky demonstrates by his own works, one can depict ugly people, or ugly themes, beautifully. Characters in the *Insulted and Injured* such as Prince Valkovsky, for example, are a variation of the theme of the underground man, a standard case of *bezobraznoe* in people. For Tolstaia's protagonist Lenechka, the appearance of the new Pushkin would be opposed to *bezobraznoe* in Soviet reality, would bring new meaning to Russia, a positive alternative to chaos. This fascination with Pushkin as a national poet is also the major theme of Dostoevsky's "Pushkin Speech".[319]

Tolstaia in her *"Limpopo"* demonstrates an irony and play with classic texts typical for postmodern writers. By using *"I v grob, skhodia blagoslovliu!"* – an imprecise quote from *Evgenii Onegin*, chapter 8, stanza 2 [*"Starik Derzhavin nas zametil i, v grob skhodia, blagoslovil"*] – Tolstaia reveals Lenechka's ambitions to be both a spiritual and a biological father to a new Pushkin. Uncle Zhenia of *"Limpopo"* – incidentally, a diminutive of Evgenii (another allusion to Pushkin's *Evgenii*

---

[316] Tolstaia, *"Limpopo"*, 337.
[317] http://www.bartleby.com/39/40.html. Accessed on July 17, 2004.
[318] D-*PSS*, 19:167.
[319] D-*PSS*, 26:129-149.

Onegin) – who was trying to keep a clear record with the Soviet bureaucracy while fighting with his nephew, the underground poet Lenechka, is torn to shreds by a wild animal in Africa. Ironically, the newspapers with his obituary are recycled and turned into cheap wallpaper, a metaphor for the underground in Tolstaia's narrative. The intertextual links to Pushkin are crowned by a postmodern mosaic of his verse; Pushkin's poems are deconstructed, given a new contemporary meaning, and supplemented with lines stylised as the language of Soviet bureaucracy. The formal elements of Pushkin verse remain: *"Esli zhizn' tebia obmanet – znachit rodina velit."*[320] A grotesque, seemingly absurd, linguistic chaos parodies both *bezobraznoe* of Soviet stereotypes and the idea of a new Pushkin, able to offer salvation through the beauty of the word. The attempt to give birth to a new Pushkin dominates this short-story. Pushkin in *"Limpopo"* is regarded as a supreme cultural achievement of humanity. Since he does not appear, the prognosis is pessimistic: there is no new Russian culture. Here Pushkin functions as does Shakespeare in Stepan Trofimovich's speech in *The Devils* – as an ideal of beauty. Since the search for Pushkin in *"Limpopo"* has no result, it becomes apparent that so there is no beauty in Russian reality but *bezobraznoe*.

Tolstaia shares an ironic attitude to Chernyshevsky's Rakhmetov with Dostoevsky, whose "Notes from Underground" are well known as a polemic against Chernyshevsky's "new people."[321] Rakhmetov, a protagonist of *What is To Be Done?*, is famous for eating raw beef and exercising his will by, for example, sleeping on a bed of nails:

At first he practised gymnastics...for with each new task, with each change, new muscles were developed. He adopted the diet of pugilists: he ate food known exclusively as strengthening, especially almost raw beef-steak, and from that time on he always lived so...he had been obliged to eat meat, much meat, and he ate it in large quantities. But he looked long at a copeck spent for any food other than meat; consequently he ordered his landlady to get the best of the meat, the best pieces for him...in the felt were

---

[320] Tolstaia, *Piatyi ugol*, 344. *Cf.* Pushkin's
Esli zhizn' tebia obmanet,
Ne pechal'sia, ne serdis'!
A.S. Pushkin, *Izbrannye proizvedeniia*, Moscow: *Detskaia literatura*, 1969, 147. Dostoevsky's narrators also have a tendency to deform sayings and phraseologisms. See V.E. Vetlovskaia, *Poetika romana "Brat'ia Karamazovy,"* Leningrad: *Nauka*, 1977, 34.
[321] Iu.K. Rudenko, *Chernyshevskii-romanist i literaturnye traditsii*, Leningrad: *LGU*, 1989, 224.

hundreds of little nails, sticking up about an inch; Rakhmetov had lain all night on this bed of his invention.[322]

[*Stal ochen' userdno zanimat'sia gimnastikoiu ...ot kazhdoi novoi raboty, s kazhdoi peremenoi poluchaiut novoe razvitie kakie-nibud' muskuly. On prinial bokserskuiu dietu: stal kormit' sebia – imenno kormit' sebia iskliuchitel'no veshchami, imeiushchimi reputatsiiu ukrepliat' fizicheskuiu silu, bol'she vsego bifshteksom, pochti syrym, i s tekh por vsegda zhil tak ...emu nuzhno bylo est' goviadiny, mnogo goviadiny, – i on el ee mnogo. No on zhalel kazhdoi kopeiki na kakuiu-nibud' pishchu, krome goviadiny; goviadiny on velel khoziaike brat' samuiu otlichnuiu, narochno dlia nego samye luchshie kuski...v voiloke byli natykany sotni melkikh gvozdei shliapkami s-ispodi, ostriiami vverkh, oni vysovyvalis' iz voiloka chut' ne na polvershka; Rakhmetov lezhal na nikh vsiu noch'.*][323]

Such achievements were regarded as proof of his masculinity, strength, and will power, eventually making him into an ideal revolutionary in the Soviet version of the nineteenth-century literature. This type was transformed into '*otvetstvennye rabotniki,*' partocrats, and a beau of the narrator in "*Limpopo*" is ridiculed for absorbing the superficial characteristics of Rakhmetov:

It was impossible, for instance, to take my suitor Valery seriously: strong and tall, and ardently admiring himself for these qualities, with the face of a policeman or an executive, Valery ate a lot of meat, kept weights, springs, a bicycle, skis, and other unnecessary thingamajigs at home...[324]

[*Nel'zia zhe bylo vser'ez otnestis', naprimer, k zhenikhu Valeriiu: krepkii, vysokii, ochen' sebia za eto uvazhavshii, s litsom militsionera ili otvetsvennogo rabotnika, Valerii el mnogo miasa, derzhal doma giri, espandery, velosiped, lyzhi i esche kakie-to neobiazatel'nye sportivnye zagoguliny...*][325]

[322] N.G. Chernyshevsky, *What Is To Be Done?*, NY: Vintage Books, 1961, 227-237.
[323] N.G. Chernyshevsky, *Chto delat'?: Iz rasskazov o novykh liudiakh*, in his *Polnoe sobranie sochinenii*, Vol. 11, Moscow: *Gosizdat. khud. lit.*, 1939, 199-200.
[324] Tolstaia, *Sleepwalker in a Fog*, 149.
[325] Tolstaia, "*Limpopo*", 340.

As well as Dostoevsky, Tolstaia writes about *bezobraznoe* in daily life, with the permanent messiness of dwellings corresponding to the chaos of thoughts, of their inner organization:

...Garik was a kind, loving, sweet, and unusually resourceful young man: he managed to feed the children, and indefatigably bustling about, he somehow quickly resurrected the papers at the same time. But I got sort of bored listening to him – everything was "vineyards" and more "vineyards," and paths, and quests, and bliss, and the sweetest and not of this world, and yet life went on – a bad life, but the only one around, and his **den** was full of rubbish, rags, dust, and glue bottles on the windowsills, and meatless porridge in a burned pot, and tatters on a wobbly nail... and could it really be that this, this puny, **ugly** world, was the one whispered about and promised, proclaimed and presaged when everything began, when the unseen gates opened and the inaudible gong sounded?[326]

[...*Garik byl dobryi, liubiashchii, milyi i na redkost' izvorotlivyi iunosha: i detei kormil, i bumazhki kak-to bystren'ko, neutomimo khlopocha, vosstanavlival, – a vot chto-to skuchno mne bylo: poslushat' ego – vse "vertograd" da "vertograd", da puti, da iskaniia, da blagodat', da vse sladchaishee da nerukotvornoe, a zhizn' idet, – plokhaia, no edinstvennaia, a v* **konure** *u nego khlam, triap'e, pyl', i butylki s kleem na podokonnike, i postnaia kashka v podgoreloi kastriul'ke, i rubishche na shatkom gvozdike...i neuzheli zhe etot, vot etot mir, tshchedushnyi i* **bezobraznyi**, *i byl obeshchan i nasheptan, vozveshchen i predchuvstvovan, kogda vse nachinalos', kogda raskryvalis' nevidimye vorota i zvuchal neslyshimyi gong?*][327]

Tolstaia contrasts the ugliness of daily existence, related to narrow and chaotic space, the false promises of the world, and the impracticality of the typical Russian '*intelligent*', with his promises of the 'Golden Age'. With sad irony she argues against Dostoevsky's ideal solution to the *bezobrazie* of daily existence – his utopian views.[328] Tolstaia's ironic attitude towards the biological explanation of

---

[326] Tolstaia, *Sleepwalker in a Fog*, 150.
[327] Tolstaia. "*Limpopo*", 341.
[328] On Dostoevsky's utopian views see K. Mochul'sky, *Dostoevsky: zhizn' i tvorchestvo*, Paris: YMCA Press, 1980, 435.

life is similar to Dostoevsky's attitude towards Darwinism. She also operates with typically Dostoevskian 'life-dream' oppositions:

> For life, as we were taught, is the form of existence of protein molecules, and what is in addition to that is empty promises, ornaments on the water, embroidery with smoke...Only one had better to dream less, since life is so cruel to the dreamers.

> [*Ibo zhizh', kak nas uchili, est' forma sushchestvovaniia belkovykh molekul, a chto sverkh togo – to sut' pustye pretenzii, uzory na vode, vyshivanie dymom...Vot tol'ko pomen'she by mechtat', ved' zhizn' tak zhestoka k mechtateliam.*][329]

Reality in "*Limpopo*" is unnatural, ugly, improper, and contrasted with the dream. The lack of private space is permanent: "There was reality: the kitchen, the shouts, the gray stubble of Spiridonov's beard diving into a glass of tea, the crowdedness and the two of them, this unnatural pair with far-flung plans"[330] [*Byla real'nost': kukhnia, kriki, sedaia shchetina Spiridonova, nyriaiushchaia v stakan s chaem, tesnota i eti dvoe, eta protivoestestvennaia parochka s daleko idushchimi planami.*][331] Tolstaia's characters have an "*ubogaia*", miserable everyday life: kitchens instead of homes; they are tiny, messy, dirty, and full of cockroaches. The private world is overcrowded; it is often limited to kitchens saturated with people who again are made analogous to insects. In this pitiful reality, when communal kitchens are functioning like homes, space is narrow and oppressive.

Bereft of personal, private space, the Russians of "*Limpopo*" are utterly homeless. We see a similar absence of home in Dostoevsky, in the context of the *bezobrazie* of family life he depicts in such works as *Brothers Karamazov*, *The Raw Youth*, and *Writer's Diary*. What sort of home could a Karamazov have? The sole example of a more or less normal family in the book seems to be that of the servant Grigorii, who also happens to be taking care of Mitia. The idea of the home/house is pivotal for Tolstaia's aesthetic system – as it is for Petrushevskaia, whose works will be discussed in the next chapter. Like Dostoevsky, they write about the metaphysical component as much as about the actual dwellings (see Chapter 2). The chaos, *bezobrazie*, and false promises of the outside world, as well as the need for the mythical house, are present in the narratives of both these female writers. This is not accidental, considering the greater degree to which women, as opposed to men, could escape into

---

[329] *Ibid.*, 359.
[330] Tolstaia, *Sleepwalker in a Fog*, 151.
[331] Tolstaia. "*Limpopo*", 341.

private life in Soviet Russia. In *"Limpopo"* the house is needed for the possibility it gives of shutting the door on that world. The house is perceived as protection from the ugly Soviet reality; and when a proper home is absent, what is left is the havoc of the outside world. [332] Although these are also viable concepts for Dostoevsky, he does not only describe the material side of the question. His accent is on the disintegrating and "accidental" families. Homelessness in Tolstaia's story is portrayed against the background of the artificial optimism of Soviet propaganda (*"druzhba narodov"*[333]); and the only salvation for her characters is in the creation of a family, an odd sort of family, including the inhabitants of the communal apartment, and not unlike happy families of Dostoevsky with their brotherly love and all being responsible for all:[334]

And then, hunkered down in our damp coats in the movie theatre, the invalid and I sullenly watched some fleetingly glimpsed factories, pig iron, awkward heroes of labor, tempered iron beams, tractors, record-setting hogs, bald, well-fed people in tweed suits rubbing ears of wheat between their fingers; we watched the stream of ideologically consistent grain flood us; we watched, waiting submissively for the friendship of **homeless people** to gel somewhere out there in the form of the illegal infant Pushkin, our last hope.[335]

[*A potom v kinozale, v podmokshikh pal'to, nakhokhlivshis', ispodlob'ia smotreli – ia i invalid – na kakoi-to mel'kaiushchii prokatnyi stan, bolvanki, koriavykh geroev truda, raskalennye brusy zheleza, traktora, svinei-rekordsmenok, na pleshivykh, khorosho pokushavshikh liudei v sheviotovykh kostiumakh, rastiraiushchikh v pal'tsakh koloski,*

---

[332] This also reveals the mythological notions Tolstaia uses in her narratives. *Cf.* Aron Gurevich, *Izbrannye trudy*, Vol. 1, Moscow/St. Petersburg: *Universitetskaia kniga*, 1999, 38-39. In Germanic languages the human realm was denoted as the "middle world:" *midjungarðs* (Goth.), *middangeard* (Old Eng.), *miðgarðr* (Old Isl.), *mittingart, mittilgart* (Old High Germ.), with the root *garðr, gart, geard* – "a fenced place." The world of people was perceived as a fenced, protected, "place in the middle," and the fact that this term occurs in all Germanic languages proves the ancient origin of the idea. Another relevant component of the cosmology and mythology of the Germanic tribes was *útgarðr* – "that which is beyond the fence." This outside space was perceived as inhabited by hostile forces, as a kingdom of monsters and giants. The opposition *miðgarðr – útgarðr* determined a whole *Weltbild*; culture was in opposition to chaos. (Grönbech, 1961, S. 183 ff.) The term *heimr* (Old Isl.; *cf.* Goth. *haims*, Old Eng. *hām*, Old Fris. *hām, hēm*, Old Sax. *hem*, Old High Germ. *heim*), which occurs mainly in mythological contexts, denoted both "world", "homeland," and "home," "dwelling," "fenced farmstead." Thus the world, cultivated and humanised, was modelled by the house and farmstead.

[333] Also the distasteful title of a 'thick' journal, another connection to Tolstaia's paper metaphor.

[334] Kenneth Lantz, *The Dostoevsky Encyclopedia*, Westport/London: Greenwood Press, 2004, 136-139.

[335] Tolstaia, *Sleepwalker in a Fog*, 152.

*na potok liushchegosia na nas, ideologicheski vyderzhannogo zerna, smotreli, pokorno ozhidaia, poka gde-to tam, iz fakta druzhby **bezdomnykh narodov**, ne zaviazhetsia bezzakonnyi mladenets Pushkin, kak posledniaia nasha nadezhda.*][336]

The version of Soviet reality which the narrator of *"Limpopo"* and her communal-apartment neighbour and kitchen-mate, the crippled soldier Spiridonov, are forced to see by Lenechka (who needs the apartment for his private needs), is ugly in its stereotypes. The screen is full of industrial dummies, pigs, pig-like people (a hint at Khrushchev), and distorted (*"koriavye"*) heroes of labour.[337]

The positive alternative of the narrator in *"Limpopo"* to the existing chaos (and one should not fail to emphasize that Tolstaia is almost unique among late twentieth-century writers in offering it) is a wooden house with washed floors, and a book in which everything is written. In the *bezobraznaia* reality of this story, books are almost as inaccessible as houses; books are distributed among the bureaucracy and party elite on holidays together with butter and sausages. Occasionally, bookstores are filled in with what seems to be the whole print run of one book in Urdu and nothing else. The idea of the book as part of a positive alternative to the ugly reality is reinforced by Lenechka's obsession with a 'new' Pushkin who is perceived as Russia's last hope, a new prophet who ultimately fails to appear in the story.

The doubling of human nature (with the emphasis on the negative component), which receives so much attention in Dostoevsky, also finds its way into Tolstaia's prose. The 'mirroring' of the protagonist is illustrated in this *bezobraznoe* description, which includes a hint of Dostoevsky's *Insulted and Injured*: "...and the shameful cold of the toilet, where the noise of the wheels is stronger and more hurtful, and from half-darkness, so close and unflattering, what is looking at you is your own reflection – insult – defeat..." [...*i sramnoi kholod sortira, gde grokhot koles sil'nei i oskorbitel'nei, i iz*

---

[336] Tolstaia, *"Limpopo"*, 342.
[337] Here Tolstaia parodies Bolshevik utopians who wanted to recover the ancient ritual/sacred aspects of the labour process. This includes the rhythm and unity of the working collective, choreographing its movements to those of machinery. As for the visual aspect of this issue, though in a certain sense the materialist Soviets insist on the physicality, the tangible and visible reality of both human flesh and the metal/machinery to which it may be compared, they still avoid emphasizing key elements of this physicality – especially those relating to the body as an object of erotic beauty, or just beauty/ugliness for its own sake (unrelated to moral/political ideals). They also avoid any representations that will make the flesh-metal link too overt, and would thus make us too aware of its dehumanising grotesqueness. See more on this in R. Hellebust, *Flesh to Metal: Soviet Literature and the Alchemy of Revolution*, Ithaca/London: Cornell U Press, 2003.

polymraka blizko i nelestno smotrit na tebia tvoe sobstvennoe otrazhenie – unizhenie – porazhenie...][338]

The burlesque ending of *"Limpopo"* recalls surrealism, with a style intended to convey the state of mind of a drunkard, alcoholism being a typical ailment of the Russian *intelligent*. The surreal ending also brings back the issue of different types of realism, as in the case of Mamleev (Chapter 3).

Tolstaia discusses relationships between the sexes in contemporary Russia in her polemical article "Notes from Underground" (*The New York Review of Books*, 31 May, 1990). She paradoxically characterises Russian women as possessing the power in society, in spite of the fact that they might happen to be road workers. The male protagonist of her parable has no name (just like Dostoevsky's underground man), comes from nowhere, and returns to nowhere. He has the noble idea of sacrificing himself in order to make a woman's daily life a holiday. As an underground dreamer he embarks upon a Dostoevskian conversation after he has done some house cleaning:

> a long, philosophical, Russian sort of conversation about morality, and whether or not one would inevitably experience a fall if one raised oneself above other people, and about how they had been exploiting him, they had been overwhelmed by proprietary instincts and negative feelings of superiority, and their souls had recognized the sin of pride.[339]

Tolstaia's underground man fails to fulfil his ideal; the moment he enslaves himself to a woman, she begins to tyrannise him, and the emphasis shifts from his ugliness to hers.

In her story "A Sleepwalker in the Fog" [*"Somnambula v tumane"*] Tolstaia portrays an ugly type of Soviet man at the top of the social hierarchy. Comrade Bakhtiiarov is referred to as *"oni"* by a waiter (an obsolete form of high respect).[340] Such a form of address is frequent among nineteenth-century servant characters (including Dostoevsky's), and artistically demonstrates that in spite of official claims traditional social strata still exist in Soviet society. In *The Brothers Karamazov* it is Smerdiakov, the evil, ugly, and stupid double of Ivan, who uses *"oni"* when speaking about him: "But

---

[338] Tolstaia, *"Limpopo"*, 343.

[339] Tatiana Tolstaia, "Notes from Underground." *The New York Review of Books*. (31 May 1990). Also published as "Women's Lives" in *Pushkin's Children*, Boston/NY: Houghton Mifflin, 2003.

[340] Sophia Wisniewska, "Narrative Structure in the Prose of Tatiana Tolstaia" (Ph.D. dissertation, Bryn Mawr College, 1992), 244, microfilm.

they [Ivan] referred about me [*sic*] that I am a stinking lackey." [*A oni pro menia otneslis', chto ia voniuchii lakei.*]³⁴¹ The servility of the waiter in Tolstaia's twentieth-century text is expressed grammatically; in Dostoevsky it is shown along with other misguided attempts at sophistication; i.e., those of Apollon in "Notes from Underground" and Smerdiakov. The ugliness of servility in "Sleepwalker in the Fog" is shown in the context of a hell-like tavern, with Comrade Bakhtiiarov as the secular Satan in charge.³⁴² Tolstaia's narrator also calls Bakhtiiarov "*Khoziain*," a Master worshipped by the dispirited people around him. Bakhtiiarov is the Eternal Evil in this story, devouring the young and tempting them with material possessions. His age is unclear: "and it was impossible to tell how old he was – could be sixty, or two hundred" [*i skol'ko emu bylo let – shesdesiat ili dvesti – skazat' bylo nel'zia*], another of his supernatural features.³⁴³

According to Sophia Wisniewska, "Tolstaia associates the people in the bar [of the tavern Bakhtiiarov is in] … with the worst criminals in the history of Moscow," by her insertion of a two-hundred-year-old gangster song into the narrative.³⁴⁴ Denisov goes to this tavern, called "Fairy-Tale," to find the mythical well-connected Bakhtiiarov and to ask for a favour on behalf of the family of a classmate of his fiancée, Lora. The favour itself is typical of late Soviet reality: a request to get a piece of furniture, accessible only to those with good connections. The farcical nature of the *sujet* and the absurdity of any attempts of Denisov, experiencing a mid-life crisis, to do good for the humanity are emphasised by the occasion on which the request is made – Lora's finding out about the death of her classmate, who died climbing a mountain, and the wedding of his sister, for which the mother of the family is asking Denisov to help to get a wardrobe. When Denisov meets Bakhtiiarov, the latter claims to be a poet, emphasising that there is nothing impossible for him. This character combines features of a criminal, devil, and a poet. The petty, ordinary ugliness of Bakhtiiarov brings him close to the 'common-place' devil-jester who appears to Ivan Karamazov. The line of 'ordinary' devil characters starts with *Brothers Karamazov* and continues through Fedor Sologub's *Petty Demon* and Mikhail Bulgakov's *Master and Margarita*, up to Tolstaia's "Sleepwalker in the Fog." Dostoevsky's *bezobraznye* criminals and writers (Raskol'nikov and the Underground Man among others) continue

---

³⁴¹ Dostoevsky, *Sobranie sochinenii*, Vol. 9, Moscow: *Khudozhestvennaia literatura*, 1958, 282.
³⁴² Bakhtiiarov is also known to frequent a bathhouse, a place often associated with low and evil spirits in Russian folklore, and portrayed as an Inferno in the *House of the Dead*. His name comes from Turk. *bakht* (happiness) and *jar* (friend, comrade), literally "following happiness" (see more at http://dictionaries.rin.ru/cgi-bin/see.pl?sel=family&wor…) The heritage of folklore in Tolstaia's texts is evident from her choice of names of Turkic origin for her villains. Denisov's name comes from Gr. *Dionisii* (*Ibid.*). Both names allude in their own way to the famous Dostoevsky scholar M.M. Bakhtin.
³⁴³ Tatiana Tolstaia, *Noch'*, Moscow: *Podkova*, 2002, 322.
³⁴⁴ Wisniewska, "Narrative Structure in the Prose of Tatiana Tolstaia", 247.

their existence in Tolstaia's prose.[345] In "Sleepwalker in the Fog," Tolstaia also seems to parody Romantic ideas of Evil being great (as opposed to petty) and Stavrogin-like demonic characters, as well as attempts to do good motivated by brotherly love.

Viacheslav Ivanov, who regarded the conceptions and plot development of Dostoevsky's novels as those of tragedy, also argued in favour of a theurgic art based on "*sobornost*'" (togetherness). Ivanov proposed medieval art (in particular, Byzantine) as a model for a future syncretic art.[346] Dostoevsky's quasi-medieval aesthetics, with their essential idea of *bezobraznoe* as a lack of God's image, fit his framework perfectly. Human beings without this image fall under the power of evil, personified by the Devil. Tolstaia reinforces the devil-like nature of Bakhtiiarov by comparing "the festivities of the bar to a witch's Sabbath."[347] Searching for a human face there, Denisov imagines that it is possible to see certain cosy and sympathetic corners on that of Bakhtiiarov, if one distorts one's vision:

...on his face there were even seen some cosy, sympathetic little corners, and if one were to squint, then it would be possible, for one little minute, to believe that here is a grandpa, elderly, loves his grandchildren... but certainly only if one were to squint.

[...*na litse ego dazhe prosmatrivalis' kakie-to uiutnye, simpatichnye ugolochki, a esli soshchuritsia, to mozhno by na minutochku poverit', chto vot – dedushka, staren'kii, liubit vnuchat ...no tol'ko esli, konechno, soshchurit'sia.*][348]

Tolstaia's concentration of diminutives within this short span of text, as well as her focus on corners/angles, recalls Dostoevsky's poetics.[349] His literary presence in the text of "Sleepwalker in the Fog" becomes evident shortly before the description of the multiple little corners of Bakhtiiarov's face: "Without suffering you won't reach anything" ("*ne postradav – ne dob''eshsia*"), says Denisov, parodying the general Dostoevskian idea of "suffering ennobling the person."[350]

---

[345] This is also the case with Mamleev, e.g. the murderer Fedor Sonnov in *Shatuny* and the protagonist *in Diary of an Individualist.*

[346]Vladimir Seduro, "Viacheslav Ivanovich Ivanov (1866-1949): An Approach to Modern Scholarship," *Dostoevsky in Russian Literary Criticism*, NY: Octagon Books, 1969, 58.

[347] Wisniewska, "Narrative Structure in the Prose of Tatiana Tolstaia", 248.

[348] Tolstaia, *Noch'*, 325.

[349] Besides those of Dostoevsky's works studied in detail in this thesis, *"Diadushkin son"* also has a description of a marionette-like face, the whole of which seems to consist of disparate corners and other elements.

[350] D-*PSS*, 28.1:164.

Wisniewska insists on the diabolical nature of the meeting at the tavern, pointing out that when Denisov attempts to escape "he sees ...silver tails, and lacquered hoofs; all demonic symbols."[351] At this meeting Denisov discovers that to suffer is to a great degree unpleasant, revealing Tolstaia's irony towards Dostoevsky's idea of suffering; but he still tries to do so for his fellow-man.[352] Bakhtiiarov and his "*ved'maki*" humiliate Denisov, forcing him to crawl under the table for their entertainment. He feels his soul weaken and cannot breathe, as there is no air. The Russian for "soul" (*dusha*), "to take a breath" (*vzdokhnut'*), and air (*vozdukh*) have the same root -*dukh-/dokh-*. Tolstaia's use of several words with this root in one emotionally-intense passage recalls Dostoevsky's emphasis on the lack of air and "*zhivaia zhizn'*." It also implies the absence of the Holy Ghost ("*Sviatogo Dukha*") among the people at the meeting, and its *bezobrazie*.

The ugliness of the demons' feast is highlighted through a variety of features, among which we have a toad's mouth, fur instead of hair, and the dead eyes of a beauty:

Others were much worse – this one, for example, a very bad woman, resembling a ski, – her front was all steeled with brocade, but her back was absolutely naked; or that one, a beauty with the eyes of a graveyard watchman; but scariest of all was that restless laugher, a disassembled Punch, and his little lilac tie, and his toad-like mouth, and fur on his head ... the dead eyes of the beauty were shedding tears.

[*Drugie byli mnogo khuzhe – vot eta, naprimer, ochen' plokhaia zhenshchina, pokhozhaia na lyzhu, – pered ee ves' zatkan parchoi, a spina sovershenno golaia; ili ta, drugaia, krasavitsa s glazami kladbishchenskogo storozha; no strashnee vsekh von tot vertliavyi khokhotun, razvinchennyi petrushka, i galstuchek ego sirenevyi, i zhabii rot, i sherst' na golove...u krasavitsy iz mertvykh glaz struilis' slezy...*][353]

The focus on death (dead eyes, the eyes of a graveyard watchman) in this passage is reminiscent of Mamleev (see Chapter 3). Death as ugliness and an opposition to beauty is depicted in Dostoevsky's *Crime and Punishment* (see Chapter 2), throughout Mamleev's works, and in Tolstaia's "Sleepwalker in the Fog" as well as some of her other stories. In "Date with a Bird" ["*Svidanie s ptitsei*]," for example, a tale of a young boy learning about death and sensuality, after reality deflates the

---

[351] Wisniewska, "Narrative Structure in the Prose of Tatiana Tolstaia", 248.
[352] Tolstaia, *Noch'*, 324, 327.
[353] *Ibid.*, 325.

121

protagonist's dreams he notes that "the dead empty world was filled with grey thick oozing depression."[354] There is also a certain surreal Gogolian *bezobrazie* (such as in *"Vii,"* for example) shared by the narratives of Dostoevsky, Mamleev, and Tolstaia: the comic *bezobrazie* of Goliadkin in Dostoevsky's "Double" (i.e., the scene with Goliadkin facing the closed door) and the *bezobrazie* of the talking corpses in his *"Bobok;"* the surreal ugliness of Mamleev's murderers and philosophers; and the description of the meeting at the bar at the bath-house in Tolstaia's "Sleepwalker in the Fog:"

> there where behind the dome a blue smoke is curling, where a chuckle strolls around like the wind blows, where champagne like a foamy **hook** jumps out onto the table-cloth, where there are heavy women's backs, where there is somebody in a little lilac tie, **puny**, dog-like, quickly fidgeting around the Master, adoring him non-stop... The guests started loudly; the lilac fidgeter, courtesy itself, was conducting with a fork...

> [...*tuda, gde za kupolom klubitsia sinii dym, gde poryvami vetra guliaet khokhotok, gde shampanskoe penistym* **kriukom** *vyskakivaet na skatert', gde tiazhelye zhenskie spiny, gde kto-to v sirenevom galstuchke,* **shchuplyi**, *sobachistyi, bystro vetritsia vokrug Khoziaina, nepreryvno ego obozhaia ...Gosti grianuli; sirenevyi vertun sama preduprediter'nost' – dirizhiroval vilkoi...*][355]

The word "hook" appears in this passage together with *"shchuplyi,"* meaning "puny," but derived from the verb *"shchupat'"* ("to probe"), which has such words as *"shchup"* ("probe") and *"shchupal'tsa"* ("tentacles") in its semantic nest. Both "probe" and "to probe" carry a negative connotation, as does *"shchupal'tsa"* when used to refer to a human being. *"Shchupal'tsa"* and *"sobachistyi"* suggest an ugly and surreal transformation of the lilac person into something animal-like. The notion of the "hook" also brings in the demonic element, since it is the tool by which devils drag the *bezobraznyi* human being into the abyss of Hell. Both *"shchup"* ("probe") and *"kriuk"* ("hook") are used interchangeably to denote the devils' tool. These references, along with those to bewitched, animal-like creatures, reinforce the satanic image of Bakhtiiarov, and constitute Tolstaia's poetic means of introducing the ugly into her narrative.

---

[354] *Dictionary of Literary Biography*, 285:319.
[355] Tolstaia, *Noch'*,, 321-322, 325.

Hooks and transformations into half-animals reappear in Tolstaia's latest work, a novel entitled *Slynx* (*Kys'*). In this anti-utopia, we find what is left of Moscow after the Explosion (an unspecified apocalyptic event, presumably nuclear). Tolstaia's nostalgic tendency to portray the old (mainly pre-revolutionary) times in her short-stories (i.e. "Darling Shura" ["*Milaia Shura*"], "Most Beloved" ["*Samaia liubimaia*"], "Sitting on the Golden Porch They Were" ["*Na zolotom kryl'tse sideli*"]) as having a charm and beauty nobody can find in the present day is also evident in *Slynx*. In this novel, in some sense a parable, the world is peopled by mutants displaying the features of animals and leading a primitive life. Time has been turned back to the pre-historic era; the novel's characters are having to learn to live in primordial conditions. Politically, however, the city of Fedor-Kuz'michsk is a surreal version of Stalin's Moscow. This horror fairy-tale has its Master (*Murza*) Fedor-Kuz'mich, assisted by a hierarchy of *murzas* of lesser status; and old printed books are believed to bring disease. An organisation similar to the KGB is in charge of purges, carried out by the *Sanitary*, whose name evokes both their animal nature (scavengers: e.g., *ptitsy-sanitary*) and the medical orderlies of 1970s Soviet psychiatric hospitals. The protagonist of *Slynx*, the "Cro-Magnon philosopher" Benedikt, is unaware of his own transformation into a *Sanitar*; his motivation is to get books and he denies the fact of his killing their owners.[356] Like any other *Sanitar* in the novel, he uses a hook both to fetch books[357] and murder people. His physical appearance changes; his hook and cloak come to feel like bodily attributes:

> All by itself, as if it were my main, magic skin, the cloak lay down upon my shoulders, the hood flew onto my face as a reliable defence; one cannot see me, I myself see everybody, right through! The weapon, strong, nimble, grew onto my hand by itself – the faithful hook, bent like the letter "*glagol*!"

> [*Sam soboiu, tochno glavnaia, volshebnaia kozha, leg na plechi balakhon, nadezhnoi zashchitoi vsporkhnul na litso kolpak; videt' menia nel'zia, ia sam vsekh vizhu, naskvoz'! Oruzhie, krepkoe, vertkoe, samo priroslo k ruke – vernyi kriuk, zagnutyi, kak bukva "glagol"!*][358]

---

[356] Benedikt comes from Lat. *benedictus* (blessed). The usual Russian version of this name is "Venedikt." Tolstaia's unusual form draws attention to the etymology. As a classisist, she is bound to select Greek and Latin names (corrupt, or not) purposefully.

[357] Here Tolstaia's fascination with the printed word surfaces again.

[358] Tatiana Tolstaia, *Kys'*, Moscow: *Podkova/Inostranka*, 2001, 326.

Here again Tolstaya uses hooks as the sign of a demonic connection – in this case, the transformation of a character into a devil-like creature. The cloak and hood together with the hook also form an iconic representation of death, with the hook substituting the scythe. In this representation the face of death cannot be seen (or is depicted as a skull). Correspondingly, the death-like, devil-like face of Benedikt remains concealed. Death, a central concept in Mamleev's *oeuvre*, is also in the focus of attention of both Dostoevsky and Tolstaia in her *Slynx*.[359]

Benedikt himself does not notice his further metamorphoses. He is horrified to learn from Kudeiar Kudeiarych, his father-in law and the chief *Sanitar*, that in his search for books, for an escape into their ideal world, he has become what he himself fears most, the legendary monster known as the *slynx*:

And, having tensed his eyes [sic], [he] started to burn Benedikt with a **yellow**, coldish, lacerating fire.

"Stop the *bezobrazie*! With children around!" yelled the mother-in-law.

"Control yourself, papá!"

"What is it with you? You yourself are …you …you…you are a slynx, that's what you are!!!" yelled Benedikt, scaring himself: a word will fly out and you won't catch it; he got scared, but yelled. "Slynx! Slynx!"

"Me?.. Me?.." the father-in-law started laughing, and suddenly loosened his grip and stepped aside. "There's a mistake here. In fact, you are the slynx."

"ME?!?!?!"

"Who else? Pushkin? You. You are the one."

[*I, natuzhiv glaza, nachal zhech' Benedikta **zheltym**, kholodnovatym, tsarapaiushchim plamenem.*

– *Konchaite **bezobrazie**! Pri detiakh! – prikriknula teshcha.*

– *Kontroliruite sebia, papen'ka!*

– *Chego vy voobshche?.. Vy voobshche…vy…vy…vy – kys', vot vy kto!!! – kriknul Benedikt, sam pugaias': vyletit slovo i ne poimaesh; ispugalsia, no kriknul. – Kys'! Kys'!*

---

[359] See Chapter 3 on death in Dostoevsky and Mamleev.

124

–   *Ia-to?..Ia?.. – zasmeialsia test' i vdrug razzhal pal'tsy i otstupil. – Oboznachka vyshla...Kys'-to – ty.*

–   *Ia-a?!?!?!*

–   *A kto zhe? Pushkin, chto li? Ty! Ty i est' ...*][360]

The scene starts with the yellow fire used by Benedikt's father-in-law to burn him, and ends with Benedikt's getting sick, with references to cheese, canaries, and yellow vomit: "Suddenly nausea came, as if he had had some **cheese**...he threw up onto the door frame. Something **yellow**...must be from **canaries**." [*Vdrug podstupila toshnota, kak esli by **syru** poel...vyrvalo na kosiak. **Zheltym** chem-to...ot kanareek, dolzhno.*][361] The colour yellow appears four times in this scene, which deals with the ugliness and moral degradation of Benedikt. Yellow in the poetics of Tolstaia's novel *Kys'* functions as it does in Dostoevsky's narratives, to signal *bezobrazie*.

Another significant detail that brings Tolstaia's and Dostoevsky's poetics of the ugly together is the image of the mouse. What was a metaphor for Dostoevsky – the underground mouse – becomes the basic food source for the inhabitants of Fedor-Kuzmichsk.[362] In this post-Explosion city, mice are used for food and clothing; and the majority of the survivors' lives also mirror that of the underground mice, emphasising their loss of the human image.

Mirroring as a Dostoevskian feature also figures in Tolstaia's short-story "Night" ["*Noch'*"] portraying lives of an elderly mother and her mentally-ill son, Aleksei Petrovich, in a communal apartment. Aleksei Petrovich occasionally finds himself existing as two different people, inner and outer doubles:

> When Aleksei Petrovich lies in bed and wants to go to sleep, his legs start growing on their own, down, down, and his head grows up, up, to the black dome, up, and sways like the top of a tree in a storm, while the stars scrape his scull like sand. And the second Aleksei Petrovich, inside, keeps shrinking and shrinking, compressing, he disappears in a poppy seed, in a sharp needle tip, in a microbe, in nothingness, and if he's not stopped, he'll vanish there completely. But the outside, giant Aleksei Petrovich

---

[360] Tolstaia, *Kys'*, 365.
[361] *Ibid.*, 366.
[362] Besides the reference to this animal in "Notes from Underground", Dostoevsky also remarks about the character of Versilov that "people are mice for him" ["*Liudi dlia nego – myshi.*"]. Mochul'sky, *Dostoevsky: zhizn' i tvorchestvo*, 404.

sways like a pine long mast, grows, scratches his bald spot against the night dome, doesn't allow the little one to disappear into a dot. And these two Aleksei Petroviches are one and the same.[363]

[*Kogda Aleksei Petrovich lezhit v posteli i khochet zasnut', nogi u nego sami nachinaiut rasti vniz, vniz, a golova – vverkh, vverkh, do chernogo kupola, vse vverkh, i raskachivaetsia, kak verkhushka dereva v grozu, a zvezdy peskom skrebutsia o ego cherep. A vtoroi Aleksei Petrovich, vnutri, vse s''ezhivaetsia, s''ezhivaetsia, szhimaetsia, propadaet v makovoe zernyshko, v ostryi konchik igolki, v mikrobchika, v nichto, i esli ego ne ostanovit', on sovsem tuda uidet. No vneshnii, gigantskii Aleksei Petrovich korabel'noi sosnoi raskachivaetsia, rastet, chirkaet lysinoi po nochnomu kupolu, ne puskaet malen'kogo uiti v tochku. I eti dva Alekseia Petrovicha – odno i to zhe.*][364]

The name Aleksei belongs to the meekest of the brothers Karamazov, and also alludes to Russian Orthodox writings: to the Vita of Saint Alexis, the Man of God.[365] In Dostoevsky's narratives the mentally-ill and crippled are often portrayed as God's people, holy fools, suffering for everyone's sins (Mar'ia Timofeevna Lebiadkina-Stavrogina, Elizaveta Smerdiashchaia, M-me Snegireva and her paralysed daughter). A similarly suffering and innocent mentally-ill person is portrayed in Tolstaia's "*Noch'*." A mentally-ill protagonist is not such a common type of character for either nineteenth- or twentieth-century literature and the fact that it occurs in the works of both Dostoevsky and Tolstaia raises the issue of influence. The name of the mentally-ill protagonist, although common, is nonetheless the name of a key character of Dostoevsky. In addition, Dostoevskian 'doubling' occurs in the same passage with two different Aleksei Petroviches. The combination of Dostoevskian elements that Tolstaia consciously uses in her short-story demonstrates a definite similarity between the two authors. The pre-sleep fantasies about the inner Aleksei vanishing into a poppy seed, the eye of a needle, a microbe, escaping into nothing, recall Tolstaia's view of Stalin's purges. Escape into the inner self existed as a defence mechanism for people in this era. In Tolstaia's article "History in Photographs," she discusses Stalin's motives for eliminating people from pictures, relating them to

---

[363] Tolstaia, *Sleepwalker in a Fog*, 73-4.
[364] Tolstaia, *Noch'*, 124-5.
[365] On the hagiographic character of Dostoevsky's narrative see Vetlovskaia, *Poetika romana "Brat'ia Karamazovy"*.

mystical, irrational notions that recall "an old rule of magic: evocation calls forth epiphanies."[366] The necessity to prove that enemies never existed originates from the same mystical sources as "the ban on depicting God, and the source of blasphemy when God's image is destroyed or distorted; this explains the jealous destruction of icons after the 1917 revolution, and their equally jealous conservation."[367] Similarly, Aleksei attempts to eliminate his own image, to minimise it as much as possible, to bring it to the point of full stop. As the lines of the outer Aleksei grow towards infinity, his inner self tries to reduce itself to a dot, a geometric point – which would bring relaxation to his troubled consciousness. Another geometric or architectural detail that appears in *"Noch'"* is the parallelepiped of the little paper boxes Aleksei makes for a living and feels sorry to part with. These boxes have a stable structure; and Aleksei wants obsessively to possess or acquire some structure, some form, looking for it in the chaos of everyday life. This chaos is accentuated, as the reader is confronted with a diseased consciousness.[368]

In his search for God's image, Aleksei aims to be a writer. At the end of the story, he is writing in an almost conceptualist fashion: "Night. Night. Night. Night. Night. Night. Night. Night. Night. Night."[369] Goscilo insists on "night" as being the state of Aleksei's "cognitive darkness;" but he writes these lines after his unfortunate experience on the streets of the city, which shows that he has simply understood the infernal qualities of the outside world. Quite the opposite of a "cognitive darkness," it is the chaotic and ugly reality of the outside world that he is trying to put down on paper. Aleksei suddenly understands "the laws of connecting the millions of shreds of disparate things" [*zakony stseplenia millionov obryvkov razroznennykh veshchei*];[370] he attempts to overcome the chaos of these things by using the power of the written word. This is one of many instances in which Tolstaia demonstrates her aesthetic views: beautiful language functions as a means of defeating ugly reality; beauty becomes the characteristic of Logos, ugliness – of the Universe. However, mentally-ill Aleksei is incapable of writing coherent sentences and beautiful texts, and his minimalist, disrupted passage depicts his experience of the ugly outside reality. Tolstaia's luscious language descends in style when she describes *bezobraznoe*, for which she adopts Dostoevsky's poetics of the ugly. She describes the ugly scenes in the ugly manner, but she does it beautifully, that is, artistically well.

---

[366] Tolstaia, *Pushkin's Children*, 201.
[367] *Ibid.*
[368] Tolstaia, *Noch'* , 121-2.
[369] *Ibid.*, 127.
[370] *Ibid.*

Despite the complete external ugliness of the protagonists of Tolstaia's *"Noch',"* by the end of this story the author's sympathy towards them becomes particularly acute. The narrative turns almost sentimental, and we see the love of Aleksei's mother, this old woman in her grotesque body, for her "long-awaited, suffered for," [*dolgozhdannoe, vystradannoe*][371] only, late child born with Down's syndrome and grown up into Aleksei Petrovich, lost in the streets. Aleksei desperately tries to understand the world, to obtain a regular, normal form. The superficial ugliness of both protagonists does not prevent Tolstaia from showing these attempts of Aleksei as a search for beauty, or the love of his old mother as an ennobling feature. The ugly themes of the story – mental illness and old age – were not appreciated by the Soviet authorities, who denied the very existence of such problems in a supposedly perfect state:

> They [the censors] asked me not to write about old people because old people have problems. It is unpleasant to speak about problems. They are old and that's a problem in itself …I would say "Well, why not write about old people?" And they would say "Because we have no old people."… And of course there are no crazy people at all. They don't exist. How can a crazy person exist in our socialist country?[372]

In spite of what Soviet bureaucrats may have wished for, people like Aleksei and his mother did exist, and they found their way into Tolstaia's prose.

Aleksei's syntax is peculiar; his sentences are abrupt like those of Kirillov in *The Devils*. This is particularly true when these sentences originally belong to a person other than himself: listening to Pushkin's verse (which he enjoys tremendously), Aleksei breaks the poetic lines of Pushkin's "Winter Evening"[373] according to what they sound like to him:

> A pall the storm casts on the sky,
> And whirls the twisting snow,
> First like a beast she'll howl and cry,
> Then like a child sob soft and low.

---

[371] *Ibid.,* 126.
[372] Christine D. Tomei, ed., *Russian Women Writers*, Vol. 2, NY/London: Garland, 1999, 1479. Trans. Stephan Salisbury.
[373] The title of Pushkin's poem "Devils" ["*Besy*"], written in iambic tetrameter as is "Winter Evening," may be a source of inspiration for the title of Dostoevsky's novel.

Aleksei Petrovich really loves this. He laughs heartily, baring his **yellow** teeth; happy, he stamps his foot.

> First like a beast she'll howl and cry,
> Then like a child sob soft and low.

The words get to the end – and turn around, get to the end again – and turn around again.

> Apall thus tormcas tson thus ky,
> An dwhirls thet wistings no!
> First likab eastsheel howland cry,
> Then likach ild sobs off tandlow!

Very good! Here is how it will howl: u-u-u-u-u![374]

> [*Buria mgloiu nebo kroet,*
> *Vikhri snezhnye krutia,*
> *To kak zver' ona zavoet,*
> *To zaplachet, kak ditia.*

Uzhasno eto nravitsia Alekseiu Petrovichu! On shiroko smeetsia, obnazhaia **zheltye** *zuby, raduetsia, topaet nogoi.*

> *To kak zver' ona zavoet,*
> *To zaplachet, kak ditia!*

Tak vot slova do kontsa doidut – i nazad povorachivaiut, snova doidut – i snova povorachivaiut.

---

[374] Tolstaia, *Sleepwalker in a Fog*, 73.

Buriam, gloiu, nebak, roet,

Vikhris', nezhny, ekru, tia!

Tokag, zveria, naza, voet,

Toza, plachet, kagdi, tia!]

Ochen' khorosho! Vot kak ona zavoet: u-u-u-u-u!]^{375}

Aleksei is compared to the winter storm in the poem. Both the storm and the protagonist of *"Noch'"* howl like a beast and cry like a child. In Aleksei's case, this shows that he does not quite come up to the *obraz* of normalcy, the lack of which is reinforced in the text by the occurrence of the colour yellow. On the surface, Aleksei is unable to produce normal "beautiful" language: the cut-off lines and distorted form of Pushkin's verse that become Aleksei's poetry seem a transformation of beauty into *bezobraznoe*. From a different vantage point, though, Aleksei's version of Pushkin is indeed beautiful: it looks like an incantation, a magic formula he is using to ward off his own demons. In the context of Tolstaia's narratives, rooted as they are in old and contemporary folklore, in children's stories, and *Kunstmärchen*, such a view of Aleksei's 'reading' of Pushkin is entirely justified. Goscilo insists on myths as a basis for Tolstaia's narratives; Lipovetsky demonstrates the differences between myths and fairy-tales, and shows the significance of both for Tolstaia's art:

> ...the difference between myth and fairy-tale is one of values rather than structure. Myth is founded on a belief in the authenticity of complexes of signs, while the fairy-tale uses these very same signs as material for decidedly lighthearted play. As a rule, Tolstaia's stories encompass both approaches; they are based on the conflict between fairy-tale and mythological worldviews.^{376}

The beautiful incantation and the ugly distortion of beauty – both aspects of Aleksei's poetry intertwine in the narrative of *"Noch'."* Pushkin is perceived as creator and symbol of perfect beauty and form in *"Noch',"* *"Limpopo,"* and throughout Tolstaia's *oeuvre*. This brings her close to Dostoevsky, who in his article *"G-n -bov i vopros ob iskusstve"* makes Pushkin a mediator between mundane reality and the beautiful, and an ideal of beauty himself. Dostoevsky uses the example of Pushkin to refute the views

---

^{375} Tolstaia, *"Noch'"*, 124.
^{376} *Dictionary of Literary Biography*, 285:319. Lipovetsky, *Russian Postmodernist Fiction*, 130.

of the utilitarians: *i eto znanie samym polnym, samym garmonicheskim obrazom iavilos' nam v Pushkine.*"[377] Given that for Dostoevsky harmony implies beauty (see Chapter 2), Pushkin personifies the most beautiful way that knowledge can reveal itself in a human being.[378] But it is not Pushkinian but rather Dostoevskian characters that prevail in twentieth-century Russian prose and reality, as Tolstaia reports in her "Pushkin's Children," a key article on classic Russian literature and its influence on the twentieth century:

> Who, after all, are the heroes of Russian literature? Idiots, epileptics, consumptives, thieves, murderers, drunkards, fallen women, idlers, dreamers, fools, nihilists, three sisters whining away for two hours straight on a stage. They loll about on the sofa in stained robes, cut up frogs, lose millions at cards, corrupt minors. They go off with axes to kill old ladies. They slit people's throats once, and then they do it again. Their heads are shaved and they're sent to distant farms. Their heads are shaved and they're sent to the army. They set dogs on children. They hang themselves. They drown themselves. They shoot themselves. Yes, an impressive panopticon! And then you get the Gulag. And then you get 60 million casualties.[379]

This article shows that Tolstaia associates most influential Russian literature with Turgenev, Chekhov, Goncharov, and Dostoevsky, references to the characters of the latter occurring eight times out of total of twelve. This proportion demonstrates the significance of Dostoevsky's influence in her opinion. The fragmentation of Tolstaia's narratives of the 1990s-2000s, her modernist technique, stylistic changes, and colloquialisms could be considered 'ugly' when compared to stylistically conservative narratives, i.e. those of Turgenev. Goscilo criticises Tolstaia's works after 1988 for her bad style: loss of narrative focus, repetitions, and longueurs, "revealing a clever, erudite author at a creative crossroads."[380] I would rather suggest that the seeming narrative shapelessness, amorphous style, and fragmentation of Tolstaia's most recent works are the result of a conscious choice on the part of the author, who is attempting to mirror contemporary concerns in her prose. She consciously distorts her linguistically wealthy language to represent *bezobraznoe* in her texts. The major role that she ascribes in her journalism to Dostoevsky in the whole picture of the influence of the Russian classics

---

[377] D-*PSS*, 18: 69.
[378] See also Dostoevsky's discussion of beauty in *PSS* 18: 102.
[379] Tolstaia, *Pushkin's Children*, 95.
[380] *Dictionary of Literary Biography*, 285:324.

on twentieth-century Russian literature is yet another demonstration of the significance that Dostoevsky has for her own creative process. And although Tolstaia's language is richer, more varied, and beautiful than that of Dostoevsky, her poetics of the ugly and her treatment of space are similar to his. Tolstaia shares Dostoevsky's humanistic values, but recognises the dominance of Dostoevskian ugly characters in the Russian literary scene of the end of the twentieth- and beginning of the twenty-first centuries. She attempts to oppose Pushkin and his art as an ideal of beauty to the Dostoevskian ugliness of the twentieth century, but cannot herself escape either contemporary Russian reality or Dostoevskian reverberations in her works.

Both Dostoevsky and Tolstaia write about suffocating atmosphere and the underground; in Tolstaia's texts, the underground is a means of escape, mainly from Soviet ideology. Tolstaia, like Dostoevsky, focuses on the *bezobrazie* of Russian reality. Although ugly poverty, in the manner of the Natural school, is a more acute subject for Petrushevskaia than for Tolstaia, the latter also writes about it, as well as about Soviet propaganda. Tolstaia's ideal of the beautiful word can be looked upon as humanistic or artistic idealism, if not escapism. Robert Porter compares her to "a latter-day English Romantic."[381] As does any utopian notion, Tolstaia's ideal of beautiful language has its dystopian side: it can be an entrapment, a prison – i.e. function as home does in Petrushevskaia's stories. (See Chapter 5.) Dystopian elements of the ideal of the beautiful word reveal themselves in Tolstaia's "Night" and "Loves Me – Loves Me Not" ["*Liubish – ne liubish*"], a story about a young girl and her nannies.[382] In these two texts, children, old people, and the disabled are alienated from the rest of society because of their *linguistic* differences, or incapabilities.

The similarities between Tolstaia's and Dostoevsky's poetics of the ugly are as follows: both writers favour unusual epithets, having to do with colour and ugly weather phenomena, reflecting the psychological state of the characters. Their descriptions of *bezobraznoe* operate with the image of the mouse, the colour yellow, multiple corner/angles, and lack of air. Both Tolstaia and Dostoevsky depict the ugliness of city life (often of the same city – St. Petersburg). These writers share a number of themes, such as literature, ugliness in art, Pushkin, and the *bezobraznoe* of the downtrodden and of old people. Tolstaia refers to the *Insulted and Injured, Brothers Karamazov*, "Notes from Underground," and *Notes from the House of the Dead* in the passages where she deals with ugliness.

Dostoevsky may have paved the way for creating the myth of Pushkin as 'our everything,' which points toward the solution to existing *bezobrazie*; and Tolstaia is just as fascinated with Pushkin

---

[381] Porter, *Russia's Alternative Prose*, 67.
[382] Tolstaia, *Noch'*, 26.

as Dostoevsky was. Imprecise quotes and an abundance of diminutives characterise the poetics of both prosaists; in addition, Tolstaia uses postmodern irony and play with classic texts, their deformation and deconstruction. The self-parody of Tolstaia brings her narratives close to those of Mamleev. Both twentieth-century writers demonstrate a Dostoevskian narrowing of disproportional space. In Tolstaia, the underground, for example, narrows down to cracks behind the wallpaper. Lack of space and the consequent *bezobrazie* are featured equally in the texts of both Tolstaia and Dostoevsky. Both share an ironic attitude toward Chernyshevskii's "new people," physical strength, and Darwinism.

Tolstaia and Dostoevsky write about *bezobraznoe* in daily life, about the messiness of dwellings and chaos of thoughts. Tolstaia argues against Dostoevsky's ideal solution to *bezobraznoe*, his hopes for the 'Golden Age.' She contrasts ugly reality with beautiful dreams, just as the young Dostoevsky did. In the fictional reality of both writers people are made analogous to insects (an approach which another contemporary Russian writer, Viktor Pelevin, develops further in his novel *Life of Insects* [*Zhizn' nasekomykh*]. The absence of home and the problem of dysfunctional families in Dostoevsky become an absence of home for Russians as a nation in Tolstaia. Doubling and mirroring, with an emphasis on their negative and ugly components, characterise both Dostoevsky's and Tolstaia's narratives. A rare case among late-twentieth century Russian writers, Tolstaia offers a positive alternative to *bezobraznoe* in "*Limpopo*". Like Dostoevsky, Tolstaia operates with life-dream oppositions, and shows pity for the dreamers as did the young Dostoevsky. The writings of Dostoevsky, Mamleev, and Tolstaia represent unusual types of realism – fantastic realism and Gogolian surrealism, allowing for the comic type of the ugly and grotesque. In "*Limpopo*," Tolstaia demonstrates that there is no beauty but ugliness in Russian reality, as the search for the beautiful form, associated with Pushkin, yields no positive result. She, like Dostoevsky, parodies Nekrasov's idea of saving a woman in her "Notes from Underground," with its Dostoevskian amorphic dialogical monologue. In this work, Tolstaia's characters demonstrate the ugly and tyrannical aspects of their personalities in a manner reminiscent of the Underground Man. The ugliness of servility and of hell-like taverns also can be found in both Tolstaia's and Dostoevsky's narratives. Such ugly characters as criminals, writers, and devils appear in the two writers' texts, with Tolstaia sometimes representing hers as half-animals. The ugliness of death, a major theme for Mamleev, is also in the focus of Tolstaia and Dostoevsky. Disproportionate, disparate elements are used to create the pictures of *bezobrazie* in the narratives of all three writers.

Tolstaia's attitude towards time recalls its treatment in Old Russian texts: the past with its heroes is beautiful, which for Tolstaia also means that the present is ugly. Such an attitude is also similar to

Slavophile ideas of pre-Petrine (old, Russian Orthodox, and beautiful) and post-Petrine (new, Western, and ugly) Russia that were partially shared by Dostoevsky, although in the modified form of his *pochvenichestvo* (derived from the Russian word "soil"), a social and cultural tendency which called for a return of the educated class to its Russian roots. Its representatives were not to abandon what they had learned from Western civilization, but rather synthesize the best of the ideas of the Slavophiles and the Westernizers.[383] Dostoevsky did not idealize pre-Petrine Rus': in his article "Two Camps of Theoreticians" ["*Dva lageria teoretikov*"] he criticises the narrowness of the views expressed by the Slavophile newspaper "Day" and voices his appreciation for the literary and cultural achievements of Russia after the reforms of Peter the Great.[384] However, he also criticises the Westerners, and regards the split between the peasantry with its traditional way of living and the educated masses, as well as the secularisation of the Church caused by the reforms of Peter I, as the major problems of Russian political and cultural development in his time.[385] The character of the narratives of "Night" and *The Brothers Karamazov* is hagiographic. They depict mentally-ill people in the same fashion: superficially ugly, in discord with society, but suffering for everybody else's sins. Geometric imagery and peculiar, abrupt syntax (distorted sentences as a sign of the asocial and the ugly) appear as poetic devices in Dostoevsky and Tolstaia, as does the search for harmonious form. Perfect form for both writers is associated with Pushkin. The poet, or his poetry, functions as a symbol of beauty, which Tolstaia associates with the word, Logos, as she does *bezobraznoe* with the reality of the outside world, the Universe.

Chapter V: Liudmila Petrushevskaia: Urban Dystopia: Spaces and People

This chapter will focus on similarities between the works of Fedor Dostoevsky and Liudmila Petrushevskaia, on deformities at three levels: poetics of the ugly; narrative structure and technique; and the *bezobrazie* of characters as well as their spatial surroundings, featuring home-hearth as a locus of dystopia. This chapter will also demonstrate common thematic preferences of Dostoevsky and Petrushevskaia, related to *bezobraznoe*.

Liudmila Petrushevskaia's life begins with a typical horror story of the Stalinist period; unlike that of Tatiana Tolstaia hers was not a privileged childhood. Born in 1938, Petrushevskaia survived

[383] Lantz, *The Dostoevsky Encyclopedia*, 324-327.
[384] D-*PSS*, 20:10.
[385] *Ibid.* D-*PSS*, 18: 36-37; D-*PSS*, 21: 255. *Cf.* Lantz, *The Dostoevsky Encyclopedia*, 309-310.

family traumas, extreme poverty, near starvation, and displacement, including some time in a children's home where she was put by her own mother in order to avoid desperate circumstances. The family was ruined by the purges; Petrushevskaia's father left the family before she was born. Her family history notwithstanding, Petrushevskaia "charts the daily psychic monstrosities of a spiritual wasteland populated by victims and victimizers bound by an endless chain of universal suffering and abuse."[386] Responsible for three offspring, Petrushevskaia took whatever job she could, working as a translator, journalist, editor, and radio announcer. In many ways such a lifestyle corresponds to the themes of her writing: those of fighting a "lone solitary life,"[387] of deprived childhoods, single, divorced, and widowed mothers, and of families falling apart.

Women make up the majority of the protagonists in Liudmila Petrushevskaia's texts. These mostly deal with specifically female problems, and according to Monika Katz's definition, fall under the category of "women's literature."[388] In the nineteenth century, the image of the strong woman (Turgenev's heroines, for example) was created as a complement to that of the superfluous man, self-focused and looking for his place in society. In the particular case of Liza and the Underground Man, a subtype of the superfluous man, the paragon of a strong woman is a prostitute – a traditionally weak and degraded member of society. However, despite possessing the lowest social role imaginable, she proves to have more common sense and compassion than the Underground Man.

In Russian literature of the Soviet period, women were still depicted as superheroes, or, indeed, supermen. The true Soviet woman, such as Baranskaia's heroine in "A Week Like Any Other", has to be productive for society both in the private and public sphere, and has a double load of responsibilities in comparison to those of any man.[389] In post-Soviet literature, the 'strong woman motif' still exists, although it receives a different treatment. In Liudmila Petrushevskaia's prose public life is given no emphasis whatsoever; it is the daily life of female characters that has her full attention. Petrushevskaia's heroines have to struggle to survive, to overcome numerous obstacles in order to have a decent meal for their children: "Everything was hanging in the air like a sword, all our life, ready to crash . . . Are there powers in the world that can stop a woman who has to feed a child." [*Vse viselo v vozdukhe, kak mech, vsia nasha zhizn' gotovaia obrushit'sia. Est' li sily, sposobnye ostanovit' zhenshchinu, kotoraia*

---

[386] *Dictionary of Literary Biography*, 285: 221.
[387] *Ibid.*, 222.
[388] "The Other Woman: Character Portrayal and the Narrative Voice in the Short Stories of Liudmila Petrushevskaia" in *Women and Russian Culture: Projections and Self-Perceptions*, ed. Rosalind Marsh, NY/Oxford: Berghahn Books, 1998, 189.
[389] N. Baranskaia, *A Week Like Any Other: a Novella and Stories*, London: Virago, 1989.

stremit'sia nakormit' rebenka.][390] For these women, life is a battlefield: "No, you can't move in here, again faces distorted with hatred, seen in our mirror in the hall; we always have rows in the hall, the bridgehead of military actions."[*Vselit'sia vam siuda nel'zia, opiat' iskazhennye nenevist'iu litsa, mel'kaiushchie v nashem zerkale v prikhozhei, my rugaemsia, my rugaemsia-to vsegda v prikhozhei, platsdarm boevykh deistvii.*][391] And it is not clear who is winning the battle with the 'loved ones.' In this permanent struggle family members cannot help but be effected by a dehumanized environment; they lose their capacity for compassion and consideration. Violation of human dignity becomes a norm for them as well.

The complex narrative structure of *Time: Night* goes along with a remarkably complicated plot. It pictures the family of the female narrator, Anna Andrianovna, whose mother becomes a schizophrenic, son – a criminal, and daughter – a penniless single mother of three (it is left ambiguous in the story, as to whether all three children are from different fathers, or whether the ratio is one to two). We also learn in the course of *Time: Night* that Anna Andrianovna has had affairs with married men, one of which resulted in a marriage, which was dissolved since Anna Andrianovna's husband had an affair and eventually married his mistress. The narrator is virtually unemployed and is trying to support all the members of her family, and is also bringing up her grandson Timochka herself. All this presumably happens within a short span of time, which is, however, difficult to pinpoint, as the narrative is consciously 'timeless:' the story goes back and forth in time, with no end in sight. The space in *Time: Night* is confined to a two-room flat, which, for the members of this family, is an object of residential claims. Anna Andrianovna insists "we are winning," but is unable to make the people closest to her secure, and loses everybody in the end. Her ugly and distorted dreams are similar to those of the Underground Man. Both of these characters exaggerate the effect they have on people around them. Both have a high opinion of themselves and are ugly in the celebration of their righteousness: the underground man in his speech to the prostitute Liza, and Anna Andrianovna in her real or imaginary conversations with her children, particularly her daughter Alena, who inherits some of the underground features. Alena is consistently described as being in a pit; both her psychological state and real-life accommodation belong to the underground: "What terrible dungeons (*podzemelii*) had she surfaced from if a room of eighteen square metres for four people seems a refuge to her!" [*Iz kakikh podzemelii*

---

[390] Liudmila Petrushevskaia, *Sobranie sochinenii*, Vol. 1, *Khar'kov*/Moscow: Folio/TKO Act, 1996, 340, 369. In my translation of Petrushevskaia, I have kept her language irregularities where possible, however, some sacrifices have had to be made to preserve comprehensibility.
[391] Petrushevskaia, *Sobranie sochinenii*, 1:366.

136

ona vorotilas', esli komnata vosemnadtsat' kvadratnykh metrov na chetverykh ei kazhetsia ubezhishchem!][392]

If in Tolstaia house/home – whether it is eighteen square metres for four people, or more – is a *locus* of utopia, in Petrushevskaia it does not enjoy this privilege. In fact, it performs the opposite function, localizing the dystopia. Although in some of Petrushevskaia's stories the intended destination of the heroes is a *"teplyi dom"* (warm house) – as it is, for example in her *"Cherez polia"* (Crossing the Fields) – their expectations are not met and the promised idyll does not materialize.[393] Van Baak writes that the notions of "house" and "utopia" are the most basic categories of the conceptualized understanding of culture. He suggests looking at utopia as a wide typological notion, including various ideal projections of a better world, of the world "as it is meant to be," and at the house/home (*dom*) as a utopian space in literature and culture. Evidently, not every home in literature possesses such a modeling or symbolic function. It depends on the literary and semantic context, as well as on features of the *Weltbild*.[394]

The archetypal, general cultural significance of the house/home has several aspects, which normally co-exist in literature and culture in general:

– the cosmological aspect (house as cosmos, house as the centre of cosmos, which stands out so much in a number of works by Mikhail Bulgakov, i.e. *The White Guard*);

– the social and psychological aspect (the sphere of security, sphere of identity, house/home as identity, i.e. Tatiana Tolstaia's ideal of a wooden house in *"Limpopo"*);

– the mythopoetical or literary (axiological) aspect, i.e. Ableukhov's house in Andrei Bely's *Petersburg*).

The basis of all these aspects is the myth of the home-hearth, which in all likelihood is universal for non-nomadic cultures. The myth of home-hearth embraces a wide range of values: security and refuge; warmth in the direct and the figurative sense; belonging to a family or dynasty, and the link between

---

[392] *Ibid.*, 385.
[393] *Dictionary of Literary Biography*, 285:223. Dostoevsky never portrays any good families in his fiction, but has an ideal of the good family as the foundation of society expressed in his non-fiction. D-PSS, 22:69-70. Lantz, *The Dostoevsky Encyclopedia*, 136-139.
[394] Ioost van Baak, *"Dom kak utopia v russkoi literature,"* Russkie Utopii, St. Peterburg: Corvus, 1995, 136-137.

generations; a religious centre and a moral landmark; world order; stability and guarantee of continuity; and hospitality. As every archetype is ambivalent, so the myth of home-hearth also encompasses: lack of freedom; cyclic development and stagnation; tyranny; and claustrophobia – that is, dystopia.[395] Van Baak discusses semantic and semiotic specifics of Russian variants of the myth of home as an expression of cultural and national mentality. He gives a brief history of Russian utopias from folklore to Platonov, but does not go as far as the post-Soviet literary period, and denies the myth of home its utopian significance during Brezhnev's era of stagnation. Among his nineteenth-century examples, the most relevant for our study is the image of the Crystal palace as an ideal dwelling of future humanity, created by N.G. Chernyshevsky in his novel *Chto delat'?* (1863):[396]

> The building, the huge, huge building, of the kind of which only a few exist today in the largest capitals... But this building, what is it, what is its architectural style? There is no such architecture now; no, there is a hint of it – the palace which stands on Sydenham hill ...this is just the casing of the building, these are its outside walls; but there, inside, there is a real house, a huge house; it is covered by this cast-iron and crystal building as by a case; this building forms wide galleries around it on every storey. How light is the architecture of this inner house, what a small distance there is between the windows, and the windows are huge, wide... "Here live a lot, a whole lot [of people]..." ...everywhere men and women, old men, the young and children together. But there are more of the young ones...

> [*Zdanie, gromadnoe, gromadnoe zdanie, kakikh teper' lish po neskolku v samykh bol'shikh stolitsakh...No eto zdanie, chto zh eto, kakoi ono arkhitektury? teper' net takoi; net, uzh est' odin namek na nee, – dvorets, kotoryi stoit na Saidengamskom kholme...eto lish' obolochka zdaniia, eto ego naruzhnye steny; a tam, vnutri, uzh nastoiashchii dom, gromadneishii dom: on pokryt etim chugunno-khrustal'nym zdaniem, kak futliarom; ono obrazuet vokrug nego shirokie galerei po vsem etazham. Kakaia legkaia arkhitektura etogo vnutrennego doma, kakie malen'kie prostenki mezhdu*

---

[395] *Ibid.*, 137-138. For linguistic proof of utopian nature of the home-hearth see van Baak, 138-139.
[396] Ioost van Baak, "*Dom kak utopia v russkoi literature*," 142. Van Baak mentions the works of Terts, Voinovich, and Zinov'iev, but does not analyze them.

oknami, a okna ogromnye, shirokie... "Zdes' zhivet mnogo, ochen' mnogo ..." ...vezde muzhchiny i zhenshchiny, stariki, molodye i deti vmeste. No bol'she molodykh...][397]

This image caused a strong reaction in later anti-utopian Russian literature (i.e. Dostoevsky and Zamiatin). Dostoevsky, in particular, fought against the idea of the Crystal Palace, in essence a communal dwelling, in his "Notes from Underground" and "Winter Notes on Summer Impressions:"

> Crystal Palace...'united herd'... At Crystal Palace it [suffering] cannot be thought of: suffering is doubt, is negation, but what sort of Crystal Palace is it, if one can doubt it? But meanwhile I am sure that from real suffering, that is from destruction and chaos, a human being will never turn away. Suffering is the only cause of consciousness.

> *[kristal'nyi dvorets...'edino stado' ...V khrustal'nom dvortse ono [stradanie] i nemyslimo: stradanie est' somnenie, est' otritsanie, a chto za khrustal'nyi dvorets, v kotorom mozhno usumnit'sia? A mezhdu tem ia uveren, chto chelovek ot nastoiashchego stradaniia, to est' ot razrusheniia i khaosa, nikogda ne otkazhetsia. Stradanie – da ved' eto edinstvennaia prichina soznaniia.]*[398]

He also obliquely addressed the utopian notion of the Crystal Palace in most of his fictional works, through depiction of the Petersburg dwellings of his characters. Gary Saul Morson calls "Notes from Underground" and *The Devils* "two of the most influential anti-utopias in European literature."[399] The dwellings in Dostoevsky's texts are the exact opposite of the Crystal Palace in the architectural sense: the windows in the cramped rooms of Dostoevskian St. Peterburg are small and the walls are misshapen; galleries, mentioned, for example, in *Crime and Punishment*, are narrow, dark, and labyrinth-like passages:

> Having found the entrance onto the narrow and dark staircase in the corner of the yard, he went up, finally reached the second storey and went out into a gallery, framing the storey from the side of the yard. While he wandered in darkness and confusion...

---

[397] Chernyshevsky, *Chto delat?*, 277-78.
[398] D-*PSS*, 5:69, 119.
[399] Morson, *The Boundaries of Genre*, 36-37.

[*Otyskav v uglu na dvore vkhod na uzkuiu i temnuiu lestnitsu, on podnialsia, nakonets, vo vtoroi etazh i vyshel na galereiu, obkhodivshuiu ego so storony dvora. Pokamest on brodil v temnote i nedoumenii...*][400]

Such a representation of communal dwellings is taken up by the twentieth-century narratives. These also include the direct opposite of the age group of inhabitants suggested by Chernyshevsky: communal apartments in contemporary narratives are populated by characters belonging to the most vulnerable social strata, primarily old people. One sees this frequently in narratives by Tolstaia and Petrushevskaia. The notion of the "*futliar*" (case) also has a negative connotation for Dostoevsky; it is mentioned in the Underground Man's dialogic monologue in connection with the *bezobrazie* of his asociability and self-entrapment.

The notion of home *per se* in Petrushevskaia transforms into an entrapment, an enclosure, or a defensive stronghold against those sharing that space – hence, the frequency in these publications of liminality, of thresholds (similar to Dostoevsky's use of them), and of barred and locked doors, which betray the psychological need for self-protection from ostensible inmates, while simultaneously locating people, metaphorically, on the existential edge of the precipice.[401]

Space is foregrounded in Petrushevskaia's stories, whereas time receives considerably little attention, or rather is overshadowed by space as the result of a conscious narrative strategy. The titles of her stories are often spatial, i.e. "*Strana*" (Country), "*Temnaia komnata*" (Dark Room), "*Izolirovannyi boks*" (The Isolation Box), "*Smotrovaia ploshchadka*" (The Lookout Point"), "*Novyi raion*" (The New Area), "*V malen'kom dome*" (In the Little House), "*Belye doma*" (White Houses), "*Taina doma*" (The Mystery of the House), and "*Dom devushek*" (The Girls' House). *Time: Night* is a significant exception, characterizing a metaphysical state of doom, apocalyptic night, as well as a certain indeterminate time period, bleak, dark, or black. Tolstaia uses an analogous title – "Night" – for a similar purpose, (See Chapter 4), that is, for depicting the world as nocturnal and violent. However, in Tolstaia's "Night" these are characteristics of the world outside of home-hearth.

---

[400] Dostoevsky, *Sobranie sochinenii*, Vol. 5, Moscow: *Khudozhestvennaia literatura*, 1957, 327. See also *Ibid.*, 253-54.
[401] *Dictionary of Literary Biography*, 285:223.

Woll writes that "all of Petrushevskaia's characters inhabit spaces that steadily shrink."[402] In this connection, she draws a parallel between Petrushevskaia's texts and "Dostoevsky's abrasive Underground Man, trapped in his miserable cellar flat, and Raskol'nikov, entombed in his coffinlike room in the Petersburg slums."[403] As she also notes, twentieth-century Russian writers, in depicting urban dwellings, are reflecting the actual material constraints of their time. The Soviet cramped flats are a reality of Russia of the twentieth century and beyond, yet they are "resonate within the Russian [nineteenth-century] literary tradition."[404]

In Toporov's concept of the tradition of the Petersburg text, space constitutes a major motif. Pushkin began writing the Petersburg text in the 1820s and 1830s (i.e. *"Uedinennyi domik na Vasil'evskom"* (1829), *Pikovaia dama* (1833)). Already in the 1830s, Gogol in his Petersburg tales (1835-1842) and his feuilletons, published in *Sovremennik*, and Lermontov in his fragment *"U grafa V. byl muzykal'nyi vecher"* (1839) and, particularly, in chapter seven of *Kniaginia Ligovskaia* (1836), are forerunners of Dostoevsky with their descriptions of St. Petersburg courtyards as narrow, misshapen (with multiple corners), dirty, and smelly.[405] Dostoevsky makes the ugliness of St. Petersburg space a permanent feature of his texts. The ugly colour of Dostoevsky's texts, yellow, was introduced in St. Petersburg during the reign of Catherine II (The Great) and became a dominant St. Petersburg colour at the time of Paul I. In literature, Gogol first noted it as a Petersburg colour. Yellow as a part of architectural design was meant to supplement the Petersburg light in dull weather.[406] However, in Dostoevsky it becomes the colour of the ugliest buildings (see Chapter 2), those that also realize the idea of Petersburg crookedness (*krivizna*) that one sees in the bent (*krivye*) lines of the small rivers and the *Ekaterininskii* canal (nicknamed The Crookeds (*Krivushi*)). The interiors of residential buildings also have an irregular shape. The repulsive sight of a typical Dostoevskian space often includes "a coffin-room, or a room-like miserably small box, a dirty staircase, the well courtyard, an house like Noah's Ark, a noisy narrow alleyway, a gutter, stink, slaked lime, dust, … stuffiness" [*komnata-grob, zhalkaia kamorka, griaznaia lestnitsa, kolodets dvora, dom – "Noev kovcheg," shumnyi pereulok, kanava, von', izvestka, pyl', … dukhota...*].[407] The Dostoevskian narrowing and overall ugliness of St. Petersburg space reappears in the works of twentieth-century Russian writers such as Liudmila

---

[402] Josephine Woll, "The Minotaur in the Maze: Remarks on Liudmila Petrushevskaia," *World Literature Today*, Vol. 67 (Winter 1993): 1, http://80-weblinks2.epnet.com.ezproxy. lib.ucalgary:20... [Accessed on 09/06/04].

[403] *Ibid.*

[404] *Ibid.*

[405] V.N. Toporov, *Peterburgskii tekst russkoi literatury*, St. Petersburg: *Iskusstvo-SPB*, 2003, 23.

[406] *Ibid.*, 40.

[407] *Ibid.*

Petrushevskaia (or Iurii Mamleev, see Chapter 3), and is also applied to other urban spaces (in particular Moscow).

Porter observes that Petrushevskaia's narratives "are placed in a world of overcrowded flats, police oppression, mental and physical infirmity, and general moral and economic stagnation."[408] Noting Dostoevsky's influence on Petrushevskaia's prose, he defends the work of both writers from simplistic sociological interpretations. The most salient feature of Dostoevsky's influence, in Porter's opinion, is the *nadryv*, or psychological lacerations, which "can afflict any character and can turn a child into a monster."[409] This makes the apocalyptic element in Petrushevskaia's work stronger than any intractable political or economic problems her prose may discuss.

In Petrushevskaia, families become even more dysfunctional than in Dostoevsky, as, for example, in *Time: Night*, or "Our Crowd." A Dostoevskian blackness of depiction is evident in her narratives; paradoxically, in the extreme animosity of the world behind the apartment door, parents and children become enemies in the fight for the survival of the grandchildren. The manipulative character of both female narrators and protagonists (in *Time: Night* and "Our Crowd") calls into question the virtue of their attempts at saving their kin; they rather seem to be enjoying their power to orchestrate scandals and choreograph scenes.

Porter makes a list of themes that Dostoevsky and Petrushevskaia share in *Time: Night* and "Our Crowd," among them "claustrophobia, people on the outer edge of sanity, bickering over money and material matters, scandal scenes and swings of mood, criminality."[410] He also states that Petrushevskaia "never relinquishes her grip on realism, and if there is any comedy in her vision of humanity, there is always a dark, Dostoevskian side to it."[411] There are a number of literary associations in *Time: Night*. The narrator, for example, who recommends herself as a poet, has a name – Anna Andrianovna – paralleling that of Anna Andreevna Akhmatova. Then there is the name of the nurse in a psychiatric hospital – Sonechka – which causes the narrator to bring up Dostoevsky: a **sun-like little name**, so surprising in our **times**, the name of a heroine of Dostoevsky ["*solnechnoe imechko, kakoe udivitel'noe v nashe vremia, imia geroini Dostoevskogo...*"].[412] The fact that the narrator states that sun-like names and Dostoevsky-related light-bearing ideals are surprising these days emphasizes Petrushevskaia's view of the twentieth century as a time of metaphysical darkness, which

---

[408] Porter, *Russia's Alternative Prose*, 62.
[409] *Ibid.*, 62-63.
[410] *Ibid.*, 62.
[411] *Ibid.*, 60.
[412] Petrushevskaia, *Sobranie sochinenii*, 1:390.

is also conveyed in the title of her story. The name of Dostoevsky's self-sacrificing character appears in the text when the narrator is considering whether not to take her mother home from a psychiatric hospital – that is, in a reverse from that of a self-sacrificing context. The reference to Dostoevsky and to his heroine, who becomes a prostitute to help her family financially, conveys Petrushevskaia's irony, as the narrator and protagonist of her own work fails to help her family in spite of her claims of constant self-sacrifice. Nurse Sonechka in *Time: Night* is responsible for the discharge of Anna Andrianovna's mother from a psychiatric hospital or her transfer to a mental asylum. We learn the last name – Golubeva – of grandma Serafima only at this point in the narrative.[413] The name of Anna Andrianovna's schizophrenic mother is symbolically loaded; her last name is derived from the Russian root "*golub-*," a "dove," a symbol of the Holy Ghost, as well as a contemporary secular metaphor for spirit. The root "*golub-*" is also the main formative element of the word "*goluboi*," light blue – blue being a traditional colour of hope. In addition, "*golub'*" is an old-fashioned term of address to somebody meek, recalling the Christian virtue that Dostoevsky focuses on in his story "The Meek One."

The religious associations of Serafima's surname are reinforced by the symbolism of her first name. "Serafim," a seraph, is a divine creature from the Old Testament (from the Hebrew verb "saraph" – to burn). Seraphim are considered to be fiery in nature and exist in the direct presence of God. They occupy, along with the cherubim, the highest rank in the celestial hierarchy. The seraphim are distinct from the cherubim who carry or veil God, and manifest the presence of His glory in the earthly sanctuary, whereas the seraphim stand before God as ministering servants in His heavenly court.[414] They have a dualistic nature, as they are described as angels with six wings and four heads, as well as fiery, flying serpents. Thus, the seraphim include Gabriel, who brought the annunciation to the Virgin Mary, as well as Lucifer, who tempted humans, and Eve in particular, in the guise of a serpent. The name Serafima is also closely related to the idea of punishment, as in the *Book of Numbers* seraphim are sent to punish the Israelites.[415] Thus, Serafima Golubeva's first name represents the possibility of good and evil in their greatness, as well as an immediate connection to God, the idea of "being in God" and the higher truth. Her last name emphasizes spirituality and Christian virtues. The meaning of both names is heavily religious, and for the most part represents the values of Dostoevsky, particularly of the late exile and post-exile period. The positive vs. negative in the name of Serafima

---

[413] It is also a bird-name, and Dostoevsky gives a bird-name to his mentally ill character, Lebiadkina.
[414] http://www.newadvent.org/cathn/06608a.htm [accessed June 30/04].
[415] Micha F. Lindemans, http://www.pantheon.org/articles/s/seraphim.html [accessed June 30/04], http://www.newadvent.org/cathen/13725b.htm [accessed June 30/04].

relates the idea of good vs. evil, and to the idea of duality, a pivotal one for Dostoevsky's art and philosophy. Serafima, as the seraph sent to punish humanity, has correlations in the narrative as well. At the point when her full name is mentioned, she exists as a punishment for her daughter, Anna Andrianovna, who hopes she could take care of her mother at home, realizes she has a moral obligation to do so, but understands that it would be not possible in practice. She understands that she has to choose between her little grandchildren and her mother, as it is unclear how they could all live together in a two-room flat. Moral laceration, a Dostoevskian type of punishment, is what she is left with. Dostoevsky propagated the idea of moral punishment as the only real one in his *Crime and Punishment* and *Notes from the House of the Dead*. The name Serafima Golubeva, saturated with Dostoevskian connotations, is the name of a mentally-ill person, which brings up Dostoevsky's thematic preference as well. What is openly positive or beautiful for Dostoevsky is entirely defeated in Petrushevskaia's story. Indeed, one could imagine a character with the name Serafima Golubeva in a Dostoevsky text, perhaps as a nun, a saint, or a moral ideal. In Petrushevskaia's *Time: Night* the name belongs to an old schizophrenic, of whom her daughter speaks "this smell of the beast...urine and feces..."[416] In the narrative of *Time: Night* Dostoevsky's "ideal of the Madonna" is denied existence on this earth, and what is left is the "ideal of Sodom," *bezobrazie*, ugliness. For Petrushevskaia, "the world lies in evil."[417] This is the reality, and there is nothing her characters can do about it. Moreover, Petrushevskaia belongs to the generation of the Russian intelligentsia for whom "God is dead," and for whom a human being is the measure of all things. As a result, the world is covered in metaphysical darkness, as the "ideal of Sodom" prevails in the human soul.[418] By the very fact of her arguing with Dostoevsky about the impossibility of the beautiful side of the human soul prevailing, Petrushevskaia, however, still includes his ideals into her narratives, making the ugly and the evil in her stories more defined and substantial against the weak background of positive ideals.

Irrespective of her motivations, which could range from genuine love and pity to pure egotism, Anna ruins the feeble generational links in her family. In reference to the breaking of these and to disorder in general, Petrushevskaia employs a textile metaphor in *Time: Night*:

---

[416] Petrushevskaia, *Sobranie sochinenii*, 1:380.
[417] V.A. Bachinin, *Dostoevsky: metafizika prestupleniia*, St. Petersburg: *Izdatel'stvo Sankt-Peterburgskogo universiteta*, 2001, 8.
[418] *Ibid.*, 19-23.

No, I did not lose my spirit, I was still dreaming of making myself a little skirt, or a dress, was still running through the shops selling remnants in search of a cheap fabric and was all in dreams.

[*Net, ia ne padala dukhom, ia vse eshche mechtala sshit' sebe to iubochku, to plat'e, begala po magazinam loskutov v poiskakh deshevki i vsia v mechtakh.*][419]

The erstwhile time of hope of Anna Andrianovna has been filled with dreams of fixing her image and attempts at normal daily worries. She has been looking for scraps, which she was planning to turn into a whole garment. She fails, just as she fails to put together the disparate lives of her family and to normalize them in any way whatsoever. The attempt at quilting her own disorderly life and patching the ugly lives of her closest relatives into a whole – that is, making connections among them – does not work. Anna Andrianovna's quest to make a whole form, a whole image out of disunited parts both at the practical and the higher psychological level, metaphorically represents her personal struggle with *bezobraznoe*, and her search for form, or *obraz*.

A similar metaphor used repeatedly in Anna Andrianovna's speech is that of lace-making, of weaving a beautiful pattern to create a whole. It is exactly in the midst of her family tragedies that the narrator dreams of weaving a beautiful form:

Or I wanted to knit a little top for myself from cheap cotton thread like guipure. Still such a mystery are all my dreams in the midst of tragedies! Is it up to me to make lace at the site of a fire…

[*To khotela sviazat' sebe koftochku iz deshevykh bumazhnykh nitok tipa gipiura. Vot kakaia vse-taki zagadka eti moi mechty v razgar tragedii! Mne na pepelishche viazat' kruzhevo…*][420]

Lace is mentioned twice in the narrative; the second time is it associated with hope as well. This time hope and beauty for Anna Andrianovna are personified in a new form, that of her new born grandson, who is "as beautiful as God" [*…krasiv kak Bog.*]:[421]

---

[419] Petrushevskaia, *Sobranie sochinenii*, 1:334.
[420] *Ibid.*

...then I ran into their room, found a bundle of baby rags there and all night was boiling and washing those scraps they collected from people they knew. My baby, however, came from the maternity ward all in lace, for now it was I who started methodically, in a joyful voice, to ring up all the old women I knew, informing them of the happy event and, ignoring their surprise, was asking right away, if, not necessarily they personally, but maybe their relatives had something leftover for newborns (the shops were empty, completely empty, I lied easily, there were some things there, but not for us).

[*...zatem kinulas' k nim v komnatu, nashla tam uzel detskogo rvan'ia i vsiu noch' kipiatila i stirala tu vetosh', kakuiu oni nabrali po znakomym. Moi malysh, odnako, prishel iz roddoma ves' v kruzhevakh, ibo teper' uzhe ia nachala metodicheski, radostnym golosom obzvanivat' vsekh kogo znala bab, opoveshchat' ikh o radostnom sobytii i, minuia ikh nedoumenie, srazu sprashivala, neobiazatel'no chtoby u nikh lichno, no, mozhet, u rodni ostalos' dlia novorozhdennykh (v magazinakh nichego, sharom pokati, skladno vrala ia, tam koe-chto bylo, no ne pro nashu chest'.)]*[422]

The new baby does come home in lace, but it is contrasted to what Anna Andrianovna calls "old rags," that is, the clothes that the baby's parents were able to get from their friends. Anything that does not come from her is ugly for the narrator; parental love does not exist, or is stubbornly not noticed by the new grandmother. Thus, love for a baby, the only symbol of beauty and hope in *Time: Night*, becomes the biggest motivation for maternal hatred. The upside-down relationships in her family would stabilize, in the opinion of Anna Andrianovna, if her daughter Alena would get rid of her husband and accept her mother's love as a romantic substitute. Alena's attempt at a normal family life is impossible, as it has to co-exist in the same space with Anna Andrianovna's hatred for and jealousy towards her son-in-law. Not being aware of it, and, therefore, supposedly not guilty of it, Anna Andrianovna re-creates the relationships between her own mother, herself, and her husband:

Oh, the hatred of a mother-in-law, it is jealousy and nothing else; my mother herself wanted to be the object of love of her daughter, that is of me, so that I would love only her, the object of love and trust; this is how my mother wanted to be a whole family for me, to

---

[421] *Ibid.*, 324.
[422] *Ibid.*, 337.

take the place of everything, and I have seen such female families, the mother sits at home like a wife, and reprimands her daughter if she does not come home on time, does not spend time with the child, spends money badly, and so forth, but at the same time, the mother is jealous of her daughter because of all her girl-friends, not to mention because of her men, in whom the mother sees rivals, as a result we have a total mess and mix-up, but what can one do? My mother, until everything terrible happened to her, in this very way forced my poor husband out of the house and always said at a good moment: who is the head of the family here? (cunningly) well, who is the head of the family? (she meant herself)

[*O nenavist' teshchi, ty revnost' i nichto drugoe, moia mat' sama khotela byt' ob''ektom liubvi svoei docheri, to est' menia, chtoby ia tol'ko ee liubila, ob''ektom liubvi i doveriia, eto mat' khotela byt' vsei sem'ei dlia menia, zamenit' soboiu vse, i ia videla takie zhenskie sem'i, mat' sidit doma, kak zhena, i ukoriaet doch', esli ona ne prikhodit domoi vovremia, ne udeliaet vnimaniia rebenku, plokho tratit den'gi i t.d., no v to zhe vremia mat' revnuet doch' ko vsem ee podrugam, ne govoria uzhe o muzhikakh, v kotorykh mat' tochno vidit sopernikov, i poluchaetsia v rezul'tate polnaia meshanina i kasha, a chto delat'? Moia mama, poka ne sluchilos' vse uzhasnoe, imenno tak vyzhila iz domu neschastnogo moego muzha i vse govorila v khoroshuiu minuty: kto tut glava sem'i? (lukavo) nu kto tut glava sem'i? (podrazumevaia sebia)*][423]

This is one of many examples of the members of this family inheriting ugly relationships, which demonstrates Petrushevskaia's pessimistic world outlook. If ugliness is genetic, or unavoidable in a family where the grandparents and parents have terrible relationships, there is nothing ordinary humans can do about it, at least not in *Time: Night*. The earthly struggle of Petrushevskaia's characters has no chance of success, since for Petrushevskaia the mundane world is filled with existential darkness without a possibility of beyond-the-grave salvation.

The absence of a man in her life is continually used as an argument by Anna Andrianovna against her daughter's having one. It is not so much the daughter who has a complex of an abandoned wife because her father divorced her mother (as Anna Andrianovna claims Alena feels), but the mother who substitutes her love for her husband with her love for her children and, in a monstrous fashion,

---

[423] *Ibid.*, 379.

insists that her children, particularly her daughter, do the same. The lace that Anna Andrianovna provides for Timochka is borrowed, given to her by people she knows. These people are able to find beautiful lacy baby-clothes in their families, although these clothes might be in the possession of some distant relatives, which shows that in other families of the same literary universe ties of kinship exist and function so well that even unfortunates like Anna Andrianovna can benefit from them. She lies so that she could have some connection to the lives of normal families; her beloved angelic baby grandson receives his lace, an artifact of beautiful family life stolen from strangers. Beauty achieved by means of lies and hatred brings no fruit, and cannot exist in the atmosphere of Anna Andrianovna's family; and Timochka's innocence does not remain untarnished by it. The angelic child promises to grow into a monster, as we shall see further on in the scene with the phone call.

Other attributes of family "*uiut*" (cosiness) do not seem to function for Anna Andrianovna's family either. Instead of creating the effect of cosiness, they involuntarily contribute to the scandals. A tablecloth is thrown by Alena into the face of her mother; a broken tea-pot and a blue cup are the cause of an argument between Anna Andrianovna and her mother, an argument Alena records in her diary as "she has nothing better to do:"

15th of January. I'm lying down. Since I have nothing to do I pretend to study, and I am writing, I'll write down the conversation of mother and grandma.

– You? You broke all the crockery already! (this is mother)

– What crockery, did you go nuts or what! – yells the grandma. – What, where? I'll die of fear!

– There, there, that cup has its handle broken off! Where am I going to buy it? Where will I buy the plate now?

– It wasn't me! It wasn't me! Ouch, save, help me! Ouch! My Lord, what is it now? Lord! People! What is this! Help! I shall kneel to prove it wasn't me (attempts to kneel for a long time, judging by the noise). There! I swear.

– O-o-o, get up, get up, what is it with you, why, well, you broke it, broken it is.

– (a long moan) People, help! And where is it... where is it (groaning, evidently getting up) that I broke anything?! (with tears) when it's you who broke my cup, the blue one...

– Aha, aha, try to recall your difficult childhood as well...

– And the only time I broke anything was when I broke the spout off of the teapot…(the chair is creaking. Evidently sat down to finish her tea). Now that was me, but it could be glued back… I hid the spout…

    – What ?!!

    – The spout of the blue teapot, that's all. It can be glued, it's no problem.

    – What tea-pot…What!!! Well then! Now it's starting! Broke the spout off the china set! Off the best teapot! Who can pour anything out it now? Oh-oh-oh (had a tear or two).

    – You – a cup, me – a spout.

    – Ale-na! Come here.

    – I have an exam, Ma. [424]

[*15 ianvaria. Lezhu. Ot nechego delat' iakoby gotovlius' i pishu, zapishu razgovor materi s baboi.*

    – *Ty? Ty vsiu posudu uzhe perekolotila! (eto mat')*

    – *Kakuiu, ty chto okhilela sovsem! – krichit baba. – Kakuiu, gde? Ia ot strakhu umru!*

    – *Von, von u chashki ruchka otbita! Gde ia kupliu? Tarelku teper' gde ia kupliu?*

    – *Eto ne ia! Eto ne ia! Oi, spasite, pomogite! Oi! Gospodi, da chto zhe eto! Gospodi! Liudi! Chto eto! Spasite! Ia na koleni vstanu, chto ne ia (dolgo stanovitsia na koleni, sudia po shumu). Vot! Klianus'.*

    – *O-o-o, vstavai, vstavai, nu chto ty, iz-za chego ty, nu razbila, nu i razbila.*

    – *(dolgii ston) Liudi, spasite! Da gde zhe … gde zhe (kriakhtia, vidimo, vstaet) ia chto razbila?! (so slezami) kogda ty razbila moiu chashku siniuiu…*

    – *Aga, aga, vspomni eshche tvoe tiazheloe detstvo…*

    – *A kogda ia edinstvenno chto razbila, tak eto otbila nosik u chainika…(skripit stul. Vidimo sela dopivat' chai). Eto ia, da, no eto zhe mozhno prikleit'…Ia spriatala nosik…*

    – *Kakoi?!!*

    – *Sinego chainika nosik, i vse. Prikleitsia, nichego.*

---

[424] *Ibid.*, 357-358.

– Kakogo...Chto!!! Zdraste! Nachinaetsia! U serviza nosik otkolotila! U luchshego chainika! Kto teper' iz nego chto nal'et?! Oi-oi-oi (proslezilas').

– Ty chashku, ia nosik.

– Ale-na! Idi siuda.

U menia ekzamen, mam.]

The Underground Man talks about the pleasures of torturing one's nearest and dearest in his monologue about the tooth-ache: "his moans become somewhat foul, dirty and evil, and last whole days and nights." [*stony ego stanoviatsia kakie-to skvernye, pakostno-zlye i prodolzhaiutsia po tselym dniam i nocham.*][425] And it is not just a moan, but a *long* moan that Grandma Serafima issues in the scandal. The tears she makes heard in her voice also produce a theatrically comical impression in this ugly scene. Anna Andrianovna has her part with tears, too, and the comments of Alena in parentheses look suspiciously like stage directions, making an impression of a play in which the actors know their parts very well, as the show has been on stage for quite a while. It is also unclear why Grandma Serafima would hide the spout of the teapot separately, if not to sustain the impression of chaos and farce. The comedy of the scene is also emphasized by the fact that the scandal occurs at tea-time, and, having started with Dostoevskian laceration at the table, it ends with an almost Chekhovian flare – "it is time to have tea" is not voiced here, but the tea continues and the youngest in the family is called to the table.

Both the broken cup and the broken teapot are blue, a traditional colour of hope in Russian literature and dramaturgy.[426] The blue cup is also an allusion to Arkadii Gaidar's story "The Light Blue Cup," a standard item of a child's home library in Soviet Russia. This is a significant point, given that *Time: Night* and many other Petrushevskaia texts revolve around children and the childbearing processes. "The Light Blue Cup," a charming little narrative, tells us about a young family in which the narrator-father is having doubts as to whether his wife still loves him. For him, his wife's complaint about her light blue cup having been broken provokes his fear that whatever dreams his wife Marusia might have had other than having this family have not been realized, and that she is blaming him for it. The father takes his little daughter Svetlana for a long hike, during which she points out to him that judging by how her mother looks at her father, she is still in love with him. Svetalana and her father acquire a kitten on the way home, and upon arrival there, the father sees his wife wearing a red dress

[425] D-*PSS*, 5:107.
[426] Petrushevskaia also has a play entitled *Three Girls in Blue*.

(with its obvious colour symbolism), and understands that she has been waiting for her family for a long time, and is very happy they are back. He thinks of the cause of the argument – the light blue cup – and decides that it was the evil, grey mice who broke it.[427] From Svetlana's song, it is clear that the newly-acquired little cat will be a danger for any evil mice from now on, and the story ends with the family's admission that they are most happy together, and are having a very good life.[428] The cause of the argument and its underlying motive (doubts about love in the family) are the same in "Light Blue Cup" and *Time: Night*. However, the development of the argument, which barely happens at all in the "Light Blue Cup," is in the key of a Dostoevskian scandal, as can be seen from the aforementioned passage from Alena's diary.

The allusions to "The Light Blue Cup," which shows how a loving, happy family can cope with jealousy and everyday conflicts and constitutes a Soviet stereotype of the theme of a happy family, is consciously used and parodied in *Time: Night*, with its never-ending psychological lacerations and its scandal scene at the table. There is a passage in *Time: Night* describing the New Year's Eve visit of Alena to Anna Andrianovna and Tima, in which Alena gives Tima a blue plastic cat, extraordinary in its ugliness ("...*prinesla Time plastmassovogo sinego kota, vydaiu-shchegosia po bezobraziiu...*").[429] Here the colour blue is again mentioned – along with a cat. Alena disappears quickly, having taken Christmas tree ornaments with her (two boxes of them, on account of which Anna Andrianovna mentions that Alena left "only three" of them, quite illogically since Alena has taken less than a half); but Tima plays with the toy, in spite of its ugliness, as mentioned by Anna Andrianovna. The blueness of the toy cat and the hopes of Alena and Tima for the new happy year contrast with the opinion of Anna Andrianovna that it is ugly. The *bezobrazie* of the toy demonstrates that these hopes will not be fulfilled.[430] A significant Dostoevskian epithet is used in opposition to the mention of the colour blue, which is a constituent (together with red) of violet, a reverse of yellow in the color scheme. For

---

[427] Gaidar associates the mice with evil, which is reminiscent of Dostoevsky's "underground mouse."

[428] Arkadii Gaidar, *Sobranie sochinenii*, Moscow: *Detskaia literatura*, 1964, 273-304.

[429] Petrushevskaia, *Sobranie sochinenii*, 1:327.

[430] Blue as the colour of hope is also used by Bulat Okudzhava, i.e. in his "Tango," *Arbat, moi Arbat: Stikhi i pesni*, Moscow: *Sovetskii pisatel'*, 1976, 22, which also features a light blue cup:

My fate was generous to me: tossing me hopes,
But life was flowing in its own way – it was not asking me,
I was drinking from a light blue cup – tried to drink up...
By chance, I dropped the cup – suddenly August was finished.

[*Sud'ba ko mne byla shchedra: nadezhd podbrasyvala,
Da zhizn' po-svoemu tekla – menia ne sprashivala.
Ia pil iz chashki golyboi – staralsia dochista...
Sluchaino chashku obronil – vdrug avgust konchilsia.*]

Petrushevskaia, the colour blue is symbolically opposed to yellow: blue signifies hope for harmony, and yellow – *bezobrazie*. Indirectly, blue brings up its opposite yellow, the ugly colour of Dostoevsky (see Chapter 2), the allusion to which is reinforced by the explicit mention of *bezobrazie* in the same passage.

The toy cat also functions as a reminder that elements of cosiness are failing to work for Anna Andrianovna's family: it is an animal often associated with home-hearth, but it is not accepted as a proper gift from mother to son by Anna Andrianovna. The kitten in "The Light Blue Cup" will fight off the 'evil mice' – that is, the causes of conflicts – whereas the cat in *Time: Night*, although it does appear, will not bring peace into the family. Among other details that normally make up the home-hearth image but fail to do so for the narrator's family in *Time: Night* is a tablecloth:

> She, my daughter and a mother, grabbed the tablecloth from the table and threw it two meters right at me, but a tablecloth is not a thing that can kill somebody, I knocked the tablecloth aside from my face – and that was it. And we had nothing lying on the tablecloth, not a crumb, good, not a glass covering, not an iron.

> [*Ona, moia doch-mamasha, khvat' so stola skatert' i brosila na dva metra vpered v menia, no skatert' ne takaia veshch', chtoby eiu mozhno bylo ubit' kogo-libo, ia otvela skatert' ot litsa - i vse. A na skaterti u nas nichego ne lezhit, ni tebe kroshki, khorosho, ni stekla, ni tebe utiuga.*][431]

There is no food on the table, and the whole text of *Time: Night* develops under the sign of near-starvation. The struggle for food, which at times becomes a literal one, emphasizes the animalistic ugly nature of human existence; Tima, for example is "... covered with crumbs and champing like a piglet..." [...*obsypalsia i prichavkival, kak khriushka...*].[432] Anna Andrianovna affirms that she has never reprimanded her relatives for eating too much, which was the case with her mother Serafima. Anna Andrianovna also notes anomalies related to food, or the lack of it, and greediness in her family:

> He [Andrei] in general, from his childhood, has been checking who eats how much desert at the table, and he would catch Alena, or sometimes Grandma or myself, at the scene of

[431] Petrushevskaia, *Sobranie sochinenii*, 1:318.
[432] *Ibid.*, 372.

the crime. He had to have everything divided lawfully, and sometimes he, like some sadist, put what he hadn't finished at the most visible place, in order to torture little Alena, yes! This took place! There was something wrong with food among the members of our family, poverty is to blame, some sort of accounts, reprimands, Grandma scolded my husband openly – "devours everything that his children need," etc. But I never did this, except if Shura infuriated me, he was definitely a crook and blood-sucker of his child's food [sic]...

[On [Andrei] voobshche s detstva sledil, kto skol'ko za stolom s''edal sladkogo, zastaval na meste prestupleniia Alenu, a inogda i nas s babkoi. U nego vse dolzhno bylo byt' podeleno po spravedlivosti, i inogda on, kak sadist, klal na vidnoe mesto svoe nes''edennoe, chtoby izvodit' malen'kuiu Alenu, da! Eto imelo mesto! Chto-to ne v poriadke s pishchei bylo vsegda u chlenov nashei sem'i, nishcheta tomu vinoi, kakie-to schety, pretenzii, babushka ukoriala moego muzha v otkrytuiu, "vse szhiraet u detei" i t.d. A ia tak ne delala nikogda, razve chto menia vyvodil iz sebia Shura, deistvitel'no darmoed i krovopiets u svoego rebenka pishchi[sic]...][433]

The colour yellow also occurs in *Time: Night* in the description of Andrei after he commits a crime: "This was altogether a scary period, when Andrei was called to the police all the time; I went there; the detective yelled at me; Andrei was coming home yellow and lifeless..." [*Eto voobshche byl strashnyi period, kogda Andreia taskali po povestkam v militsiiu, ia byla tam, sledovatel' nakrichal na menia, Andrei vozvrashchalsia domoi zheltyi i bezzhiznennyi...*][434] In the passage preceding the description of the yellow Andrei, the poetic means of depicting ugliness – the colour yellow – shared by Dostoevsky and Petrushevskaia is implemented together with the Dostoevskian theme of insanity. Crime and insanity, ugly themes prevalent in Dostoevsky's works, are dealt with in *Time: Night* by the same poetic means.

Another feature of Dostoevsky's poetics of the ugly in the narrative of *Time: Night* is the negative insect simile used for depicting *bezobraznye* (ugly) people:

... Ksenia and I ran into a washroom; she put her skirt up and began taking off woolen sweatpants leaving only her woolen tights; her tight belly and fat crotch were glimpsed at fleetingly. It's a horror, to what extent we are not aware of our **ugliness** and often appear in

[433] *Ibid.*, 377.
[434] *Ibid.*, 353.

front of people in a dangerous way, that is fat, flabby, dirty, come to your senses, people! **You take after insects** but demand love; and for sure, because of this Kseniia and her mother, their husband, out of horror, sleeps around ...

[... *my s Kseniei zabezhali v tualet, ona tam zadrala iubku i stala snimat' s sebia sherstianye reituzy i ostalas' v sherstianykh kolgotkakh, mel'knulo obtianytoe briukho i zhirnoe lono. Uzhas, do chego my ne vedaem svoego **bezobraziia** i chasto predstaem pered liud'mi v opasnom vide, to est' tolstye, obvisshie, griaznye, opomnites', liudi! **Vy pokhozhi na nasekomykh**, a trebuete liubvi, i naverniaka ot etoi Ksenii i ee materi ikhnii muzh guliaet na storone ot uzhasa...*][435]

The comparison of people to spiders and insects, which occurs in such passages by Dostoevsky as the description of people as spiders in a jar in *Notes from the House of the Dead*, or the introduction of Stavrogin's sins in the narrative of *The Devils* with the help of the image of a spider), creates a Dostoevskian description of *bezobrazie*; and the word itself is also used in the aforementioned passage. Petrushevskaia's exploration of bodily ugliness foreshadows the horror Kseniia causes in other ways; thus the narrative of *Time: Night* creates a complete picture of *bezobrazie* using Dostoevsky's poetics of ugliness.

The image of the mouse and the metaphoric use of the 'underground mouse' in *bezobraznye* situations in Dostoevsky's narratives also occurs in *Time: Night*. The members of Anna Andrianovna's family, falling apart again, are compared to mice making very little noise in their opposition to misfortunes:

...when Andrei was coming home from interrogations and lying with his face towards the wall, and Grandma was sitting in her little room having curtained off the windows tightly, ate almost nothing, was getting weak, and once I brought some food to her and she squinted looking at me; her eyes were absolutely scarlet in colour, the vessels had burst, and she moved her eyes heavily, like a black person. What she knew, what she understood, it is hard to say, everything happened in silence, here when we rustled like mice, and Andrei noiselessly disappeared in the jaws of the investigative machine, and I was

---

[435] *Ibid.*, 375.

noiselessly disappearing, running from the investigator to the advocate, and to the meeting with Veronica, and Alena, now by herself in her room, was crying quietly…

[… *kogda Andrei prikhodil domoi s doprosov i lozhilsia litsom k stenke, a babushka nepodvizhno sidela v svoei komnatke, plotno zavesiv okna, pochti ne ela, slabela, i odin raz ia ei prinesla poest', a ona skosila na menia glaza, absoliutno alye po tsvetu, lopnuli sosudy, i ona vorochala glazami, kak negr. Chto ona znala, chto ponimala, skazat' trudno, vse sovershilos' v tishine, vot uzh kogda my shurshali kak myshi, i Andrei ischez v pasti sledovatelskoi mashiny besshumno, i ia ischezala besshumno, nosias' ot sledovatelia k advokaty i na svidaniia k Veronike, i Alena, teper' odna v svoei komnate, plakala tikho.*][436]

As to the narrative features of Dostoevsky's works, Gary Saul Morson discusses the structure of Dostoevsky's "generically problematic and formally anomalous works" and says that

As Dostoevsky was well aware, his novels were likely to appear shapeless to most readers – "loose and baggy monsters" – as Henry James was to call them – and he therefore outlined a theory of realistic art to justify, and to aid in the development of, his aesthetic practice. Like the novels themselves, which have had such great influence on twentieth-century European literature, this theory seems remarkably modern … by the mid-1870s Dostoevsky had come to believe that social "disintegration," "fragmentation," and "dissociation"… were, in all probability, literally apocalyptic in extent …[437]

Dostoevsky finds ways to write about ugly themes; his narratives reflect fragmented social situations. Fragmentation is related to the problem of memory: we write the way we remember things, and we remember them differently every time, so there arises a question of what is truth. *Protomodern* and postmodern treatment of memory is related to a multiplicity of deviations in narrative time, an example of which is the timeline in *The Devils*.[438] This also happens in *Time: Night*, in which the narrator attempts to record her past. Fragmentation and memory are major concerns of the twentieth-century literature, also dealt with in Margaret Lawrence's *The Diviners* and Gabriel García Márquez's *Hundred Years of Solitude*, among other works.

[436] *Ibid.*, 378.
[437] Morson, *Boundaries of Genre*, 8.
[438] Arkadii Klioutchansky, "On the Chronology of *Besy*," CAS paper (2001).

The narrative structure of *Time: Night* is 'messy' in a Dostoevskian way: Alena's diary, one of its constituents, is an example of Dostoevskian confessional-type *Ich-Erzählung*(-en), interwoven into a quilted narrative consisting of the 'ten little sheets' of Alena's diary, the inclusions of Anna Andrianovna's comments on the diary contents, Anna Andrianovna's own textual shreds in verse and prose, the diary entries that she writes on behalf of her daughter, and her distorted narrative of the story of *Time: Night* dating from various times. The presence of Alena's diary makes it a two-narrator story, which, together with the voice of the editor, gives it a polyphonic nature. The text also contains short narratives which seemingly have little to do with the story of Anna Andrianovna's family; they are inserted at odd junctures. Structurally such inclusions are similar to Dostoevsky's digressions, for example, in his "Winter Notes on Summer Impressions:" "And by the way, can you possibly think that I am getting into Russian literature instead of writing about Paris? That I am writing a critical article? No, I am only doing this from nothing better to do." [*A kstati: uzh ne dumaete li vy, chto ia vmesto Parizha v russkuiu literaturu pustilsia? Kriticheskuiu stat'iu pishu? Net, eto ia tol'ko tak, ot nechego delat'.*][439]

In Petrushevskaia's *Time: Night* the digressions are shorter and are linked thematically among themselves. These narratives tell stories of children's deaths: deaths caused by a mother or another female. For example, Anna Andrianovna tells her imaginary interlocutor about a woman (this story is originally told to Anna Andrianovna by her daughter-in-law about a neighbour), who, with the help of a male medical practitioner, goes into labour three months early (a process Anna Andrianovna calls 'a late abortion') and leaves the newborn crying by an open window for six hours until he dies. To deny the baby its human nature, its crying is described by Anna Andrianovna as meowing; that is, a sound an animal would make. Another digression gives an example of the death of a baby bird in the tone of a parody of a philosophical parable, again equating human children to animals.[440] And most importantly, the story serves to express Anna Andrianovna's views not just on childbirth, but on what her daughter's actions should have been had she had more common sense. She, therefore, wishes her grandchild had been murdered. As Anna Andrianovna attempts to assume the role of mother to her grandson, this idea of murder suggests certain parallels between Anna Andrianovna and the ancient Greek tragic heroine Medea. The eponymous story, included in the section entitled "Requiems" in Petrushevskaia's

---

[439] D-*PSS*, 5:51.

[440] Following Gary Saul Morson, I would like to stress that in our discussion of 'influence,' 'references,' 'allusions,' 'dystopia,' 'parody,' and so forth, we "shall *not* be concerned with defining or regulating the proper use of those *terms*, which may as I have suggested be properly used in different senses in different contexts." Morson, *The Boundaries of Genre*, ix.

156

collected works, does indeed explore the phenomenon of a contemporary Medea.[441] The theme of the section as well as of the story itself – death – is also a major one for Iurii Mamleev (as discussed in Chapter 3). Alena finds Anna Andrianovna's diary after her death and mails it to a stranger, presumably an editor, which gives this diary entitled *"Zapiski na kraiu stola"* (Notes on the Edge of the Table) an analogous provenance with Mamleev's *Diary of An Individualist* and Gorianchikov's text in Dostoevsky's *Notes from the House of the Dead*. The title of the diary in *Time: Night* (*"Zapiski na kraiu stola"*) recalls Dostoevsky's various *Notes* and renders the meaning of fragmentation as well. There are also parallels between the presence of an 'editor' in the text of "Notes from Underground" and *Time: Night*, which include the forced interruption of the narrative caused by the death of the author in *Time: Night* and *Notes from the House of the Dead*, as well as the decision of an 'editor' in "Notes from Underground" to interrupt the narrative of the paradoxalist at random. *Time: Night* also has an apologue, a typically Dostoevskian feature, from which the reader learns that the diary was written on disparate sheets of paper, school notebooks, even telegram forms, a combination that makes this physically multi-layered narrative remarkably postmodern.

Both in *Time: Night* and "Our Crowd," families are composed of people "who rely on their socially sanctioned roles to legitimate their relentless, pragmatic abuse of those whom they proclaim to love."[442] The nameless female narrator of "Our Crowd" describes numerous parties organized by a group of friends. Socially and culturally, they all belong to the Russian *intelligentsia* of the end of the twentieth century. The story registers all the bodily functions and gives a detailed account of the sexual affairs of the new *'fin-de-siècle.'* It also contains a scheme of the carefully-planned maneuvers of the narrator, the overt final goal of which is to provide for her son's future after she dies from a genetic illness. She, however, makes her judgments about the people surrounding her with an authority of knowing the final truth and proceeds to act on them; and the reader is left to decide for himself if it is really the future of the narrator's son she is mainly concerned about. In *Time: Night* the terrible events of a family history repeat themselves: the reader gradually learns that Anna Andrianovna's scandals with her daughter Alena recall Anna Andrianovna's ugly scenes with her own mother, Serafima. The narrative also demonstrates indirect parallels between the obsessive, fleshly love of Anna Andrianovna for her grandson Timochka and the similar relationship between Grandma Serafima and her grandson Andrei. As Anna Andrianovna notes, it may well be that children sense the sinful nature of such love – in "Our Crowd" it becomes overtly incestuous – and grow up as monsters: Andrei goes to prison and

---

[441] Petrushevskaia, *Sobranie sochinenii*, 2:41-48.
[442] *Dictionary of Literary Biography*, 285:223.

comes back to steal from his mother, to drink, swear, blackmail, and survive a suicide attempt, and be incapable of holding a regular job afterwards. His language is abrupt and elliptic; by the end of the story it is reduced to the one letter he repeats responding to his mother. The syntax of Andrei's speech is distorted, just as is that of Dostoevsky's character Kirillov. Andrei is as incapable of normal social relations, including undistorted discourse, as is the Underground Man. But compared to these nineteenth-century characters, Andrei is much uglier. He is a criminal, and although he may be innocent at the time he is sent to prison, after he is released he has become a complete monster with clear criminal intentions. This turn of Petrushevskaia's narrative demonstrates Dostoevsky's point that exile and imprisonment train criminals rather than redeem them, as expressed in his *Notes from the House of the Dead*:

> ...I haven't seen, in the least, a trait of repentance, or a heavy thought about their crime among these people...Of course, prisons and the system of forced labour do not transform a criminal... In a criminal ... prison and most reinforced labour of exile develop only hatred, a thirst for forbidden pleasures, and a terrible light-mindedness.

> [...*ia ne vidal mezhdu etimi liud'mi ni maleishego priznaka raskaianiia, ni maleishei tiagostnoi dumy o svoem prestuplenii...Konechno, ostrogi i sistema nasil'nykh rabot ne ispravliaiut prestupnika...V prestupnike ... ostrog i samaia usilennaia katorzhnaia rabota razvivaiut tol'ko nenavist', zhazhdu zapreshchennykh naslazhdenii i strashnoe legkomyslie.*][443]

Timochka, portrayed as a cherub by his loving grandma, kicks her in the shin so strongly that she can barely stand, but still manages to conduct telephone negotiations about taking her mother home from the psychiatric hospital:

> Another ring. Struggle. I pull the receiver out, he roars and hits me in the shin with his little leg. What pain ... I throw him off with my hand and talk politely, and the baby sits on the floor, his eyes glitter like edged crystal, this is how he is starting up, getting his breath, three-two, one – go! A-a-a!!!

---

[443] D-*PSS*, 4:15.

[*Opiat' zvonok. Bor'ba. Ia vykhvatyvaiu trubku, on vzrevel i stuknul menia nozhkoi po goleni. Kakaia bol'... Ia otbrasyvaiu ego rukoi i vezhlivo razgovarivaiu, a malysh sidit na poly, glaza sverkaiut kak granenyi khrustal', eto on zakhoditsia, khvataet vozdukh, tri-dva, odin – pusk! A-a-a!!!*[444]]

Tima's conflict with Anna Andrianovna involves the same strategy as Andrei's conversation with her: his speech is reduced to a single sound. Anna justifies the tantrum as being caused by Tima's supposed encephalopathy and pretends not to notice either Andrei's swearing and minimal speech or Tima's wild yelling. By forgiving the worst behavioral patterns of her child and grandchild, Anna Andrianovna facilitates their growth to monstrosity.

As Goscilo notes, home in Petrushevskaia is a synonym for a prison, or a torture chamber, as any family gatherings result in scenes "of psychic evisceration, hysteria, and physiological debasement."[445] She points out the Dostoevskian spirit with which family table conversations turn into "scandals, exposés, beatings, drunken vomiting, and the dissolution of marriages."[446] "Our Crowd," one of Petrushevskaia's narratives which she herself characterized as "marking the end of love,"[447] demonstrates the ugly nature of friends and family gatherings to the full extent. Most of such gatherings in Petrushevskaia's works end up with the disintegration of relationships and with descriptions of the physiological details that accompany this disintegration.

Porter agrees that "Helena Goscilo is perfectly justified in detecting an echo of Dostoevsky's Underground Man in the way ... ["Our Crowd"] opens."[448] The similarities in the opening passages of "Notes from Underground" and "Our Crowd" are evident for any reader of Russian literature. Not only does the narrative of "Our Crowd" start in *medias res*, but it also strongly recalls the beginning of "Notes from Underground" in its syntactic structure and general tone (which is the case with Iurii Mamleev's *Diary of an Individualist*, discussed in Chapter 3, as well):

> I am a coarse person, a cruel person, always with a smile on my full, rosy lips, always with a snigger at all of them...In short, not for my understanding, and I am very smart. What I do not understand does not exist at all.

[444] Petrushevskaia, *Sobranie sochinenii*, 1:369.
[445] *Dictionary of Literary Biography*, 285:224.
[446] *Ibid.*
[447] *Ibid.*
[448] H. Goscilo and B. Lindsey (eds.), *Glasnost: An Anthology of Russian Literature under Gorbachev*, Ann Arbor, 1990, pp. xl-xli. Porter, *Russia's Alternative Prose*, 55.

[*Ia chelovek zhestkii, zhestokii, vsegda s ulybkoi na polnykh, rumianykh gubakh, vsegda ko vsem s nasmeshkoi...Ne dlia moego, koroche govoria, ponimaniia, a ia ochen' umnaia. To, chto ne ponimaiu, togo ne sushchestvuet voobshche.*][449]

Just as space is cramped and deformed in Petrushevskaia's stories, so her focus on physicality in her portrayal of people reflects the violation of the body. Goscilo postulates that this may be the reason why Petrushevskaia was not published before the era of glasnost'.[450] Petrushevskaia's works give accounts of people urinating, vomiting, involved in sexual intercourse, and the like. "Our Crowd," in particular, exposes the reader to a variety of ugly deformities of the narrated body. It pictures "false eyes rolling out of sockets, knocked-out teeth, a ripped-up body with a hole in the stomach, a bleeding nose, a ruptured maidenhead, dildos, D-cup breasts, impotence, one-night stands, incestuous relations between parents and children, group sex, sexual experimentation between children, near rape, bed-wetting, and child beating."[451] The final scene of "Our Crowd," choreographed by the nameless female protagonist, is a Dostoevskian culmination – a scandal – which concludes with a child beating. This scene uniting bodily and spiritual violation is conveyed in the bland narrative tone typical of Petrushevskaia. Goscilo suggests that the deformed body in Petrushevskaia is a metaphor for the violation of the psyche, for suffering, and the devastation of the soul.[452] Both ugly corporeality – suicides, prostitutes, murderers, corpses – and, in particular, spiritual deformities were captured by Dostoevsky in his narratives, which makes the nineteenth- and the twentieth-century writers thematically close. In Petrushevskaia's texts, prostitutes, suicides, and alcoholics talk neutrally about such ugly body-related details as miscarriages, abortions, sickness, bodies rotting alive in hospitals, rape, and beatings, while masking with irony, or not mentioning at all the emotional side of existence, and the psychological motivation behind physical violence. Petrushevskaia thus inverts the taboo, laying bare corporeal ugliness and leaving moral and psychological monstrosity in the background. For example, Anna Andrianovna is fixated on Alena's dirty hair, but does not express concern for the psychological state of her daughter, who is obviously going through a very tough time. Alena thinks of suicide, does not get out of bed for weeks, and cries all the time. The absence of words on such topics becomes in effect a loud yell, "what in reality the East means by "silence." It is opposed to the "word,"

---

[449] Petrushevskaia, *Sobranie sochinenii*, 1:45-46.
[450] *Dictionary of Literary Biography*, 285:224.
[451] *Ibid.*
[452] *Ibid.*, 225.

for it itself is the word – this "thunder-like silence…" [*…chto v deistvitel'nosti imeet v vidu Vostok pod "molchaniem". Ono ne protivostoit "slovu", ibo samo ono est' slovo – eto "gromopodobnoe molchanie…*][453] Non-participation in one another's emotional life is a conscious strategy – 'I don't want to know, or I won't survive myself' – an instinct of self-preservation, animalistic and rudimentary. The sacrificial side of human nature, honored by Dostoevsky (in such characters as, for example, Sonia Marmeladova in *Crime and Punishment*), is what would be required for the world of Petrushevskaia's characters to cease being chaotic and ugly. This is impossible, however, as Petrushevskaia views earthly existence as a punishment, and her characters are lacking the same moral and religious grounds as the Underground Man.

Similar to Tolstaia, Petrushevskaia practices the technique of *skaz*, rendered in first-person narratives, with narrators – "women Homers…who tell their stories orally, just like that, without inventing anything"[454] – predominantly attempting to aggressively exculpate themselves, in the same fashion as the Underground Man does:

> …there appeared a hysterical urge for contradictions, contrasts, and there I went to debase myself. And I totally did not say all this to exculpate myself… But, on the other hand, no! I lied! What I wanted to do was to exculpate myself.

> [*…iavlialas' istericheskaia zhazhda protivorechii, kontrastov, i vot ia i puskalsia razvratnichat'. Ia ved' vovse ne dlia opravdaniia moego seichas stol'ko nagovoril…A vprochem, net! sovral! Ia imenno sebia opravdat' khotel.*][455]

Like Dostoevsky's "Notes from Underground," most of Petrushevskaia's stories begin in *medias res*, with the narrator resuming a presupposed dialogue, i.e. in *Time: Night*:

He is not aware of the fact that, when visiting, he may not run to a vanity cabinet and grab everything: little vases, statuettes, little flacons, and especially little boxes with fake jewelry. Of the fact that, when at the table, he may not ask for a second helping. He, having come to somebody's home, searches everywhere, a child of starvation…

---

[453] Daizettsu Sudzuki, "*Lektsii o dzen-buddizme*," in E. Fromm, D. Sudzuki, R. de Martino, *Dzen-buddizm i psikhoanaliz*, Moscow: *Ves' mir*, 1997, 84.
[454] Sally Laird, "Liudmila Petrushevskaia" in *Voices of Russian Literature: Interviews with Ten Contemporary Writers*, Oxford: Oxford U Press, 1999, 23-48.
[455] D-*PSS*, 5:127.

[On ne vedaet, chto v gostiakh nel'zia zhadno kidat'sia k podzerkal'niku i tsapat' vse, vazochki, statuetki, flakonchiki i osobenno korobochki s bizhuteriei. Nel'zia za stolom prosit' dat' eshche. On, pridia v chuzhoi dom, sharit vsiudu, ditia goloda...][456]

Given the narrative tone and the number of misfortunes happening to the characters, one imagines the family living in a time of revolution or war. Neither is there a war in Russia at the time the novella is set, nor have the members of this family started out their lives in a Voronezh-area orphanage of the 1930s. However, food is a major issue for them; *"oborona"* is the word used by Anna Andrianovna in reference to it (Night. The baby has fallen asleep. I hold the defenses, although my daughter is in charge of assault and battery from time to time ... *[Noch'. Malysh usnul. Ia derzhu oboronu, khotia doch' vremia ot vremeni nanosit udary...]*[457]). And the family fights are so serious and long-lasting that they resemble a war.

The female characters in *Time: Night* are educated people, university graduates; Grandma Serafima belonged to a high party echelon; both Anna Andrianovna and Alena had normal jobs at respected institutions. The romantic entanglements of these two women are so bizarre and radical that they both end up unemployed and penniless. Anna Andrianovna becomes a free-lance part-time journalist (and calls herself a poet, perhaps emphasizing that her sufferings have a romantic reason). It is unclear as to whether Alena would be able to keep her position, which she officially still has, though she is on a third maternity leave. All the children are small, and being a single mother she would most probably not be able to go to work and care for her offspring if they became ill. Her misfortunes invoke those of Katerina Ivanovna Marmeladova, despairing in total poverty with three children in spite of a noble background and education sufficient for a woman of her times. Raskol'nikov's affirmation – Polen'ka will go the same way *[Polen'ka po toi zhe doroge poidet]* – in *Crime and Punishment* can be recalled in connection with the fate of Alena, who repeats the mistakes and misfortunes of her mother, Anna Andrianovna. The reader can imagine the fate of Alena trying to cure the sicknesses of her children and barely managing to do it, as the same incident occurs in the narrative with Anna Andrianovna and the coughing and choking Timochka:

---

[456] Petrushevskaia, *Sobranie sochinenii*, 1:311.
[457] *Ibid.*, 327.

That night, I remember, Timochka started coughing in a somewhat strange way, I woke up, and he was simply barking: khav! khav! And couldn't breath the air in, this was scary, he went on breathing out and out, crouched into a little ball, turned hare-gray, the air went out of him with this barking, he turned blue and couldn't sigh, and kept on barking and barking, and started crying from fear. We know this, we have learned this, nothing special, the swelling of the throat, and false croup, acute pharyngitis, I have survived this with my children, and the first thing: one has to sit him up and calm him down, his feet in hot water with mustard, and call an ambulance, but everything cannot be done at once, the ambulance line is busy all the time, there has to be another person around...

[*V tot vecher, ia pomniu, Timochka stal kak-to stranno kashliat', ia prosnulas', a on prosto laial: khav! khav! I ne mog vdokhnut' vozdukh, eto bylo strashno, on vse vydykhal, vydykhal, s''ezhivalsia v komok, stanovilsia seren'kim, vozdukh vykhodil iz nego s etim laem, on posinel i ne mog vzdokhnut', a vse tol'ko laial i laial i ot ispuga nachal plakat'. My eto znaem, my eto prokhodili, nichego, eto otek gortani i lozhnyi krup, ostryi faringit, ia eto perezhila s det'mi, i pervoe: nado usadit' i uspokoit', nogi v goriachuiu vodu s gorchitsei i vyzvat' "Skoruiu pomoshch'", no vse srazu ne sdelaesh, v "Skoruiu" ne dozvonishsia, nuzhen vtoroi chelovek...*][458]

Timochka needs to breath in air but cannot do so, which shows both the degree of his actual physical illness and, metaphorically, the lack of spirituality and love in the family. Dostoevsky's metaphor of air appears together with another comparison of Tima with an animal; his breathing is like barking. Tima, missing his supply of air, demonstrates his animalistic side.

When Anna Andrianovna complains about the absence of a second person in the family at a time when immediate help for the sick child is needed, she is primarily complaining about Alena. It is, however, clear that Alena is going through the same crises but with a different child, and will be in the same situation with all three of them later. The Greek tragedy of this family, with fate seemingly determining the life of these women, affects them in spite of the positive potential they have, including their belonging to the middle-class and intelligentsia.

---

[458] *Ibid.*, 321.

Mirroring, a characteristic of Dostoevsky's prose, also occurs in *Time: Night*. The mirror in the hall reflects the distorted faces of members of Anna Andrianovna's family; the misfortunes of her children mirror her own and those of her mother. The doubling of Anna Andrianovna with Alena, and Anna Andrianovna with Grandma Serafima, as well as the doubling of the males in this family, demonstrates the inescapable pattern of *bezobrazie* prevalent in *Time: Night*. Characters in this novella, particularly the narrator, bear a strong resemblance to the Underground Man type, with their dialogic monologues, graphomania, lack of humility, and desire to manipulate the lives of those who are more vulnerable than they are. *Time: Night* and "Our Crowd" are dystopias with Dostoevskian characters and locus. The house/home is a place of dystopia for both Dostoevsky and Petrushevskaia; its oppressive nature is represented in the narrowing of space and the tyranny taking place within that home. This distinguishes Tolstaia from Petrushevskaia, as for the former the home-hearth functions as a utopian space. In Dostoevsky and Petrushevskaia, home is as an entrapment, an enclosure, influencing the psyche of characters in a claustrophobic fashion.

Psychological laceration, *nadryv*, is a salient feature of Dostoevsky's influence on Petrushevskaia's prose. In the works of both authors, lacerations often occur in descriptions of table scenes or scandal scenes in dysfunctional families. These scenes are also ugly in the manner of Bakhtin's carnivalesque. Bodily and spiritual deformities are present in the *oevres* of both Dostoevsky and Petrushevskaia. Yet Petrushevskaia's narratives are profoundly gynocentric. Her ugly characters recall anti-heroes like the Underground Man, but they are women. Men are either the cause of misfortunes – job losses, unwanted children, lack of psychological stability, and the like – or are not represented in Petrushevskaia's narratives. She explores animalistic and corporeal ugliness in detail, yet is intentionally silent about spiritual *bezobrazie*. This creates such a contrast that spiritual ugliness is in fact foregrounded. The representatives of the Russian intelligentsia in *Time: Night* possess some logic, even if fantastic at times, but no practical reason in the Western sense of the word. The absence of reason is combined with self-destruction. In "Our Crowd," the narrator's practical reason is dominant; the story is an exercise in showing what practical reasoning alone can do to a human being. The utilitarian approach the narrator of "Our Crowd" takes in planning her son's life for the better recalls the ideas of *What is to Be Done*, as the boy is placed under the care of the collective, her 'circle of friends.' Given the *bezobrazie* of this circle, the reader is left to doubt whether the narrator's plan is ultimately in her son's best interests, or is actually a part of a vicious vendetta. Petrushevskaia demonstrates the flaws of the intelligentsia in her works; her anti-heroines, like the Underground Man, have some education and a chance for a career. Dostoevsky's anti-hero becomes a productive type for his own writing, twentieth-century Russian literature (particularly, of the end of it), and for modern European literature as well.

Petrushevskaia uses Dostoevsky's ideals to defy them; for Petrushevskaia God is dead, and any utopian or religious salvation is impossible. As Victor Terras says, "Dostoevsky certainly defined the condition of man *without* God with great power... Those of Dostoevsky's characters who are *with* God, holy men, simple souls, or humble sinners, are less compelling."[459] *Bezobrazie* prevails in the godless literary universe of Petrushevskaia as the beautiful cannot. Petrushevskaia employs textile metaphors to symbolize unattainable beauty and wholeness. Jealousy prevails over love, which, particularly in its maternal variant, is what ignites evil in *Time: Night* and "Our Crowd." The Dostoevskian epithet "*bezobraznyi*" comes up in the parts of the narrative of *Time: Night* having to do with jealousy, moral evil, and ugliness in general. The colour yellow has a connotation of *bezobraznoe* in both Dostoevsky and Petrushevskaia. These writers also share 'ugly' themes such as insanity, criminality, and death, and express particular concern about the fate of young children in accidental families. Among other poetic means the use of which Petrushevskaia owes to Dostoevsky are his negative insect metaphor, the image of the underground mouse, and the lack of air as lack of "*zhivaia zhizn'*."

As to narrative structure: digressions, dialogic monologues, beginning in *medias res*, the presence of an editor, and an inclusion of an apologue are found in both Dostoevsky and the narrative of *Time: Night*, which also features at least three diaries. These structural features allow us to consider Dostoevsky's fragmented narratives *protomodern*; but Petrushevskaia goes further than this; i.e. the omnivorous postmodern structure of *Time: Night* includes references to the various media the story has been recorded on. The distorted language of the anti-heroes, in particular their syntax, is a common feature for Dostoevsky and Petrushevskaia. The use of *skaz* is another parallel between these writers as well as with Tatiana Tolstaia, who like Petrushevskaia re-creates a private world in her writing. The general tone, narrative similarities, poetics of the ugly, and treatment of characters and space with home-hearth as a locale of dystopia create a complete picture of Dostoevsky's heritage in the works of Liudmila Petrushevskaia. This heritage is so visible in her work because of Dostoevsky's discussion of *bezobraznoe*, which, in her view, is the dominant characteristic of the world. She uses Dostoevsky as a bitter reminder of his utopian ideals that do not materialize in Soviet and post-Soviet reality.

Literariness is a significant characteristic of the text of Petrushevskaia's *Time: Night*, which contains references to Tolstoi, Agniia Barto, Arkadii Gaidar, Marina Tsvetaeva, Anna Akhmatova, and

---

[459] Victor Terras, "*Samoe Glavnoe*," *Dostoevsky and the Twentieth Century*, Nottingham: Astra Press, 1993, 4.

Anton Chekhov, in addition to the prevailing allusions to Dostoevsky. The narrative of *Time: Night* includes a parody of the Soviet classic Gaidar, which is realized with the help of Dostoevskian devices, i.e. scandal at the table and psychological lacerations. The question of Chekhov's influence on Petrushevskaia's work appears fruitful for a topic for future investigation.

A literary tradition, in this case that of Dostoevsky (and Gogol') "is equally the product of a conscious creative effort on the part of participants in the literary process, and the result of transpersonal evolutionary forces within and without the artistic sphere."[460] Such a tradition leads us from proto-modern protean Dostoevsky to the omnivorous postmodern end of the twentieth century, with Mamleev's writings inclining towards surrealism, Tolstaia's magic realism, and Petrushevskaia's dark realism. Each of these twentieth-century writers has benefited from the Russian nineteenth-century canon and, in particular, from the Gogol-Dostoevsky tradition with the latter's Underground Man, ideal of Sodom, and fragmented narratives. As Rozenblium writes on aesthetics, its characteristic feature is

... in the interpermeation of the tragic and comical and it is enveloped in the nature of things, and this is why the depiction of the laughable even in the deeply gloomiest situations does not become a sacrilege.

[...*vzaimoproniknovenie tragicheskogo i komicheskogo zakliucheno v samoi prirode veshchei, a potomu izobrazhenie smeshnogo dazhe v samykh gluboko mrachnykh situatsiiakh ne stanovitsia koshchunstvennym.*][461]

Gogol's grotesque and Dostoevsky's *bezobraznoe*, reappearing in late twentieth-century prose, allow for comic relief in ugly, at times tragic, writings and reality. As Sally Dalton-Brown suggests, the problem of the new literature in Russia is "its desire for variety within a form of definitive unity,"[462] a desire that the ugly, by Croce's definition, satisfies.

---

[460] Rolf E. Hellebust, "The Pushkinian Tradition as Narrative and Intertext," Ph.D. dissertation, U of Toronto, 1993, 5.
[461] L. Rozenblium, "*Iumor Dostoevskogo*," *Voprosy literatury* 1(January-February 1999): 145.
[462] Sally Dalton-Brown, *Voices from the Void: The Genres of Liudmila Petrushevskaia*, NY: Berghahn, 2000, 10.

Conclusion: Afterthoughts on Poetics, Genre, and Culture

This book begins by demonstrating the poetic devices employed by Dostoevsky to convey the notion of the ugly (*bezobraznoe*): the abundance of yellow in the narrative colour palette, images of the spider and the mouse, polyphonic monologues, and the broken geometry of lines in sculptural and spatial depictions. The variety of meanings of *bezobraznoe* in "Notes from the Underground" embraces overindulgence in sentimentality and romanticism, alienation from society and 'living life,' interiors of St. Petersburg and its climate, the Underground man's messiness, amorality, and averbality. The ugly in the "Notes" is related to the problem of the individual's 'formlessness' in his irrational search for freedom, and to the chaos and existential disorder of Russian society.

The conscious use of Dostoevsky's poetics of the ugly by twentieth-century authors testifies to his heritage in their works, but also illustrates their intertextual technique. Mamleev's grotesque, humour, and solipsistic characters continue the line of Gogol' and Dostoevsky in twentieth-century Russian literature. The comic relief and minimal or non-existent didacticism allowed for by this tradition may explain its flourishing in post-Soviet times. The egotistic tendencies of Dostoevsky's anti-heroes are reflected in Mamleev's works; contemporary egotists reach harmony and order by eliminating the surrounding world and obtain stability at the expense of external chaos. The *Diary of an Individualist* features the underground as a psychological or psychopathological phenomenon, and *Shatuny* represents the underground as the nether world.

Mamleev's "Diary of an Individualist" and *Shatuny* reveal elements borrowed from Dostoevsky's *Notes from the House of the Dead*, "Notes from the Underground," "*Polzunkov*," "*Mr. Prokharchin*," "*Bobok*," and *Crime and Punishment*. The term *bezobraznyi* frequently occurs in Mamleev's works. In these texts, it serves as the basis for neologisms, the meaning of which is related to ugliness and Dostoevsky's aesthetics and poetics of the ugly. Mamleev's multiple diminutives and preference for the prefix "*polu-*" reflect Dostoevsky's influence as well. Works by Dostoevsky and Mamleev feature the same characteristics of the ugly *topos* such as corners/angles, disproportionate houses and windows, mirrors and doubles, taverns, dumpsters, and the underground. The twentieth-century writer transposes underground nature onto the whole cosmos, but also into physical cracks and cervices. Mamleev attempts to create an underground of the underground, perhaps, reacting to the late-Soviet idea of the cultural and intellectual underground as "the voice of truth," and ultimately, criticising the intelligentsia. This brings him close to Tolstaia's and Petrushevskaia's critical portrayal of 'the educated' and 'the cultured.'

Postmodern literature uses Russian as well as world classics and prominent authors such as Dostoevsky are at the epicentre of this process. Intertextuality and quotation link texts and cultures of several temporal periods and assist in creating the cento of the postmodern world. Irony, parody, and pastiche also participate in quilting intertextual fields of contemporary literature and culture. The end of the twentieth century in Russia, the period of wild capitalism, disintegration and lack of faith gave birth to an abundance of "black" literary texts, whose authors frequently relate their works to those of Dostoevsky, his philosophy and poetics. As opposed to Dostoevsky they do not necessarily keep the measure of the beautiful and the ugly; the latter becomes foregrounded. The borders between these notions have shifted in the modern and postmodern eras, just as have the geographical borders of many Central and Eastern European states. The ugly is viewed as a new, more dynamic category by modernists and substitutes for beauty in postmodern times.

The concept of ugliness as a subject for art, and its relation to the city, become major issues for both the nineteenth and twentieth centuries. In the latter, what the traditionalists called chaotic and ugly is already viewed by the Futurists as a fresh contribution towards the revival of art, who thus emphasize the creative side of the ugly in its multiplicity. Even earlier on, in his attempt to discredit the Austrian artist Klimt's "eroticized, organic representations of reality," one stalwart defender of rationalism stated: "It is not against nude art, nor against free art that we struggle but against ugly art."[463] As incredible it seems now, Klimt had to defend his highly aestheticized portrayal of the female body from being criticized as ugly. This debate, however, gave rise to the Vienna School of Art History and Franz Wickhoff's new view of art history as tolerant to innovation.

Dostoevsky and his *homo duplex* were the focus of attention of Symbolists who, like Futurists and other avant-garde poets and painters, searched for a new beauty, a new philosophy of art and poetics. The study of the provenance of Dostoevsky's heritage in Tolstaia's works shows that in addition to direct parallels between the two writers, there are connections with Dostoevsky via the Modernists, whose significance for her the author openly acknowledges.[464] (Tolstaia's texts, especially the latest ones and those related to the theme of St. Petersburg, demonstrate direct allusions to Blok's use of yellow, for example.) Tolstaia affirms that she values pre-revolutionary culture (over that of the USSR) and calls this "elitist, rich time" – that of Modernism – "the 'golden age' of twentieth-century Russian

[463] Carl E. Schorske, *Fin-de-Siècle Vienna: Politics and Culture*, NY: Vintage Books, 1981, 234.
[464] Serafima Roll, *Contextualizing Transition: Interviews with Contemporary Russian Writers and Critics*, NY/Washington: Peter Lang, 1998, 112.

literature."[465] She also discusses her own prose in the context of the artistic tradition of the 1920s in a newspaper interview:

> But the prose of the 20s gives one a feeling of a hall half-empty. This is a principally new prose: in its style, vocabulary, metaphors, syntax, *sujet*, narrative structure. Everything is different, everything is changing, hundreds of new opportunities appear, and only a small part of them gets realized. For this literature, for this tradition that is only starting to develop itself, I feel a certain tenderness. There, in the ruins of this half-constructed poetics, there could be treasures hidden... And it is somehow very easy to imagine that at that time there was one more writer, about whom nobody knows anything, who never published a single line, and then he died, and all who knew him died, too, and his work remained unfinished. You may consider that I am instead of him.

> [*A vot proza dvadtsatykh godov daet oshchushchenie polupustogo zala. Eto printsipial'no novaia proza – stil', leksika, metaforika, sintaksis, siuzhet, postroenie – vse drugoe, vse meniaetsia, poiavliaiutsia sotni vozmozhnostei, i lish malaia chast' ikh osushchestvliaetsia. Vot k etoi literature, k etoi tol'ko nachavsheisia [sic] razvivat'sia traditsii u menia lezhit serdtse. Tam, v razvalinakh etoi nedostroennoi poetiki, mogut tait'sia klady... I kak-to ochen' legko predstavit' sebe, chto byl v eto vremia eshche odin pisatel', o kotorom nikto nichego ne znaet, kotoryi ni strochki ne napechatal, a potom on umer, i vse, kto znal ego, tozhe umerli, i delo ego ostalos' nesdelannym. Schitaite, chto ia za nego.]*[466]

The postmodern in Tolstaia's texts includes irony and multiplication of individual, unique artistic worlds that are characteristic of modernism.[467] The modernist era also covers a large part of the literary career of her grandfather Aleksei Tolstoi, whom she admires and with whom she associates herself. The reception of Dostoevsky and the modernist trends of the beginning of the twentieth century overlap in late-Soviet and post-communist Russia, and the generic ugliness of the modern city appears to express the crisis of national identity, particularly during the politically-unstable times of the creation and dissolution of the Soviet empire. City spaces represented as ugly in nineteenth-century

---

[465] *Ibid.*, 98.
[466] *Literaturnaia gazeta* (23 July 1986): 7.
[467] See Lipovetsky, *Russkii postmodernizm*, 227.

Russian literature, and Dostoevsky in particular, continue to be described similarly in late twentieth-century narratives, in which this tendency becomes even more visible. Mamleev's and Petrushevskaia's works, for example, depict Moscow as ugly under the influence of the ugliness of Dostoevskian St. Petersburg.

Dostoevsky's study of individualism has inspired numerous works of late twentieth-century Russian and European writers, whose egotistic and solipsistic characters often exist within polyphonic narratives. The mentally-ill people of Dostoevsky's works – both genuinely-ill holy fools and murderers with a supposed mental illness due to a lack of morality – give rise to the theme of schizophrenia, mythical and real, both a poetic practice and the actual disease, explored in Russian postmodernist works. Post-Soviet writers are free to dedicate their works to the low and the monstrous, to fill in the niche left by the socialist realism of the previous era. Romanticism aestheticized ugliness, emphasizing its tragic and horrible aspects. This is reflected in Dostoevsky's romantic and realistic texts (e.g. Stavrogin in *The Devils*); but this tendency did not persist through time – late twentieth-century Russian writers are not Romantics in the sense that Dostoevsky was. Romanticism is parodied by these writers; postmodern irony plays with romantic ideas as it does with all others. By the end of the twentieth century, literature strives for fragmentation rather than congruency, a tendency that one can trace back to Dostoevsky's art and aesthetics. The emphasis in contemporary works is on multi-layered narratives: "loose and baggy monsters" become the artistic norm; fragments become whole works.

A modern cultural icon, Umberto Eco, writes on literature's thaumaturgic potential: "By changing the letters of the book, we change the world."[468] In Russia at the end of the twentieth century, demythologizing of literary context and tradition (the idea of throwing the ideals of Woman and Beauty, like that of Pushkin, from the steamship of the modern era) occurs at the same time as a mythologizing of the debris of these ideals.[469] Such deconstruction and immediate construction create an effect of self-estrangement of the whole cultural language, happening from within the cultural context. Mikhail Epstein thinks that such self-estrangement is the salient function of cultural studies as an independent branch of the humanities, and the flourishing of this branch in Russia coincides with the postmodern era.[470] Cultural studies thus become a critique of any cultural situation from the outsider's

---

[468] Umberto Eco, *Foucault's Pendulum*, quoted in Lipovetsky, *Russkii postmodernizm*, 297. See also Umberto Eco, ed., *On Ugliness*, New York: Rizzoli, 2007.

[469] Lipovetsky, *Russkii postmodernizm*, 284.

[470] Mikhail Epstein, *After the Future: The Paradoxes of Postmodernism in Contemporary Russian Culture*, Amherst: U of Massachusetts Press, 1994, 281-306.

point of view (*vnenakhodimost'*, the Bakhtinian term used by Gurevich in reference to the study of mediaeval culture.)[471] This facilitates the participation of writers and their creations in not just literary, but also cultural polyphony. Postmodern writers use other authors' contexts to create their own texts and turn any image into a culturological formula. It is the culturological semantics of the image that gains primary importance and substitutes for the original literary one. Such transformations of semantics characterize Tolstaia's stories as well as works of other contemporary writers, the discussion of whom is beyond the scope of this book (Sorokin, Sokolov, P'etsukh, and Viktor Erofeev, for example).

In their quest for form, late twentieth-century Russian writers seek ways to fulfill a dual task: to mythologize the signs of context and to deprive them of their hierarchical qualities, thus becoming material for play. In this search for a form meeting these criteria, new Russian prose (and Ukrainian, e.g. Iurii Andrukhovich's *Perverziia*) turns to the traditions of fairy-tale magic and the carnivalesque. Tolstaia's fairy-tale style, enticing us to believe in its magic, comes together with the carnivalesque, for example in her stories *Limpopo* and "Sleepwalker in the Fog." The carnivalesque – and the related category of ugliness – are revealed in Tolstaia's changes, and dissonances in style, and are often expressed through theatricality and irony (Petrushevskaia and Tolstaia), parody (Mamleev and Petrushevskaia), and pastiche (Mamleev). Both fairy-tale magic and the carnivalesque are stylistic techniques for the creation of cultural myths that lay at the basis of the postmodern model of the world; they are elements of play with and interpretation of mythologized cultural contexts that occur at the surface level. Fairy-tale magic and the carnivalesque provide a demythologizing background full of ambivalent critical evaluations for these cultural contexts. A deeper level of artistic play, restructuring the mythology of cultural context from the inside, is that of the meta-genre, such as the drama for Classicism, or the poem for Romanticism.[472] I suggest that for Russian postmodernism such a meta-genre is that of the fragment, another form favoured by the Romantics. Fragmentation is evident in the writings of all three late-twentieth century writers studied in this book, and the fragmented (and from the point of view of classical form – ugly) narratives of Dostoevsky are at the roots of this tradition.

I find "Diary of An Individualist" and *Shatuny*, in particular, to parallel *menippea* with their depiction of death. Hell and Purgatory, life after death, the nether world – these are among prominent

[471] Aron Gurevich, *Kategorii srednevekovoi kul'tury* in *Izbrannye trudy*, Vol. 2, Moscow/St. Petersburg: *Universitetskaia kniga*, 1999, 19.
[472] N.L. Leiderman, "*Zhanrovye sistemy literaturnykh napravlenii i techenii,*" *Vzaimodeistviia metoda, stilia i zhanra v sovetskoi literature*, Sverdlovsk: *Sverdlovskii gosudarsvennyi pedagogicheskii institut*, 1988, 4-17.

themes of *menippea*.[473] Mamleev with his chicken-corpse and characters coming to life after they have been murdered in *Shatuny*, and the confessional dialogicity of "The Diary of An Individualist," continues the line of conversations from beyond the grave.

Bakhtin points out that the *menippea* has always been, from ancient times, a self-parody; it is one of its characteristics as a genre and a reason for its unusual popularity.[474] *Menippean* self-parody is evident in the works of Mamleev and self-irony in those of Tolstaia. In her *Limpopo* the *menippea* of the ending is close to burlesque and the mystery play (see Chapter IV).

Another scholar of *menippea*, Joel Relihan, writes that this genre represents the first self-criticism of philosophical thought and literature per se in the history of culture.[475] Tolstaia's anti-utopia *Kys'*, with its self-destructive disillusionment regarding book culture, provides an example of such self-criticism. Relihan also remarks that the style of *menippea* often involves a use of language – vocabulary and grammar – as fantastic as the events it describes.[476] Such fantastic style can be found in all three contemporary writers studied in this book, and to some extent to Dostoevsky as well. Kristeva discusses poetics "falling apart" in her works on modern literature and culture.[477] Chaos of poetics within the cosmos of text can be found both in Dostoevsky's art and, more explicitly, in late-twentieth century writings. This textual situation in a logocentric country like Russia becomes what Lipovetsky calls the *chaosmos* (borrowing Joyce's term) of Russian postmodernism, and transforms from the literary to the cultural plane.[478]

The naturalist side of the ugly is well-represented in the works of Mamleev, and even more so in those of Tolstaia and Petrushevskaia. The theme of the little man (taking its roots from Pushkin's "Station Master" [*Stantsionnyi smotritel'*], Gogol''s "Overcoat" [*Shinel'*], and continuing in Dostoevsky) is a major topic of Soviet and post-Soviet works by Tolstaia and Petrushevskaia. This theme is among the reasons for the Soviet authorities' not publishing – or severely editing – stories about such "little people" as children, the old, ill, poor, and lonely people.

The idea of the underground which Dostoevsky claimed to introduce (but which probably started out with Gogol''s "Overcoat") becomes very popular with late twentieth-century writers: witness the feeding on underground mice in Tolstaia's *Kys'*, her "Notes from Underground," and the

---

[473] One of the most popular classic *menippeas* is "Menipp, or a Trip to the Nether World" by Lucian. Bakhtin states that Dostoevsky was most likely familiar with it. Bakhtin, *Problemy poetiki Dostoevskogo*, 190.
[474] Bakhtin, *Problemy poetiki Dostoevskogo*, 189.
[475] Joel C. Relihan, *Ancient Menippean Satire*, Baltimore/London: John Hopkins U Press, 1993, 10-11, 24.
[476] *Ibid.*, 26.
[477] Iuliia Kristeva, *Izbrannye trudy: razrushenie poetiki*, Moscow: Rosspen, 2004.
[478] Lipovetsky, *Russkii postmodernizm*, 317.

underground creatures in "Sleepwalker in the Fog"; Mamleev's underground individualists, poets, and murderers in "Diary of An Individualist" and *Shatuny*; Petrushevskaia's underground women and space in *Time: Night* and "Our Crowd." Starting with the philosophical and psychological underground depicted by Dostoevsky, late twentieth-century Russian writers develop the concept in three differing ways: Mamleev creates a metaphysical underground, the underground of the underground, Tolstaia – the ironic underground of the cultural isolation of the reader and, primarily, of the writer from the 'simple folk,' and Petrushevskaia – multi-layered polyphonic confessional narratives featuring the underground of psychological isolation with a gender twist.

Dostoevsky explores the relationship between the ugly and the comic, which becomes the monstrosity plus comic relief of the narratives of Mamleev, Petrushevskaia, and Tolstaia. The nineteenth-century writer also studies evil in connection with violence, and readers can find excesses of violence and the most refined torture, both bodily and spiritual, in Petrushevskaia, Mamleev, and Tolstaia. This tendency is prevailing in contemporary cinema as well in the 2004 film *Nochnoi dozor* [Night Watch], among many others.

Of the clear and dim states of mind and moral consciousness that Dostoevsky explored in his works, twentieth-century narratives prefer the dim part: authors depict their characters in horrible and confused stages of mind and moral consciousness. This especially applies to Petrushevskaia. The dim stages of *bezobraznoe* depicted by all four writers include sensualism and tyranny. Tolstaia's works in particular present interesting complexities. The mood of her works is pessimistic and her dreamers are ugly in a Dostoevskian fashion. She emphasizes petty ugliness and enjoys the carnival of words and things that organize chaos into form in her texts. For her Gogol' exemplifies "true cultural chaos" and she believes that, compared to him, those occupying themselves with cultural chaos in the late twentieth-century are writing ineptly.[479] I suggest that Tolstaia herself is an example of a talented contemporary writer dealing with chaos in a Gogolian fashion. This adds another dimension to the problem of literary influences in her works: that of Gogol' (recalling the question of the influence of Dostoevsky and the Symbolists) is both direct and also the indirect result of reading Dostoevsky. When asked what kind of writers attract or interest her as a reader, she briefly acknowledges her "hysteria" for Pushkin's verse. In contrast, she describes her interest – but dislike – for Dostoevsky in a lengthy passage, from which one gathers that she reads and re-reads the author of *Crime and Punishment*, quotes him, and obviously knows his texts very well.[480] This is of course not sufficient evidence by

---

[479] Roll, *Contextualizing Transition*, 111.
[480] *Ibid.*

itself. It is a question to what extent interview replies can be trusted and whether, because of their subjectivity, they are at all relevant to historical and critical study of a writer. The textual evidence may contradict or confirm the opinions expressed in interviews, but it is the text that needs to be the primary object of study. In the case of Tolstaia, however, it is helpful that her interviews tell us about her interest in and knowledge of Dostoevsky, as her texts demonstrate strong similarity to Dostoevsky's poetics and most likely influence. The texts studied in this book reveal connections to Dostoevsky's poetics of the ugly; however, the proportion of Tolstaia's *ouevre* that does so may be less than in the case of Mamleev, or Petrushevskaia.

The varieties of Tolstaia's artistic production embrace short, highly polished, and beautiful forms; the long and sloppy narrative of *Kys'*; and essayistic writings. Tolstaia's talent allows her to weave ugly scenes into beautiful narratives subtly; it involves the power of contrast rather than the bold universal ugliness of Mamleev's texts. The reader and critic may not notice the ugliness in Tolstaia's works at first, as the immediate impression is that of her luscious language. The effect Tolstaia's texts make is that of a represented author's intention to depict beauty; however, the narration often reverts to depicting the ugly – a lowering of the genre in the Ancient fashion. This incongruence between the author's intention and the impression made on critics is not unlike that of Dostoevsky and his impression of a "cruel talent," despite his religious and utopian ideals. Dostoevsky's influence on Tolstaia's is not so much in the aesthetics of the ugly – hers is rather the aesthetics of the beautiful – but in the poetics of the ugly, bequeathed to her by the Russian classics, Dostoevsky among them.

I think that ugliness in art, in particular, the fine arts, is a way of expressing tragedy, or crisis. In static arts such as painting, for example, tragedy would be depicted by means of twisted lines of the face, broken lines of the body, structures being destroyed. Tragic painting would have to be one of maximal disharmony and disproportion. Petrushevskaia has a well-defined interest in the fine arts and recently was engaged in professional painting, which explains the focus on the visual in her narratives. Bearing in mind Ivanov's idea of Dostoevsky's novels being tragedies and my study of Dostoevsky's focus on the visual, one could transpose the abovementioned theory onto Dostoevsky's writings, and use it as an explanation of the specifics of the depiction of his Underground characters (distortion, disfigurement, etc.). As Helena Goscilo points out, Dostoevsky and Petrushevskaia share an anatomizing of "the heritage of evil and its infinitely subtle variations through the resonant trope of the family," like the Greek tragedians.[481] In addition to her prose, highly dramatic prose as lacking in

---

[481] *Dictionary of Literary Biography*, 285:285.

catharsis, Petrushevskaia writes drama pieces per se. Critical reception of her prose is not unlike that of Dostoevsky's 'cruel talent:'

> The intensity and frequency of abuse and suffering in her works are so great that she is considered by some to be simply a repulsive distorter of the Russian scene. However, her knowledge of that scene is so intimate and detailed, and her ability to evoke the social and moral atmosphere so impressive, that she has commanded increasingly enthusiastic and respectful attention.[482]

The response of Petrushevskaia to the contemporary cultural crisis in Russia can be characterized as shock therapy. Mamleev's writings fall under the same category, while Tolstaia combines shock with retro therapy. Epstein suggests that in postmodern Russian culture objects are deconstructed in the process of their construction and says that: "In Russia, nothingness comes to light…as the self-erasure of the positive form."[483] It seems to me, though, that the first part of this statement is only true if one reverses its structure, i.e. the objects are being constructed in the process of deconstruction. Otherwise writers would have stopped writing altogether and all gone to dental schools. Various attempts to avoid discredited cultural symbols, to go beyond the literary word, include Petrushevskaia's recent preoccupation with operatic singing and painting, and involvement in politics on the part of Mamleev (in his non-fiction) and Tolstaia (in her polemical articles and essays). Such social and political criticism, however, is also in the spirit of classic Russian literature, with writers like Dostoevsky dedicating his publications to recent political events, or the social criticism in his *Writer's Diary*. Among the writers trying to re-work the Russian contemporary literary and cultural situation are authors like Viacheslav P'etsukh, whom I intend to include in a future monograph on Dostoevsky and late twentieth-century Russian literature. P'etsukh, together with Boris Akunin, develops the genres of the detective story and the mystery novel, with clear allusions to Dostoevsky. (Other parts of this future work would address the philosophical science-fiction narratives of Viktor Pelevin and the black pornography of the texts of Vladimir Sorokin.)

The fragmented narratives of postmodern literature, its self-referentiality, skepticism, and chaotic character illustrate "a game played within hyperreality according to consciously artificial

---

[482] Dalton-Brown, *Voices from the Void*, 6.
[483] Mikhail Epstein, "The Origins and Meaning of Russian Postmodernism" in *Re-Entering the Sign: Articulating New Russian Culture*, Ellen E. Berry and Anesa Miller-Pogacar, eds., Ann Arbor: U of Michigan Press, 1995, 35.

rules."[484] Lyotard, in his book *The Postmodern Condition*, affirms that proper narratives (that is, in their performative function) in fact no longer exist, as they became a part of a language game a la Wittgenstein.[485] Articulation, according to Derrida, embraces "connection, intertextuality, joining while preserving division."[486] Such articulation seems to be the underlying phenomenon of contemporary Russian literature and its desire to relate to the Russian classics while preserving its own individual traits.

The search of the characters of postmodern fiction for form, wholeness, *"blagoobrazie,"* and moral structure within *chaosmos* is pointless and absurd; the world is depicted as irrational, and the author merges with the discredited narrator. I suggest that the next stage in the literary and cultural situation will be a tendency of the humanities to attempt to become a science, in a more radical fashion than previously promoted by Jakobson and Lotman, perhaps, in the way some performance trends involve the use of genetics to create glowing cacti and rabbits, or display bacteria at art exhibits. It seems to me that a desire to formalize the *chaosmos* would drive the urge for a scientific approach in the artistic community. All this strongly resembles the tendency of Romanticism to combine art and science, and post-postmodernism would, thus, remain close to the art of Dostoevsky, an irreversible Romantic in his realist fiction.

Works Cited:

Russian Literature

Baranskaia, N. *A Week Like Any Other: A Novella and Stories*. London: Virago, 1989.

Chernyshevskii, N.G. *What Is To Be Done?*. NY: Vintage Books, 1961, 227-237.

---

[484] Dalton-Brown, *Voices from the Void*, 9.
[485] Jean-François Lyotard, *The Postmodern Condition: A Report on Knowledge*, Minneapolis: U of Minnesota Press, 1991, 41.
[486] Dalton-Brown, *Voices from the Void*, 10.

_____. *Chto delat'?: Iz rasskazov o novykh liudiakh. Polnoe sobranie sochinenii*. Vol. 11. Moscow: *Gosudarstvennoe izdatel'stvo khudozhevstvennoi literatury*, 1939.

_____. *"Esteticheskie otnosheniia iskusstva k deistvitel'nosti." Polnoe sobranie sochinenii*, Vol. 2. Moscow: *Gosudarstvennoe izdatel'stvo khudozhevstvennoi literatury*, 1949.

_____. *Izbrannye filosofskie sochineniia*, Vol. 1, Moscow: *Gosudarstvennoe izdatel'stvo politicheskoi literatury*, 1950.

Dostoevskii, F. M. *Polnoe sobranie sochinenii*. Leningrad: *Nauka*, 1973. [D-*PSS*]

_____. *Sobranie sochinenii*. Moscow: *Khudozhestvennaia literatura*, 1957.

_____. *Crime and Punishment*. NY/London: W.W. Norton and Co., 1989.

_____. *Notes from Underground: Poor People: The Friend of the Family*. Translated by Constance Garnett. Dell Publishing Co., 1960.

_____. *The Best Short Stories of Dostoevskii*. NY: The Modern Library, 1992.

_____. *Winter Notes on Summer Impressions*. Translated by David Patterson, Evanston, IL: Northwestern U Press, 1988.

_____. *Notes from Underground*. A Norton Critical Edition. New York/London: W.W. Norton and Company, 2001.

Gaidar, Arkadii. *Sobranie sochinenii*. Moscow: *Detskaia literatura*, 1964.

Makanin, V. *"Laz."* Moscow: Vagrius, 1998.

Mamleev, Iurii. *Shatuny*. Moscow: Terra, 1996.

_____. *"Tetrad' individualista"* in Viktor Erofeev, *Tzvety zla*. Moscow: *Podkova*, 1997.

_____. *The Sky Above Hell and Other Stories*. Translated by H.W. Tjalsma. New York: Taplinger Publishing Company, 1980.

_____. *Bunt luny*. Moscow: Vagrius, 2000.

Okudzhava, Bulat. *Arbat, moi Arbat: Stikhi i pesni*. Moscow: *Sovetskii pisatel'*, 1976.

Petrushevskaia, Liudmila. *Sobranie sochinenii. Khar'kov*/Moscow: Folio/TKO Act, 1996.

Pushkin, A.S. *Izbrannye proizvedeniia*. Moscow: *Detskaia literatura*, 1969.

_____. Sleepwalker in a Fog. Translated by Jamey Gambrell. NY: Alfred A. Knopf, 1992.

_____. *"Limpopo"* in *Piatyi ugol: Sbornik sovremennoi prozy*. M: *Knizhnaia palata*, 1991.

_____. *Noch'*. Moscow: *Podkova*, 2002.

_____. "Notes from Underground." *The New York Review of Books*. (31 May, 1990).

_____. *Kys'*. Moscow: *Podkova/Inostranka*, 2001: 326.

_____. "Women's Lives." In *Pushkin's Children: Writings on Russia and Russians*. Boston/NY: Houghton Mifflin, 2003.

Other Sources

Dictionary of Literary Biography. Vol. 285, Detroit: Gale, 2003.

Encyclopaedia Britannica: A New Survey of Universal Knowledge. Vol. 10, Chicago/London/Toronto: William Benton, 1956.

Estetika, Beliaev, A.A. et al. eds. Moscow: *Politizdat*, 1989.

Etimologicheskii slovar' russkogo iazyka. Fasmer, M. Vol. 1, 2, Moscow: Progress, 1964.

Filosofskaia entsiklopediia, Konstantinov, F.V., ed.-in-chief. Moscow: *Sovetskaia entsiklopediia* 1960-1970.

Filosofskii entsiklopedicheskii slovar', Il'ichev, L.F., P.N. Fedoseev, S.M. Kovalev, and V.G. Panov, eds. Moscow: *Sovetskaia entsiklopediia*, 1983.

Filosofskii slovar', Frolov, I.T., ed. English edition. Moscow: Progress, 1984.

Literaturnyi entsiklopedicheskii slovar'. Moscow: *Sovetskaia entsiklopediia*, 1987.

Allen, Elizabeth Cheresh. *Beyond Realism: Turgenev's Poetics of Secular Salvation*. Stanford: Stanford U Press, 1992.

Aristotle, *Poetics*. Translated by Kenneth McLeish. New York: Theatre Communications Group, 1999.

Arkhipova, A.V. *"Dostoevskii i estetika bezobraznogo"* in *Dostoevskii: Materialy i issledovaniia*. Vol.12, St. Petersburg: DB, 1996.

Art in Theory: 1900-1990: An Anthology of Changing Ideas, Oxford, UK/Cambridge, USA: Blackwell, 1996, 941.

Baak, Ioost van. *"Dom kak utopia v russkoi literature."* *Russkie Utopii*, St. Petersburg: Corvus, 1995, 136-137.

Bachinin, V.A. *Dostoevskii: metafizika prestupleniia*. St. Petersburg: *Izdatel'stvo Sankt-Peterburgskogo universiteta*, 2001.

Bakhtin, Mikhail. Problemy poetiki Dostoevskogo, Moscow: Sovetskii pisatel', 1963.

_____. *Problemy poetiki Dostoevskogo*. Moscow: *Khudozhestvennaia literatura*, 1972.

Barsht, Konstantin. *"Goticheskii ieroglif Dostoevskogo."* *Novoe literaturnoe obozrenie*, 39 (1999).

Belinskii, V.G. *"Vzgliad na russkuiu literatury 1847 goda."* *Estetika i literaturnaia kritika*. Vol. 2, Moscow: *Khudozhestvennaia literatura*, 1959.

Berdiaev, N. *Mirosozertsanie Dostoevskogo*. Moscow: *Zakharov*, 2001.

Bibler, V.S. *Nravstvennost': Kul'tura: Sovremennost'*. Moscow: *Znanie*, 1991.

Biriukov, S. *"Ia napisal stikhotvoren'e,"* *Zevgma: Russkaia poeziia*, Moscow: *Nauka*, 1994, 183.

Bulatov, D., ed. *Eksperimental'naia poeziia: Izbrannye stat'i*. Königsberg/Malbork: *Simplitsii*, 1996.

Catteau, Jacques. Dostoevsky and the Process of Literary Creation. Cambridge: Cambridge U Press, 1989.

Croce, Benedetto. "The Beautiful and the Ugly" in *The Aesthetic as the Science of Expression and of the Linguistic in General*. Cambridge: Cambridge U Press: 1992.

Dalton-Brown, Sally. *Voices from the Void: The Genres of Liudmila Petrushevskaia*. NY/Oxford: Berghahn Books, 2000.

Dark, O. *"Mir mozhet byt' liuboi: razmyshleniia o novoi prose."* *Druzhba narodov* 6 (1990).

Dobroliubov, N. A. *"O stepeni uchastiia narodnosti v razvitii russkoi literatury." Izbrannoe.* Moscow: *Iskusstvo*, 1986.

Eco, Umberto, ed. *On Ugliness.* New York: Rizzoli, 2007.

Epstein, Mikhail. *After the Future: The Paradoxes of Postmodernism in Contemporary Russian Culture.* Amherst: U of Massachusetts Press, 1994.

_____. *"Posle budushchego: o novom soznanii v literature." Znamia* 1 (1991).

_____. "The Origins and Meaning of Russian Postmodernism" in *Re-Entering the Sign: Articulating New Russian Culture.* Ellen E. Berry and Anesa Miller-Pogacar, eds. Ann Arbor: U of Michigan Press, 1995.

Fanger, Donald. *Dostoevskii and Romantic Realism: A Study of Dostoevsky in Relation to Balzac, Dickens, and Gogol'.* Cambridge: Harvard U Press, 1965.

Frank, Joseph. *The Stir of Liberation: 1860-1865.* Princeton: Princeton U Press, 1986.

Gaut, Berys and Dominic McIver Lopes, eds. *The Routledge Companion to Aesthetics.* London and New York: Routledge, 2001.

Goldfarb, David A. "Kant's Aesthetics in Dostoevskii's *Notes from Undergound.*" Mid-Atlantic Slavic Conference, Columbia U, 18 March 1995, http://www.echonyc.com/~goldfarb/u-ground.htm.

Goscilo, H. and B. Lindsey, eds. *Glasnost: An Anthology of Russian Literature under Gorbachev.* Ann Arbor, 1990.

Grois, B. *"Polutornyi stil': sotsialisticheskii realizm mezhdu modernizmom i postmodernizmom. NLO* 15 (1995).

Gurevich, Aron. *Izbrannye trudy.* Vols. 1, 2. Moscow/St. Petersburg: *Universitetskaia kniga*, 1999.

Hellebust, Rolf. *Flesh to Metal: Soviet Literature and the Alchemy of Revolution*. Ithaca/London: Cornell U Press, 2003.

_____. "The Pushkinian Tradition as Narrative and Intertext." (Ph.D. dissertation, U of Toronto, 1993).

Higgins, Lesley. *The Modernist Cult of Ugliness: Aesthetic and Gender Politics*. NY: Palgrave Macmillan, 2002.

Holman, C. Hugh. *A Handbook to Literature*. N/Y: Bobbs-Merrill, 1972.

Ivanov, Viacheslav. *"Dostoevskii i roman-tragediia."* *Russkaia mysl'* April (1914), http://www.vehi.net/dostoevsky/ivanov.html, accessed on October 16, 2004.

Jackson, Robert Louis. *The Art of Dostoevsky: Deliriums and Nocturnes*. Princeton, New Jersey: Princeton U Press, 1981.

_____. *Dialogues with Dostoevsky: The Overwhelming Questions*. Stanford U Press: Stanford, 1993.

_____. *Dostoevsky's Quest for Form: A Study of His Philosophy of Art*, New Haven: Yale U Press, 1966.

_____. *Dostoevskii's Underground Man in Russian Literature*. The Hague: Mouton & Co, 1958.

Kabakov, Il'ia. "On Emptiness" in *Re-Entering the Sign*. Ann Arbor: U of Michigan Press, 1995.

Kant, I. *Sochineniia v 6-ti tomakh*. Vol. 5. Moscow: *Mysl'*, 1963-1966.

Katz, Monika. "The Other Woman: Character Portrayal and the Narrative Voice in the Short Stories of Liudmila Petrushevskaia" in *Women and Russian Culture: Projections and Self-Perceptions*, ed. By Rosalind Marsh. NY/Oxford: Berghahn Books, 1998.

Khrustaleva, O. *"Konets veka." Mitin zhurnal*, 1993 (50).

Klimontovich, Nikolai. *"Dalee vezde". Oktiabr'* (2000) 11.

Klioutchanskii, Arkadii. "On the Chronology of Besy." CAS paper (2001).

Kostka, Edmund K. *Schiller in Russian Literature*. Philadelphia: U of Pennsylvania Press, 1965.

Kristeva, Iuliia. *Izbrannye trudy: razrushenie poetiki*. Moscow: Rosspen, 2004.

Kudriavtsev, Iu.G. *Tri kruga Dostoevskogo*. Moscow: *Izdatel'stvo Moskovskogo universiteta*, 1979.

Kuritsyn, V. *Russkii literaturnyi postmodernism*. Moscow: *OGI*, 2000.

Laird, Sally. "Liudmila Petrushevskaia" in *Voices of Russian Literature: Interviews with Ten Contemporary Writers*. Oxford: Oxford U Press, 1999.

Lantz, Kenneth. *The Dostoevsky Encyclopedia*. Westport/London: Greenwood Press, 2004.

Lebrun, David. *Proteus*, USA, 2004. Film.

Leiderman, N.L. *"Zhanrovye sistemy literaturnykh napravlenii i techenii." Vzaimodeistviia metoda, stilia i zhanra v sovetskoi literature*. Sverdlovsk: *Sverdlovskii gosudarsvennyi pedagogicheskii institut*, 1988.

Lindemans, Micha F. http://www.pantheon.org/articles/s/seraphim.html [accessed June 30/04], http://www.newadvent.org/cathen/13725b.htm [accessed June 30/04].

Lipovetskii, Mark. *Russian Postmodernist Fiction: Dialogue with Chaos*. Armonk/London: M.E. Sharpe, 1999.

_____. *Russkii postmodernism: ocherki istoricheskoi poetiki.* Ekaterinburg: *Ural'skii gosudarstvennyi pedagogicheskii universitet*, 1997.

Lowe, David. *Russian Writing Since 1953: A Critical Survey.* NY: *Ungar*, 1987.

Lyotard, Jean-François. *The Postmodern Condition: A Report on Knowledge.* Minneapolis: U of Minnesota Press, 1991.

Mamleev, Iurii. *Iznanka Gogena.* Paris/NY: *Tret'ia volna*, 1982.

_____. *"Mezhdu bezumiem i magiei." Beseda* 6 (1987).

_____. *"Moi geroi zadaiutsia voprosami, na kotorye razum ne v sostoianii otvetit'. " Literaturnaia gazeta.* 16.11.94. No. 7 (5487).

_____. *"O Esenine." Nash Sovremennik* 10 (1990).

_____. *Rossiia vechnaia: Rossiia v proshlom, nastoiashchem, budushchem.* Moscow: *AiF* Print, 2002.

Mazur, Natalia. *"Kobob." Literaturnoe obozrenie*, 7-8 (1992).

Mikhailov, Sergei. *"O pisatele Iurii Mamleeve." Skrizhali* (1999).

Mikhailovsky, N.K. "Dostoevsky's Cruel Talent." In *Fyodor Dostoevsky: "Notes from Underground,"* A Norton Critical Edition. New York/London: Norton & Company, 2001.

Mochul'skii, K. *Dostoevskii: zhizn' i tvorchestvo.* Paris: YMCA Press, 1980.

Morson, Gary Saul. *The Boundaries of Genre: Dostoevskii's "Diary of a Writer" and the Traditions of Literary Utopia.* Austin: U of Texas Press, 1981.

Nietzsche, Friedrich. *The Birth of Tragedy*. Translated by Francis Golffing. Garden City, NY, 1956.

Odesskii vestnik. 1875 (March 13). No.58.

O Dostoevskom: Tvorchestvo Dostoevskogo v russkoi mysli 1881-1931 godov, Moscow: *Kniga*, 1990.

Parts, Liudmila. "Pushkin and Company: from Myth to Text in Today's Russia." *Russian Literature* I.II (2002), North-Holland.

Pope, Richard. "Peter Verkhovensky and the Banality of Evil." *Dostoevsky and the Twentieth Century*, Nottingham: Astra Press, 1993.

Porter, Robert. Russia's Alternative Prose. Oxford/Providence: Berg, 1994.

Relihan, Joel C. Ancient Menippean Satire. Baltimore/London: John Hopkins U Press, 1993.

Revue d'esthètique. 1954 (7), No.2.

Roll, Serafima. *Contextualizing Transition: Interviews with Contemporary Russian Writers and Critics*. NY/Washington: Peter Lang, 1998.

Rosenkranz, Karl. *Ästhetik des Hässlichen*. 1853, 463.

_____. *Ästhetik des Hässlichen*. Leipzig: Reclam-Verlag, 1990.

Rozenblium, L. *"Iumor Dostoevskogo." Voprosy literatury* 1(January-February 1999): 141-188.

Rudenko, Iu.K. *Chernyshevskii-romanist i literaturnye traditsii*. Leningrad: *LGU*, 1989.

Ruge, A. *Neue Vorschule der Ästhetik*. 1837.

Russkii mir. 1875 (February 27). No.55.

Schiller, Friedrich. *Ausgewählte Kostbarkeiten.* Lahr: SKV-Edition, 1981.

_____. "Über die notwendigen Grenzen beim Gebrauch schöner Formen," *Ausgewählte Werke.* Vol. 5, Darmstadt: Wissenschaftliche Buchgemeinschaft E. V., 1954.

Schmid, Ulrich. "Flowers of Evil: The Poetics of Monstrosity in Contemporary Russian Literature (Erofeev, Mamleev, Sokolov, Sorokin)." *Russian Literature* XLVIII (2000).

Seduro, Vladimir. *Dostoevskii in Russian Literary Criticism: 1846-1956.* NY: Octagon Books, 1969.

Selden, Raman and Peter Widdowson. *A Reader's Guide to Contemporary Literary Theory.* NY/London: Harvester/Wheatsheaf, 1993.

Schorske, Carl E. *Fin-de-Siècle Vienna: Politics and Culture.* NY: Vintage Books, 1981.

Shklovskii, Viktor. *O teorii prozy.* Ann Arbor: Ardis, 1985.

Smirnov, Igor P. *"Evoliutsiia chudovishchnosti: Mamleev i dr."* *NLO* 3 (1993).

_____. "Geschichte der Nachgeschichte: Zur russisch-sprachigen Prosa der Postmoderne," in *Modelle des literarischen Strukturwandels*, Michael Titzmann, ed. Tübingen: Max Niemeyer, 1991.

Sokolov, S. Interview. *Iunost'*, (12) 1989: 66-68.

Spencer, Francis. "Form and Disorder in Dostoevsky's A Raw Youth" in *F.M. Dostoevsky (1821-1881): A Centenary Collection*, ed. by Leon Burnett. University of Essex: Department of Literature, 1981.

Sudzuki, Daizettsu. *"Lektsii o dzen-buddizme"* in E. Fromm, D. Sudzuki, R. de Martino, *Dzen-buddizm i psikhoanaliz*. Moscow: *Ves' mir*, 1997.

Suslov, Alexander V. *The New Art Tradition in Modern Russian Prose*. Dissertation Abstracts International, Vol. 47, No. 1 (July 1986), 175-A.

Terras, Victor. *"Samoe Glavnoe"* in *Dostoevsky and the Twentieth Century*. Nottingham: Astra Press, 1993.

Tolstaia, Tatiana. *Literaturnaia gazeta* (23 July 1986): 7.

Tomei, Christine D., ed. *Russian Women Writers*. Vol. 2, NY/London: Garland, 1999.

Toporov, V.N. *Peterburgskii tekst russkoi literatury*. St. Petersburg: *Iskusstvo-SPB*, 2003.

Vetlovskaia, V.E. *Poetika romana "Brat'ia Karamazovy."* Leningrad: *Nauka*, 1977.

Vischer, F.T. *Ästhetik*. Vol. 1, 1846.

Wisniewska, Sophia. "Narrative Structure in the Prose of Tatiana Tolstaia." (Ph.D. dissertation, Bryn Mawr College, 1992). Microform.

Woll, Josephine. "The Minotaur in the Maze: Remarks on Liudmila Petrushevskaia." *World Literature Today*, Vol. 67 (Winter 1993): 1, http://80-weblinks2.epnet.com.ezproxy. lib.ucalgary:20... [Accessed on 09/06/04].

Zelinskii, V., ed. *Istoriko-kriticheskii kommentarii k sochineniam F.M. Dostoevskogo*. Moscow, 1885, pp. 1, 91. Microform.

Zen'kovskii, V.V. *"Problema krasoty v mirosozertsanii Dostoevskogo,"* *Russkie emigranty o Dostoevskom*, ed. Belov, S.V. St. Peterburg: *Andreev i synov'ia*, 1994.

187

Zubova, L.V. *Sovremennaia russkaia poeziia v kontekste istorii iazyka.* Moscow: *NLO*, 2000.

http://www.newadvent.org/cathen/06608a.htm [accessed June 30/04].

http://www.bartleby.com/39/40.html [accessed July 17/04].

I want morebooks!

Buy your books fast and straightforward online - at one of the world's
fastest growing online book stores! Environmentally sound due to
Print-on-Demand technologies.

Buy your books online at
www.get-morebooks.com

Kaufen Sie Ihre Bücher schnell und unkompliziert online – auf einer der am
schnellsten wachsenden Buchhandelsplattformen weltweit!
Dank Print-On-Demand umwelt- und ressourcenschonend produziert.

Bücher schneller online kaufen
www.morebooks.de

SIA OmniScriptum Publishing
Brivibas gatve 1 97
LV-103 9 Riga, Latvia
Telefax: +371 68620455

info@omniscriptum.com
www.omniscriptum.com

Scriptum

Printed in Great Britain
by Amazon

75094423R00111